IT STARTED WITH COFFEE IN THE VESTRY:

The History of Kingston and Surbiton
Young Men's Christian Association
1858–1908

Audrey C. Giles

Front cover illustration: Warwick Lodge, Eden Street, Kingston upon Thames circa 1900

Kingston University Press
Kingston University
Penrhyn Road
Kingston upon Thames
Surrey, KT1 2EE

British Library Cataloguing in Publication Data available.

ISBN: 978-1-899999-75-0

Printed in the UK
Cover design: Ditte Loekkegaard

KU
PRESS
KINGSTON UNIVERSITY
PRESS

FOREWORD

In this study of local history in Kingston and Surbiton from 1858 to 1908, Audrey Giles reminds us of the important and at times influential role played by the YMCA in England and also more widely. Set up in London in 1844 by businessman and Evangelical nonconformist George Williams, the YMCA expanded rapidly to become an international and world organisation. (The YWCA, founded in the mid-1850s, followed a not dissimilar trajectory.) Concerned about the detrimental impact of urban society on young men's lives, George Williams promoted personal and civic improvement through individual and shared activities such as prayer, Bible reading and physical recreation. Historians of the organisation have noted that its growth relied heavily on networks of transport and communication; as cities expanded in Britain, Europe, the US and parts of the British Empire, so the YMCA expanded also. Its establishment in Kingston and Surbiton was indicative of much broader trends in the mid-to-late nineteenth century.

The YMCA was also dependent on other well-established networks; churches and church representatives played a vital role. Audrey reveals that the first meeting of the Kingston branch took place on a date earlier than previously supposed: in March 1848, at the local Congregational Church. Not long after that, another important early YMCA characteristic manifested itself: Protestant inter-denominationalism; members of the Congregational Church co-operated with their Baptist counterparts. Two visits to Kingston in 1859 by the eminent Baptist preacher Charles Haddon Spurgeon further strengthened relations between the churches. However, Williams and his co-founders took the view that the organisation should not be too closely tied to a particular church or churches. Therefore, as they sought to further expand the movement's reach in the 1860s, members of the Kingston branch undertook what would become a protracted search for suitable premises.

As Audrey makes clear, there were many vicissitudes, and membership – and therefore income – fluctuated. Those men whom the YMCA sought to attract typically worked long and unsocial hours. For that reason branch officials and members took particular interest in the Early Closing Movement – as they also did in the question of temperance. In 1874 there was a 'fresh start' in new premises.

There was also reconstitution of the organisation, with an additional emphasis on education, through provision of evening classes. Progress was difficult, however, and in the 1870s and 1880s membership grew slowly.

The Surbiton branch of the YMCA appears to have been formed in 1868. It continued in existence for 11 years before closing in 1879. It then reopened in 1882 and amalgamated with Kingston three years later, finally bringing into being the Kingston and Surbiton Young Men's Christian Association.

Little remains of early branch records. Only some minute books from subsequent years are still extant. Audrey has augmented careful research of these records with study of local newspaper reports and other sources. Her book provides new insight into the YMCA in Kingston and Surbiton. It sheds light on the lives of its officials, members, sponsors and supporters. More than a meeting place and a venue for education and recreation, the YMCA also facilitated local debate on social and theological issues. It attracted the interest and the participation of many people, among them Wilberforce Bryant, of Bryant & May. Audrey describes vividly the challenges that constantly faced this local, suburban branch of an international and worldwide movement. She notes its capacity for adaptability and change, characteristics that served it well up to and beyond 1908. Her fine book contributes to our historical knowledge of Kingston and Surbiton and of much else besides.

John Stuart

Associate Professor of History

Kingston University

In memory of all past volunteers

No human practice ever stands still; all demand a historical perspective, which uncovers the dynamics of change over time.

Whereas the starting point for most popular forms of knowledge about the past is the requirements of the present, the starting point of historicism is the aspiration to re-enter or re-create the past.

John Tosh, *The Pursuit of History*, 3rd ed. (Longman, Harlow: 2000) pp.9, 15.

CONTENTS

Foreword

Contents

Acknowledgements

Figure Acknowledgements

Appendix and Tables List

Map of Kingston and Surbiton

ACKNOWLEDGEMENTS

A debt of gratitude must be extended to many people, in particular to:

Richard James, Chief Executive of the Y.M.C.A. London South West for permission to use this material and for reading and commenting on the original work.

Dr. Christopher French, Emeritus Reader in History at Kingston University, for reading, commenting and scholarly advice before, during and after completion.

Leslie Feast, current Vice-president and former Director of YMCA London South West for proofreading.

Clyde Binfield the author of *George Williams and the Y.M.C.A.: A Study in Victorian Social Attitudes* for his astute, in-depth study of the 'life and times' of the founder of the movement.

Former Borough Archivist Jill Lamb, and Amy Graham, Local History Officer for their help over many months, in particular for locating and lifting heavy ledgers and for providing many photocopies of the *Surrey Comet* newspaper.

The nineteenth century *Surrey Comet* journalists without whom the details of the Kingston Y.M.C.A. meetings between 1858 and 1871 would have vanished without trace. The reporting of the meetings and events from 1872 to 1890 has continued to be a very helpful addition to the information contained within the Association minutes.

Members of the Kingston United Reformed Church (formerly Kingston Congregational Church) for allowing the picture of the Rev. Lawrence Byrnes to be included in the work and in particular to John Fisher, the U.R.C. Archivist for his interest, help and ongoing encouragement.

Neil Greenough for the basic map of Kingston upon Thames.

Ann Gillespie for lending a very helpful book, giving the writer a detailed tour of the stained glass windows of Christ Church, Surbiton and for sharing her research relating to some of the nineteenth century church members. Thanks are also extended to the members of the church for giving permission to photograph the stained glass windows and to Sue d'Albertanson who found and provided the photograph of Canon Garbett.

Graham and Pat Lavers for lending a book and helping to find the Wesleyan Chapel in Ewell Road.

Christopher Rayner for allowing the publication of a considerable number of his extensive postcard collection.

Dr. David Kennedy for his advice on the location of buildings in Kingston, for his interest and support.

The former Centre for Local History Studies, Kingston University, for developing the Kingston Local History Project under the direction of Dr. Christopher French and Peter Tilley. To Annie Sullivan, former Project Coordinator, Juliet Warren, former Database Manager, and more than 30 voluntary data inputters and checkers who produced the Kingston upon Thames Database, 1851 to 1891.

Juliet Warren, former Database Manager, Local History Studies, Kingston University, currently Heritage Projects Officer, Surrey History Centre, a special thank you, for giving me permission to use the Database to produce the tables and graphs in this book and for good advice and help throughout the project.

Dr. Sue Hawkins, Senior Lecturer, History and Dr. Helen Goepel, History Researcher, Kingston University London for their ongoing help.

Thelma Cripps who listened with patience to numerous accounts and details of what had been found in the minutes; to Fiona Cook who introduced the writer to her friends in Christ Church and sought permission for taking photographs within the church.

An enormous thank-you to Peter Giles for rescuing most of the Y.M.C.A. archive from oblivion during the 1970s; for his invaluable help during the 'skimming' of the *Surrey Comet* from 1858 to 1890; his good humour whilst providing numerous cups of tea; for transport facilities, and general support throughout the three years taken to write the first edition and a further year to complete the current work.

A special thank-you to Dr. John Stuart, Head of History, Kingston University London, for his advice and interest. To Judith Watts, Senior Lecturer, Publishing and Managing Director, Kingston University Press who made publication of the work a reality. Sincere thanks are also expressed to my Copy Editor, Lewis Parker and to my Cover Designer, Ditte Loekkegaard for their hard work and expertise. Finally a very big thank-you to Dr. David Rogers, Director of Kingston Writing School, for his help, advice and support during the revision and to several members of Kingston Writing School who have shown interest in the work.

FIGURE ACKNOWLEDGEMENTS

Abbreviations used to accredit pictures and graphs, referred to as Figures in the text:

AG   Photographs taken and graphs produced by Audrey Giles

CCS   By kind permission of Christ Church Surbiton

CF   Memorial from Teddington Public School supplied by Christopher French

CR   By kind permission of Christopher Rayner taken from his postcard collection

NG   Basic Map produced and supplied by Neil Greenough

SC   Copied from Surrey Comet

URC   By kind permission of the United Reformed Church Kingston upon Thames

YMCA   Pictures supplied from the Y.M.C.A. Archive.

APPENDIX pages 216 - 230

TABLES pages 231 - 242

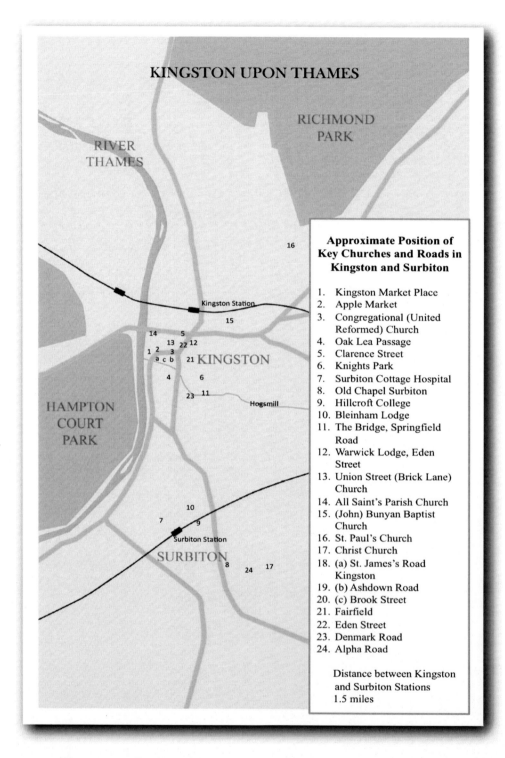

KINGSTON UPON THAMES

RICHMOND
PARK

RIVER
THAMES

16

Kingston Station

15

14   5
    13 22 12
1 2   3
  a c b   21 KINGSTON

4   6
      23 11
            Hogsmill

HAMPTON
COURT
PARK

10
7   9
Surbiton Station

SURBITON
        8   24   17

**Approximate Position of
Key Churches and Roads in
Kingston and Surbiton**

1. Kingston Market Place
2. Apple Market
3. Congregational (United
   Reformed) Church
4. Oak Lea Passage
5. Clarence Street
6. Knights Park
7. Surbiton Cottage Hospital
8. Old Chapel Surbiton
9. Hillcroft College
10. Bleinham Lodge
11. The Bridge, Springfield
    Road
12. Warwick Lodge, Eden
    Street
13. Union Street (Brick Lane)
    Church
14. All Saint's Parish Church
15. (John) Bunyan Baptist
    Church
16. St. Paul's Church
17. Christ Church
18. (a) St. James's Road
    Kingston
19. (b) Ashdown Road
20. (c) Brook Street
21. Fairfield
22. Eden Street
23. Denmark Road
24. Alpha Road

Distance between Kingston
and Surbiton Stations
1.5 miles

Map of Kingston and Surbiton showing the approximate position of churches and roads
mentioned in the text.   (**NG**)

INTRODUCTION

George Williams

Every young man who joined the Young Men's Christian Association during the nineteenth century would have been familiar with the story of how the movement began as it is related in the Surbiton Branch Report for 1871-72:

> The London Young Men's Christian Association owes its rise to a young man, now the treasurer of the Association, who in 1842 came from a large provincial town to London. The house of business to which he came, employed about 80 young men, amongst whom there were no signs of religious feeling, the majority being indifferent to all such considerations, and many very profligate. For some time his one work was prayer. He asked that God would open a way of usefulness for him amongst these his ungodly companions, and especially that one like-minded might be sent into the establishment. In due time the companion came; subsequently others were induced to join them in prayer, and ultimately, by a meeting held at 72, St Paul's Churchyard, on the 6th June 1844, it was decided to form "The Young Men's Christian A$_6$ sociation," in order to the improvement of the character and social condition of young men.[1]

George Williams, the founder of the movement, was born on October 11, 1821, on the borders of Devon and Somerset, at the family home of Ashway Farm. Baptised into the Church of England, he was educated at a Dame's school in the nearby town of Dulverton and later attended a private school in Tiverton. At the age of thirteen he left school to work on the family farm. Two years later he was apprenticed to a draper in Bridgewater where he became a member of the Zion Congregational Church. By the autumn of 1841, aged twenty, George had moved to London and was employed in the draper's shop of Hitchcock and Rogers situated at 72-74 St. Paul's Churchyard.[2] Migration into the town from the country was not unusual, and during the 1840s many young people flocked into London with the aim of finding work. George probably arrived in the city soon after the line from Bridgewater to Bristol Temple Meads opened on June 30, 1841. From Bristol he most likely travelled by the Great Western main line through to Paddington. Once the railway had been laid, and the length of the journey had been cut to 152 miles, it would not have been sensible to travel by stagecoach along twisting country roads.[3] Arriving at the old Paddington Station in 1841,

George would have seemed a very ordinary twenty-year-old, one of many young men arriving in the city. It is therefore remarkable that within three years of this journey he, together with a few of his colleagues, formed an association that in the words of Clyde Binfield, 'encircled the world rather more successfully than the British Empire did.'[4]

Kingston & Surbiton Young Men's Christian Association
In 1974 the Kingston and Surbiton Young Men's Christian Association held its centenary celebrations, believing the movement had started in Kingston a hundred years before. The early minute books show that on January 10, 1874, arrangements were made to open a reading room for young men in the Gospel Hall, Kingston Apple Market, and the group affiliated with the parent group of the Association on July 14 of that year.[5] Recently the assumption that this was the first Y.M.C.A. in Kingston has been revised. The *Surrey Comet*, in an article dated June 1, 1861, reported that a Young Men's Christian Association had been formed in March 1858 in Kingston Congregational Church by their pastor the Rev. Lawrence Byrnes.[6] After Byrnes left Kingston in 1869 this movement faltered and an association formed in the Brick Lane Baptist Church in 1872. It is now obvious that the Association that started in the market place in 1874 was a breakaway group, deliberately reformed with the intention of being re-affiliated with the parent group and seeking to provide improvement for young men not only spiritually but also through education.

By 1900 the number of Y.M.C.A.s, associated unions and auxiliaries in the United Kingdom had reached 1,490 with a membership of 105,196. Worldwide the Associations totalled 7,226 with a membership of more than half a million.[7] However, the growth of the movement both in Kingston and Surbiton was slow. It frequently faltered and experienced many difficulties, and its continuation in the locality relied mainly on the dedication of key individuals. A comparison with the New York movement, which began in 1852, reveals obvious differences. These were not the result of different interpretations of the movement, rather they evolved out of the wide diversity of life experience of individual members within the different Associations. These variations and contrasts, together with the distinctiveness of the various places, make the story of the Y.M.C.A. in the context of local history, very interesting.[8]

The aim of this book has been to write a history of the Kingston Association, but also to consider what one of our eminent local historians, Kate Tiller has called 'the interaction between local circumstances and wider factors which together produce the particular local experience.'[9] The result is an account of the life experiences of the members, their failures as well as successes, disagreements as well as harmony. On occasions outside events take centre stage. It relies on Clyde Binfield's book *George Williams and the Y.M.C.A* as well as articles and letters from local newspapers. Eighty per cent of the work is based on primary sources. Nevertheless, although I have taken care to identify individuals correctly, inaccuracies may have occurred, and if so, they are of course, my own.

Finally I make no apology for quoting a considerable number of reports and letters from association minutes and local newspapers. Verbatim reporting is a means whereby it is possible to listen to voices from the past and to share the values and doubts retained within the written word. Nineteenth century society was culturally and socially very different. Individuals then did not behave and think exactly as we do.[10] For this reason, although authorial comment is occasionally included, my aim has been to let individuals speak for themselves. I hope that what emerges is not only the history of a local Association in the context of a Victorian market town, but also an 'unwitting testimony' of some of the fears and aspirations of ordinary people living in nineteenth century Kingston.[11]

Audrey C. Giles
Revised January 2015

1. The Rev. Lawrence Henry Byrnes B.A. Minister of the Kingston upon Thames Congregational Church 1851—1869. Engraved by J. Cochran, from a photograph by Mayall. By kind permission of Kingston United Reformed Church.   **(KURC)**

THE YOUNG MEN'S CHRISTIAN

ASSOCIATION

1858 – 1862

The Rev. Lawrence Henry Byrnes

In 1850, the year before the Great Exhibition in Hyde Park, the Congregational Church in Kingston chose the Rev. Lawrence Henry Byrnes to be its new minister. Byrnes, a young man of twenty-eight, had just finished a degree course at the theological college in Cheshunt.[12] In seeking his first position as a minister he had received two calls, one from a congregational church in Lincoln and another from the church in Kingston.[13]

Why did Byrnes choose the market town of Kingston and not the cathedral city of Lincoln? A.C. Sturney described the Congregational Chapel in Kingston as 'a little, obscure, building,' where there was 'practically no institutional work except that of the Sunday School.' He also wrote that there had been no special attempt to meet the needs of youth, and evangelical work amongst the poor and degraded was almost unknown.[14] It is possible that Byrnes felt called to administer help where it was most needed. In September 1862 he:

> found that there were no less than 82 taverns and public houses in Kingston and Surbiton. Yet on the other hand how few were the associations of a religious character. The young men who attended the churches and chapels were but a sprinkling of those in the town; he did not know what became of the young men on a Sunday. The mass of young men in the town, he did not say it censoriously, were ungodly young men. There was not even a mechanics institute to take a medium course…[15]

Lawrence Henry Byrnes was born in Swaffham in Norfolk in 1822. He was a year younger than George Williams, but whereas Williams had been brought up in the Anglican Church but later became a member of the Independent Church, Byrnes had been brought up in a Roman Catholic household but later became a Congregational minister. This change occurred when Byrnes' family moved to Wisbech. There was no Roman Catholic Church in the area, so he attended the

Independent Sunday School. At his ordination he told the story of how this decision was taken. Although his parents had a great dislike of the established church, they thought that the Independents were 'less bigoted.' They even occasionally attended services themselves, although his mother was displeased when one of Isaac Watts' hymns that included the line, 'nor fear the wrath of Rome and Hell' was sung during one of the services.[16] Despite this reservation, Byrnes continued to attend and eventually entered into membership.

2. The 'New Kingston Station' the Old Station in Surbiton and the Horse Bus circa 1900.   (CR)

Here the similarity with the founder of the Y.M.C.A. ends. George Williams left school at thirteen years of age whilst Lawrence Byrnes left home in 1845, at the age of twenty-three, to continue his studies at Cheshunt Theological College leaving in 1850 with a B.A. (London) qualification.[17] (We can detect his scholarship from the summaries of the lectures he gave and which are recorded in the *Surrey Comet*.) Included in his pastoral care were lectures on William Paley's *A View of the Evidences of Christianity* published in 1794. These lectures included an exposition of Paley's chapter on the 'Morality of the Gospel.' He also advised the young men when he left them in 1869 to read Paley.[18] Cambridge University and possibly Cheshunt College required theology students to read *The Evidences*. At the centre of Paley's argument was the concept that a universe with order and design must have a Designer.[19] Arriving at New Kingston Station—

now called Surbiton Station—to take up 'the Pastoral Office', Lawrence Byrnes preached his first sermon on Sunday, January 12, 1851, was introduced to the church members and occasional communicants ten days later, and can be found on the 1851 census living at an address in Westfield Road, Kingston.[20]

Anxiety and Change

For many individuals in Britain the early period of the nineteenth century was one of deep anxiety. Many thousands, through no fault of their own, were without work, being victims not only of the new technological processes in agriculture and industry but also the vagaries of trade. In 1839, 1842 and 1848 the Chartist riots caused by hunger, hatred of the workhouses and a lack of representation in parliament, were put down by the military. In 1846 and 1847 the potato blight in Ireland killed over one million people with a further million emigrating to England, Scotland and North America. Although there was in some areas of Kingston extreme poverty, and there is evidence that Kingston residents were concerned about the events in the world outside their town, few were physically affected by them. A market town by the side of the Thames, Kingston continued to produce sufficient food to feed an increasing population, enjoyed an expanding retail market and retained an established brewing industry.[21] What later affected those living in Kingston was the railway coming through Surbiton in 1838.[22] By 1850 a new town had started to emerge with more educated residents, many of whom worked in London, and had found homes among the Surbiton villas. By contrast in Kingston little had changed, and the local brewers, retailers and boot-makers remained typical members of the Corporation of Kingston.[23]

The Great Exhibition; 1851

By the beginning of the 1850s, an increasing awareness of the importance of new discoveries and processes, started to pervade the country. Supported by Prince Albert, the Queen's consort, there was a growing resolve to showcase Britain's manufacturing superiority. The result was the Great Exhibition of 1851, the first international exposition, displaying manufactured goods, works of art and inventions from all over the known world. To house the exhibits a prefabricated building, made of iron and glass, 1,851 feet long and 100 feet high, was erected in Hyde Park, London. It encased several trees and covered 26 acres. Designed by Joseph Paxton, head gardener to the sixth Duke of Devonshire, it was initially ridiculed by critics and called 'a giant cucumber frame.' Once constructed it became the most famous new building of its time and when aptly described by

Punch magazine as the 'Crystal Palace,' the name stuck. The size and design of Paxton's construction with exhibits from as far away as India, Russia, Turkey and Egypt, encouraged international interest. Between May and October 1851, about 100 thousand exhibits from 14 thousand exhibitors had been seen by 6 million people. Although travel was difficult and expensive over 58 thousand foreigners arrived in the country during the six months of the Exhibition. Before 1851 the estimated yearly rate had been between 21 and 22 thousand.[24]

The first copy of the *Surrey Comet* was not printed until 1854, and the *London and South Western Railway Traffic Minutes* for the period 1850 to 1857 are missing. (This is believed to be due to Waterloo Station being bombed in 1941.) Consequently there are few details of Kingston's reaction to this event, but many hundreds would have taken the train from the station in Surbiton to travel up the line to Waterloo and then on to the exhibition in London's Hyde Park.

The Great Exhibition provided the catalyst for the extraordinary growth of the Y.M.C.A. The young men planned a tract campaign. They divided London into thirty-six districts, each district being covered by two young men with a printed plan. The content of the tracts, which included details of their mission statement and an invitation to visit their rooms in 7 Gresham Street, inspired a large number of young men. During the period of the Exhibition members distributed an estimated sixteen thousand tracts each Sunday to visitors entering Hyde Park. One recipient was the Duke of Wellington who, it is said, courteously received a tract; another was George H. Petrie, a twenty-four-year-old merchant who had come to London from New York. Petrie later visited Gresham Street, and by 1852 had become involved in the formation of the New York Y.M.C.A. As he learned later, the New York Association was not the first to be formed in North America; the Y.M.C.A.s in Boston and Montreal were founded the previous year.[25]

The Rev. Lawrence Byrnes probably did not attend the exhibition. He was ordained in May 1851, and would have been involved with pastoral duties. Large numbers attended his ordination service and it was said to be 'a day to be remembered with satisfaction and devout gratitude.' Forty-eight people joined the church in 1851, and, by the end of Byrnes' second year, the membership had almost doubled.[26] During the next few years and mainly through his initiative, a Congregational church in Maple Road was built, and later Byrnes reformed the church in Cobham approximately nine miles from Kingston. In 1855 a committee was appointed to oversee the pulling down of the old Congregational chapel in Kingston to replace it with the building that still stands in Eden Street today. In

October when a public tea-meeting was held to bid farewell to the old chapel the church minutes recorded:

> About 400 took tea … the old walls resounded for the last time to the praise of God. It was a meeting full of hallowed associations and references and radiant with hopes of prosperity to come.[27]

The new church could accommodate seven hundred and fifty people when it opened in July 1856. The first stage of the building took only nine months, but a second stage was added, the church reopening on November 8, 1863. The entire cost of £4,550 was met in eight years.[28]

Darwin's *Origin of the Species*; 1859

The 1850s were eventful for another reason. In October 1859 Charles Darwin produced his book *The Origin of the Species*. Darwin's book was not the first to challenge the basic foundations upon which Christianity had been structured. During 1830 to 1833 Charles Lyell published his *Principles of Geology*. Victorians bought and read Lyell's book 'as if it were a novel,' with geologists flocking to look at the earthworks revealed by the explosions when the navvies laid the tracks of the railway lines.[29] Robert Chambers' *Vestiges of Creation* closely followed in 1844, although, possibly because Chambers was concerned about public reaction to his work, the authorship of his book remained secret until after his death in 1871. Darwin is reputed to have remarked that *Vestiges* was important as it prepared the public to accept his own theory of evolution; but Darwin's book was a much more chilling picture of nature than that put forward by geologists and natural philosophers.[30] Natural selection presented a fearful idea for those who had previously considered the Old Testament story of creation sacrosanct, and Darwin himself worried about the reception of his research. The decline of Christianity and the prospect of a society devoid of religious faith was seen by many nineteenth century thinkers as the route to the destruction of a responsible, orderly, moral society. Without Christianity, many argued, society would disintegrate because people would not fear wrongdoing and once the working classes moved away from Christianity, bad behaviour would increase and riots and disturbance ensue.[31]

The Y.M.C.A. in Kingston; 1858

The Young Men's Christian Association was formed in the premises of the new Congregational Church in Kingston in March 1858. The Rev. Lawrence Byrnes invited young men in the local area to take coffee with him in his vestry, and forty or fifty arrived in response to this invitation.[32] The church minutes do not mention the meeting.[33] We do know from the reports in the newspaper that meetings were held in the winter months on Wednesday evenings. On the first Wednesday of the month there was a prayer meeting, on the second Bible study, on the third conversation or discussion and the fourth a lecture. At some of these meetings essays and papers were read on various subjects, and amicably discussed; at others brief addresses were delivered and adapted to meet the interests of young men. Mr. Byrnes gave pastoral care whilst Mr. Garner, a church member who lived in Thames Street, attended all the meetings.[34]

3. Kingston Congregational Church circa 1907   **(KURC)**

During the summer of 1862 the meetings were on a Thursday evening. In May the subject for discussion was 'The pursuit of religion under difficulties,' which covered 'the obstacles met within our daily intercourse with the world in our different callings.'[35] In June, a Mr. Penfold gave a lecture called 'Haunted Houses,' the report in the Surrey Comet reads: 'these haunted houses in reality turned out to be haunted men.'[36] In July the meeting discussed the subject, 'Is it consistent for a Christian to join the Rifle Corps?'[37] This question continued on to the next Thursday evening before it was closed.

In the mid 1850s, certain events enhanced the spirit of co-operation between the members of the Eden Street Congregational Church and their neighbours the Brick Lane (later called the Union Street) Baptists. Thomas William Medhurst, a young man who had been converted by the evangelical Baptist the Rev. Charles Haddon Spurgeon, became a temporary minister at the Baptist Chapel, a chapel that lay only a very short distance from the Congregational Church.[38] This situation brought Spurgeon, on several occasions, to Kingston.

4. Kingston United Reformed Church   (AG 2014)

Charles Haddon Spurgeon

By the time Charles Haddon Spurgeon was twenty-one he was the most popular preacher in London. Born in Kelvedon, Essex in 1834, he was converted in January 1850 and worked initially as an articled pupil at a school in Newmarket, moved to Cambridge in August where he worked without payment as an assistant in a school there. Towards the end of October 1851 when he was seventeen he became the pastor of a small chapel in Waterbeach. This fen-edged village, was thirty-four miles from Wisbech where Lawrence Byrnes had lived before attending Cheshunt Theological College, but unlike Byrnes, Spurgeon never undertook formal theological training. At the age of nineteen, he preached in the Guildhall at a Cambridge Sunday School Union. There was a vacancy at the New Park Baptist Church in Southwark, and a deacon from a church in Loughton, Essex, who heard his Cambridge sermon, mentioned his name to another deacon at the New Park Street Church. When he was invited to preach in London, Spurgeon thought they had invited the wrong man. Although not happy about the visit, he eventually agreed to preach on December 18, 1853.

The New Park Street Baptist Church could accommodate one thousand two hundred people, but the first time Spurgeon preached at the church the congregation was only about eighty. Yet his impact was immediate and a much larger congregation came to the evening service. Before he left the building he was asked to return and he preached again on alternate Sundays in January 1854. Afterwards he was invited to occupy the pulpit for six months and in April was asked to settle as a pastor permanently and accepted the invitation. As so many people wanted to hear him preach, during 1855 and 1856 the New Park Lane Church occasionally used Exeter Hall in the Strand for their services. In 1856 to 1859 the Music Hall in the Royal Surrey Gardens was used. It had three galleries and was filled each Sunday with ten thousand people wanting to hear his sermon. He remained as pastor of the church for thirty-eight years; during this time he founded a pastors' college, an orphanage and a Christian literature society.[39]

Thomas William Medhurst

Thomas Medhurst was converted at one of the New Park Street evening meetings. Two months after his conversion he started preaching in the open air. Some of the New Park Street Chapel congregation did not approve and complained that it was obvious he lacked education. Spurgeon took note of this and in July 1855, Medhurst was sent to a collegiate school in Bexley Heath but spent several hours with Spurgeon every week. During the last months of 1856 Medhurst became the temporary pastor of the Brick Lane Baptist Church in Kingston. Spurgeon arranged that apart from the payment for his services, money should be paid for his tuition. At the end of the first quarter this money was paid to Spurgeon, but when offered to Medhurst it was refused and

Spurgeon used the money to train a second student. It was said that this was the start of Spurgeon's College currently situated at South Norwood Hill in Croydon.[40]

In January 1859 Spurgeon came to preach in the Brick Lane Baptist Church, and the collection following the service was given to the Congregational Church to reduce the debt outstanding on their buildings.[41] In May 1859 Spurgeon returned to marry Thomas Medhurst to his bride Miss Mary Ann Cranfield of London. Spurgeon presented the bride and groom with a sum of £38.10s 0d. collected from friends, church members and possibly also Spurgeon's own family, whilst the Congregational Church lent their facilities for the occasion.[42] In June of the same year Spurgeon preached twice, after which he said from the pulpit that he would, at any time, return the kindness of the Rev. Lawrence Byrnes for lending his chapel on this occasion.[43] This co-operation continued into the 1860s when the Baptist Chapel was rebuilt, with Mr. Byrnes present at the ceremonies. Unfortunately the Rev. Charles Spurgeon failed to attend the co-operation tea held in July 1863 as he missed his train.[44]

The Early Closing Movement; 1859

By 1859 it had become obvious that the Y.M.C.A. meetings had become sparsely attended due to the long hours many of the members were expected to work. Extensive hours had always been a feature of working class employment, and in the retail trades the hours were particularly long as employers took advantage of employees living on the premises. Most had to work between fifteen and sixteen hours a day, 'from half-past six or seven o'clock in the morning till ten or eleven at night.'[45]

When George Williams began work for Hitchcock and Rogers, some improvement had occurred from the 1820s and 1830s when employees were 'herded together, ten or fifteen in a room, at night.'[46] Even in 1841 life in 72 St. Paul's Churchyard continued to be frugal. Hitchcock and Rogers was a profitable business and the forerunner of the later department store. It sold a large number of expensive items such as silk mercery, haberdashery, jewellery, perfume, French flowers, horlogerie, fancy porcelain, boys' caps, French and German manufactures, ostrich plumes, china, footwear, writing desks, cravats, mirrors and fans. A Parisian milliner was in 'constant attendance to receive orders and to effect any alterations which ladies may suggest.'[47] The extravagance of the merchandise and ostentation of the premises existed in stark contrast to the cramped conditions experienced by the employees. Most dormitories had only

three beds in them, but each bed had two occupants. Working hours were from
seven a.m. to nine p.m. although eight p.m. in the winter. Workers received only
a short break for meals and had to continue after the shop closed, with street
doors being bolted at eleven p.m.[48] Many retail premises throughout England
housed and used young people in similar fashion. In Kingston Market Place in
1861 there were thirty-two young men and thirty-eight young women between
the ages of fourteen and twenty-five classified as assistants and servants who
would have worked in similar conditions as those experienced by George
Williams.[49]

It was not surprising that George Williams was one of the many supporters
of the Early Closing Movement, a movement that had been started in the 1830s.
Those who didn't support it argued that it would let loose onto the streets young
men who might behave badly, and closing early would be bad for trade.[50] The
Surrey Comet reported that, while some outdoor workers were striking for a nine
hour day, in the retail trades circumstances were much worse.[51]   Byrnes
continually voiced concern about the hours young people in Kingston had to
work. He frequently mentioned this issue at the meetings, and he continued to
object until he left Kingston. It was, however, Medhurst who wrote the letter to
the *Surrey Comet* printed on September 10, 1859:

> In London and the large towns of England the question has gained the
> serious attention of the great and good, and the effect may be seen by the
> closed shutters of the houses of business by 8 o'clock in the evening.
> Notwithstanding this, Kingston still clings to the customs of the DARK ages.
> … Were our shops closed by 8 o'clock there would be a saving in gas, an
> improvement in those who are our hope for the future, and a consequent
> addition to the improvement of our neighbourhood.

The letter continued urging that ladies should not shop after seven o'clock.[52] The
Surrey Comet took up this matter in an editorial comment on September 17,
reminding its readers that a London society called the Early Closing Association
had been in existence for several years:

> The statistics collected by this society from sources so reliable as to place
> their accuracy beyond all question, have revealed such an amount of
> suffering and disease, so many premature deaths, and so much moral evil,
> among those young men and women, clearly resulting from the too
> prolonged hours of business, that they had only to be made known to bring
> out statesmen, clergymen, physicians, and even the most eminent employers
> themselves, in numbers as opponents of the late hour system; and to array
> them as determined champions of sweeping reform.

The paper then quoted Lord John Russell, who became Prime Minister during 1865 to 1866, and other prominent persons, continuing:

> the testimony of such men as these, and hundreds more like them cannot be set aside. ... There is no time for reading or thought to benefit the soul, none for outdoor exercise to benefit the body, none for innocent amusement and relaxation, so necessary for the welfare of both. ... Profit so acquired would in reality be the 'price of blood.'[53]

On September 24, the *Surrey Comet* printed the following letter:

> Sir – We the undersigned Drapers' Assistants of Kingston beg to tender our sincere thanks for your able and excellent article on Early Closure, in the last week's impression of the *Surrey Comet*, also to those Employers who have already shown themselves favourable to the movement.
>
> Trusting your labours in this good cause may be crowned with success, we are sir,
>
> Your obliged Servants,
>
> T. Hill, H. Kelly, H. Baker, E. Tucker, E. Allen, R. Southby, R. Flatman, J. Miller, R. Benn, J. Waters, C. Woodall, E. Bubb, J. Sands[54]

In September 1860 a meeting took place in the Assize Courts for those involved in the drapery trade. Those in attendance agreed that they should encourage the closing of shops at seven p.m. for six months of the year and at eight p.m. for the other six months. The opinion was that some of the shops held back because they were afraid that others might continue to open late. There was also another difficulty 'in as much as some of the drapers deal in ready-made goods, which are also dealt in by the boot and shoe makers, and other branches of trade, who it is alleged, ought in justice to the drapers to close at the same time.'[55] In November the paper made the following announcement:

> In every direction shutters were being rattled cheerily up, and settled into their places with a good hearty bang, the pavement rang with the clanking of iron bars, and an observer standing in the Market-place might have fancied he was listening to an explosion of fireworks in honour of some event; the glare and twinkling of gas disappeared with the closing of one shop after another, as you see the sparks die out from a piece of burnt paper, and a few moments the town sunk into quietude and left off business for the night... The butchers and bakers, we are sorry to say, have as yet taken no part in this desirable movement though what they can gain by continuing open we are at a loss to comprehend...[56]

Although the *Surrey Comet* waxed lyrical, the move in favour of early closing appears to have been short lived.

Removal to Neutral Ground; 1862

On June 1, 1861, a meeting in the Eden Street School Rooms considered whether the usefulness of the Young Men's Christian Association could be extended. The Association meetings were described as a rendezvous for young men who 'owing to the late hours of business were prevented from attending any evening service during the week.' A nineteen-year-old, Mr. Walter H. Fry who was in 1861, the secretary of the local Association, endorsed this description. Mr. Fry, who had been born in Plymouth, worked as a corn dealer's apprentice, lodging in Kingston Market Place. In a short speech at the end of the meeting he spoke of the benefit he had received through the Association: 'when he came to the town there was nothing of the kind, and when the invitation to meet the minister was first issued, he felt it was just the thing that was wanted. He knew that many young men were greatly indebted to the Association.'[57]

The founding date for the 'neutral ground,' the accommodation outside the Congregational Church, remains uncertain, but it is probable that it was at the same time as the early Kingston Y.M.C.A. affiliated with the main body of the Association, at the beginning of 1862. The mayor who found the room was the brewer Mr. Joseph East. Mr. East arrived in Kingston after buying the Tudor brewery called Flint & Shaw in Church Street sometime in 1846. Thereafter the name of the brewery was changed to Joseph East's Albion and Star Brewery. Joseph East was the first nonconformist mayor of Kingston and served as mayor in 1865 and 1866. During his tenure as mayor he abolished the traditional Shrove Tuesday football game in the town.[58] In 1867 his brewery moved to Oil Mill Lane (later called Villiers Road).

Why did the young Association have to leave the Congregational church? From the beginning George Williams and the other founders of the organisation never intended that the Association should exist in a particular church, the aim being that the movement should be interdenominational. Originally membership was restricted to church members (assumed to be converted persons) and later depended on evidence of conversion, referred to by 1849 as the London Rule of Membership.[59] The Association's premises would be a place where young Christians of all denominations could meet during the week, have devotional evenings, read books, newspapers, write home and thereby be kept away from beer shops and taverns.

The Paris Basis — The Y.M.C.A. Foundation Statement — 1855

At the 1855 First World Conference of the Y.M.C.A.s, ninety delegates from nine countries met in Paris, and adopted a somewhat more flexible view of who could become a member. This new view became known as the 'Paris Basis' and remains the ongoing foundation statement of the mission of the YMCA:

> **The Young Men's Christian Associations seek to unite those young men who, regarding Jesus Christ as their God and Saviour, according to the Holy Scriptures, desire to be his disciples in their faith and in their life, and to associate their efforts for the extension of his Kingdom amongst young men.**
>
> **Any differences of opinion on other subjects, however important in themselves, shall not interfere with the harmonious relations of the constituent members and associates of the World Alliance.**[60]

English leaders may have preferred the London Rule, but the Paris Basis provided the basis on which national Y.M.C.A.s became affiliated to the World Alliance, and the movement became an 'international federation of affiliated societies,' each branch being independent but each branch being held together by a Christian core.[61]

The decision to move the Kingston group away from the church would have been made from the beginning, and confining the movement in church premises between 1858 to 1861 was a means whereby Byrnes could nurture the young movement until it could stand alone.

FINDING A PLACE IN KINGSTON
SOCIETY
1862−1869

Lack of Support

Newspaper reports give the impression that the Kingston Y.M.C.A. during the early 1860s experienced no difficulty finding a place in wider society. Nevertheless, from the beginning glimpses of the problems that, by the end of 1865 appeared to overwhelm the young Association, emerged. These included the lack of interest shown by the local tradesmen and initially the lack of interest shown by the local clergy and ministers. Although they employed many of the young men, most local tradesmen gave little or no financial support, and as many of the young men worked late into the evenings, they could not attend the meetings. In the first few years the churches, in particular the Anglican Church, showed little interest. There was also the mobility of the members, this remained problematic not only during the early period of the movement but also throughout the nineteenth century and into the twentieth. Once the movement grew, with many towns having an association in their boundaries, the loss of personnel from one association meant a gain for another. Unfortunately during the early years, this situation did not apply.

Although the Promotional Meeting held in the Assize Courts in September 1862 attracted about two hundred individuals, the lack of support soon became obvious. The meeting began with Mr. James Morgan Strachan, a J.P. who lived in Teddington, expressing his sorrow that the young Association should have gone out of town to find a president. He had, he said, 'gladly accepted the office, the nature of the Association inducing him to do so, though he made it a rule no longer to undertake any public duties.'[62] Strachan was born in 1789 and would have been 73 years of age when he took over as the president of the Kingston Association. He was a leading figure in setting up the Teddington Public School during 1831 to 1832 and had been part of the school's management committee. The school later became St. Mary's and St. Peter's Church of England Primary School.[63] Strachan died, age 85, in 1874.[64]

Why did the various associations need a president? A president ensured that the meetings of an association ran according to the rules. He would also have acted as a figurehead, someone with influence who could speak for the group. Once the young Association had left the protection of the Congregational Church someone other than the Rev. Lawrence Byrnes had to assume this position. Nobody in Kingston during the early 1860s wanted to accept this role as it meant a degree of commitment and possibly some financial backing. Several notable people had agreed to be a vice-president but only Mr. Strachan had agreed to be the president.

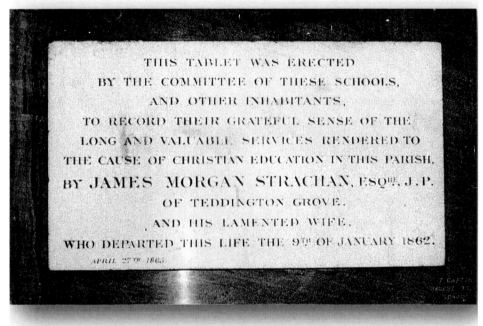

5. Memorial to Mr. J.M. Strachan placed on a wall of the Teddington Public School. The school was demolished in the 1970s. **(CF)**

Only five churchmen attended the Promotional Meeting in September 1862: the Rev. T.G.P. Hough, whose church was in Ham; the Rev. T. Pyne, from Hook, were Anglican vicars; the Rev. A. Mackennal and the Rev. L.H. Byrnes, were Congregational ministers and Mr. Medhurst, having left the area, the fifth churchman was the new minister of the Baptist Chapel in Brick Lane, the Rev. H. Bayley. Before the end of the meeting, Mr. Bayley noted that the vicar of All Saints Parish Church in the Kingston Market Place had not attended, and he testified from his own experience in Liverpool to the value of the Young Men's Christian Association. He said:

Ministers, both of the Established Church and Nonconformists, met on the same platform, similarly as they had witnessed that night. He rejoiced to see so many new persons.[65]

The Association throughout most of the nineteenth century may have lacked support from some of the ministers and clergy, but others were generous with their time. The Rev. Alfred Williams, the vicar of All Saints Parish Church from April 10, 1867, until his death on April 26, 1877, was a good friend to the Y.M.C.A. and deeply mourned when he died.[66] Later the Rev. Edward Garbett M.A, the vicar of Christ Church Surbiton, became president of the Surbiton branch of the Association. In 1862 neither of these clergymen had arrived in the town, and the Rev. H. Bayley voiced what others must have felt. An even greater problem was the long hours the young men in the town had to work. Mr. C. Dann, the secretary in 1862, in his report for the preceding nine months, mentioned that despite meetings now taking place on both Mondays and Wednesdays, the attendance, satisfactory at first, had fallen off during the summer months, principally due to late closing hours. He said:

> The number of members received had been 33, of whom three had left the neighbourhood. The Committee desired to establish a reading room and library, and acknowledged the liberal spirit with which the Mayor of Kingston had subscribed a large and useful Bible – an example which they trusted would be followed by many.

A cash statement appended to Mr. Dann's report showed that the Association's expenditure had exceeded income by a sum of £2.19s 8d. The major reason for the Promotional Meeting was obviously an attempt to acquaint those in the locality that this worthy Association needed support and extra funding.[67] Although the amount of the collection was in excess of the deficit, being £3. 1s 7d, as there were two hundred people at the meeting, the average amount collected was small. Nevertheless the members of the young Association felt sufficiently confident to organise a reading room, as was announced on January 31, 1863, together with a list of those who had given subscriptions and donations (see Figure 6). Mr. Samuel Ranyard, the candle maker living in Claremont Road, who by 1881 was a county magistrate, gave ten shillings. Benjamin Looker the brick and tile manufacturer, gave the same amount, and both Mr. George Nuthall and his son, also called George, who were both confectioners, one living in Clarence Street, the other in Thames Street, gave ten shillings each. The mayor who gave the Association 'a large and useful Bible' was the Brewer William F. Hodgson, who had been mayor of Kingston in 1861.

Young Men's Christian Association
Subscriptions and Donations 31 January 1863

J.M. Strachan Esq., P, Annual Subscription	£2	2	0
Do. Donation		10	
do. Books for Library			
R.W. Lack Esq.			
V.P., Annual Subscription	£1	1	
W.F. Hodgson Esq., large Bible			
G. Constable Esq. Annual Subscription	£1	1	
J. King, Esq., do.		10	
S. Ranyard Esq., do		10	
F. Gould Esq., do		10	
B. Looker, Esq., do		10	
W.S. Roots, Esq. do		10	
Du Croz. Esq. do		10	
R. Horne, Esq., do		10	
S. Gray, Esq., do		5	
Kermock, Esq.		10	
J. Williams, Esq. donation		2	
Mr. Wheatly Annl Subscription		2	6
Windsor Esq.		10	
N.W. Lavers Esq., donation		10	
G. Nuthall Esq., Senr. Annual Subscription		10	
P. Jones, Esq., do		10	
Mr. Longhurst donation		2	6
Mr. Terry, do		1	
Collected at Public Meeting	3	1	7
C. Simpson, Esq., Annual Subscription		10	
G. Nuthall, Junr. Esq., do		10	
A. Friend, per Mr. Marshall		2	
Mrs. W.B. Jones Annual Subscription		5	
T.T. Walker Esq., donation		2	6
Mrs. Saunders, Annual Subscription		5	

Subscription and Donations will be thankfully
received and acknowledged by Mr. J. East, junr.,
Church Street, Treasurer; Mr. Marshall, junr.,
Market Place; and by the Secretary, Mr. C. Dann,
Apple Market, Kingston on Thames.

6. Subscriptions and Donations—January 31, 1863, page 1.   **(SC)**

Only six out of the fifty-one trades and businesses in Kingston Market Place on the 1861 census can be found on the subscription and donation list in 1863, although some may have donated at the public meeting. The Nuthalls did not live in the market place, but their shop was in this location. (Figure 8 shows the shop.) The Nuthalls gave ten shillings each. Mr. Frederick Gould the chemist also gave ten shillings; J. Williams, one of the five victuallers, gave two shillings; Mrs. W.B. Jones, the wife of W.B. Jones the magistrate and chemist, gave the same amount; Mrs. Saunders, who gave five shillings, was probably Sarah Saunders the pawnbroker.[68]

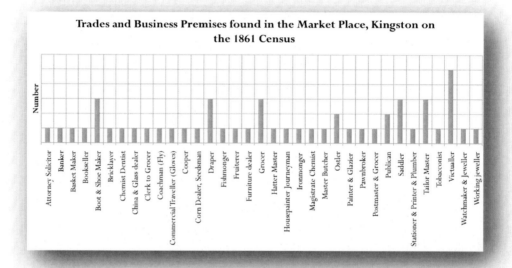

7. Calculated from the 1861 Census   (AG)

The list of subscriptions and donations dated April 9, 1864, shown in the *Surrey Comet* in that year, reveals a small increase in the prominent individuals who had donated. Among the new donations were Abraham Le Blond, the engraver and printer; William Wadbrook, the brewer; Charles Walter, the solicitor; and G. Phillipson the bookseller who also lived in the market place. All gave 10s, and J. Shrubsole gave 2s 6d. Overall the subscriptions and donations totalled just under £18 and £1 more than the previous year. The donation lists had very few names compared with the number of tradesmen in Kingston.[69] Mr. Joseph East, the brewer who lived in Church Street, provided the initial room and an additional room under the same roof for the library and reading room in the market place. The number of churchmen involved did increase after the first year and in 1868, five years after Christ Church Surbiton Hill was established, this church too supported a Y.M.C.A.

The Rev. Lawrence Byrnes had not appreciated the quick turnover of the members, in particular the secretaries, during the early stages of the Association. By the end of 1865 only forty-five members remained out of the eighty-eight who had joined since the beginning.[70] This was not peculiar to Kingston, during the nineteenth century a continuous migration of people, many under twenty years of age, moved from the countryside into the towns. By 1851 in most of the great towns newcomers outnumbered the indigenous population.[71] In the same way that George Williams started work in Bridgwater before travelling to London, by the end of the 1860s many of the early members had moved away from Kingston, one or two had died through ill-health and in 1865 one member had drowned in the Thames. Badly attended meetings, a direct result of the late closing of the shops also dogged those trying to nurture the young Association into a self-sustaining group. As we shall see later, the apparent lack of regard for the wellbeing of their young employees by those in business both irritated and enraged the Rev. Lawrence Byrnes.

8. Kingston Market Place and Thames Street circa 1898 – Nuthall's Shop is on the right of the picture.   (**CR**)

9. Kingston Market Place in November—Nuthall's Shop remains but not
timbered.   (AG 2012)

John De Fraine; March 1863

The movement appeared to succeed during 1863 until the early part of 1864. On
March 21 the 'popular young orator' Mr. John De Fraine came to Kingston to
speak to the Y.M.C.A. Although only twenty-four years of age, Mr. De Fraine was
very well known as he had featured in the press on several occasions. At
nineteen he had begun to travel and had started to address open-air meetings.
Although originally employed as a clerk by the National Temperance League, he
had begun to lecture on the beneficial affects of being a total abstainer from
alcohol. He had previously lectured in places such as Leamington Spa, Jersey,
Belfast and Newcastle before coming to Kingston. The *Newcastle Daily Chronicle*
wrote that, 'all who listen to him will be the better for his teaching.'[72] In the Eden
Street lecture room he spoke on the subject of 'How to Get On in the World.' The
Surrey Comet noted that:

> he illustrated the follies of those young men, not having the means, would
> be gentlemen; contrasting the same with the humble, plodding, steady, self-
> persevering young man. From the latter qualities, such men had risen to
> eminence and greatness. Neither was he more lenient in his remarks

towards the gentler sex and their failings, especially 'servant-girlism', exposing their frivolous and extravagant ideas in the present day, with their crinoline absurdities. And again going a step higher, among the middling classes of young women – assuming the lady-like, in the occupation of fancy work, novel reading, or spoiling good music on a very bad piano; leaving the aged mother in the back kitchen to fulfil the harder duties of the household.

The writer in the *Surrey Comet* concluded that it was 'one of the most brilliant lectures ever delivered in the town of Kingston.'[73] The Rev. Lawrence Byrnes may have hoped that some of the young men in the Kingston Association would also display a gift of oratory and on many occasions, the *Surrey Comet* reported that members gave short lectures in Association meetings.

Mr. Strachan chaired the second annual meeting of the Association held in September 1863. The report also gave the impression that the group was making headway. The *Surrey Comet* reporter wrote that, 'Mr. C. Dann read the report for the past year, which breathed throughout a Christian and unsectarian spirit. Instead of falling to the ground, as had been predicted of it, the Society had made steady progress.' A small reading room had been established but, because they could only use it for three nights a week, the arrangement did not answer their needs. Mr. Joseph East therefore found another room in the same building that could be used as a reading room and library every evening except Sundays. The Association reduced the subscription from 1s 6d to 1s per quarter and to 6d per quarter for members, and 'the committee were sanguine of success.' The funds were healthier than they had been at the last annual meeting as 'an appeal to their friends then present had extricated them from debt.' However the report continued: 'as they were incurring additional expense all voluntary subscriptions and donations would be gratefully received and books thankfully accepted.'[74]

Henry Vincent; January 1864

In January 1864 the Association invited the celebrated orator Henry Vincent to speak. Vincent was a Chartist who had been born in 1813 in High Holborn. At fifteen he had been apprenticed to a printer, joining Spottiswoode's the King's printers in London in 1833. He left the firm in 1836 after a dispute and joined the London Working Men's Association, lecturing successfully as he travelled to promote the People's Charter. Chartism emerged in the late 1830s, as part of a flood of working class dissent, the result of enormous social disruption, and industrial change with no right to protest. The Charter, with its demand for six changes, lay at the heart of Chartism. Its demands consisted of voting rights for every man aged twenty-one years of age, secret ballots, the elimination of property qualifications for members of parliament, payment for members of parliament, equal constituencies, and annual parliaments. His skill as an orator had led to the selection of Vincent as the chief speaker at the great Chartist meeting held in London in the autumn of 1838. Reports claim that he exercised a remarkable command over an audience. In December 1838, Vincent founded the *Western Vindicator* newspaper. In May the following year he was arrested and charged with having participated in 'a riotous assemblage.' He was taken to Bow Street and committed to Monmouth prison to stand trial at the ensuing assizes. Outside the court the mayor apparently had to read the Riot Act. In August 1839 Vincent was sentenced to twelve months' imprisonment. The intense feeling among the Welsh miners about Vincent's treatment in prison helped spark an armed rising of the Chartists in South Wales.

Vincent married Lucy Chappell following his release from prison, and they lived together in Bath. There he lectured, published and became associated with teetotal Chartism. He advocated popular education, free trade, and religious tolerance and frequently conducted services on Sundays in free churches and chapels as a lay preacher.[75] On January 22, 1864, invited by the young men of the Y.M.C.A., Henry Vincent lectured on 'The philosophy of true manliness' in the Kingston Assize Courts, lecture hall. The paper notes that crowds gathered in the Assize Courts long before the lecture began, and Alderman Edward Phillips, the Thames Street chemist and druggist, took the chair and introduced Mr. Vincent. The *Surrey Comet* commented:

> the highest expectations were fully realized, the gratified audience proving it by the most unusual demonstrations of approval from first to last during the evening. It would be impossible to convey any adequate conception of the brilliance, power, effect, of the oration, even by a verbatim report.

Mr. Philpott, the principal of Beamham House School in Southsea Road, proposed a vote of thanks, which Mr. Frederick Gould, the chemist and dentist, seconded, and Mr. Benjamin Looker the brick and tile manufacturer, supported.[76]

A Low State of Affairs and a Lecture from Signor Gavazzi; April 1864

The young Association appeared to flounder following Vincent's visit. The Rev. T. P. Hough spoke about the labourers in the vineyard at a Wednesday meeting in April 1864 held at the members' room in the apple market. Forty young men attended, and he said that he had 'great sympathy for his hearers, who he knew could not attend such meetings at the present except after a hard day's work.'[77]

The poor attendance continued during the latter half of 1864 through to the third annual meeting in October.[78]

Despite the problem Signor Gavazzi came to lecture on Garibaldi in November 1864.[79] It was said of Garibaldi when he came to London in 1864 that hundreds of eager admirers and curious lookers-on lined the road from the station to the house of his host, '... No King, no Emperor, had ever been thus honoured...'[80] Signor Alessandro Gavazzi had been a Barnabite monk who had left the Catholic Church to join the Italian Protestant community and became Giuseppe Garibaldi's army chaplain.[81] At the Y.M.C.A. meeting in Kingston Mr. Ranyard took the chair, and the *Surrey Comet* reporter commented 'the lecture was a good one but unfortunately the accent of the lecturer's words was unmistakably foreign, and so that at least half of it was not understood.' The reporter also wrote that, 'the earnestness of the man was undeniable...'[82] Later in 1870 Gavazzi became head of the Free Church of Italy and in 1875 founded a theological college in Rome, where he taught dogmatics, apologetics and polemics.[83]

The Rev. Lawrence Byrnes' Anger; November 4, 1865
Only half the room was filled for a public meeting at the Assize Courts on the fourth anniversary of the young Association when an angry Rev. Lawrence Byrnes rose to second the motion for the adoption of the annual report and said:

> he was ashamed of Kingston because there was not a greater meeting to encourage the young men of the town. He was ashamed of the tradesmen when he saw there was no one to take the chair at their meetings; they had to go to Teddington to get a chairman. He was happy to see Mr. Wilson (the current President) and meant no disrespect to him, but it was not proper to go year after year out of town to obtain a chairman. He also thought it a shame to think that when they wanted the presence of the clergy they had to go to Ham or Hook to obtain it, there being but one or two out of the eight or ten to come forward. He considered they ought to have the presence of the chief tradesmen. His remarks were not made in a capricious or disrespectful spirit but he felt bound to say so to show the difficulties thrown in the way of young men in maintaining their society. It was a great credit to them to go on as they did, by themselves, and increasing. He was sorry so many of the best young men left the town just when they were getting most useful; he wished they would stay so as to improve their class. His desire was that when the present race of tradesmen were gone, for they must go in time, they should be followed by Christian young men.[84]

The *Surrey Comet* only mentioned the Y.M.C.A. once during 1866, reporting in September that the young men were holding 'penny readings,' and no anniversary had been observed that year because, 'the affairs of the society were so low that it was considered expedient to dispense with the annual meeting.' [85]

Long Hours and an Unhealthy Year; 1866

On September 29, 1866, the *Surrey Comet* printed a letter to the editor entitled 'The White Slaves of Kingston' that read as follows:

> Dear Sir – Will you kindly give your influence on behalf of the white slaves of Kingston. During the past six months we have as assistants been engaged most of us from 14 to 15 hours a day in continuous toil relieved only for an hour during the whole day. As the Winter months are now arriving we are anxious to have some time for relaxation, recreation, and mental improvement, and as this can be accomplished without injury to any class we earnestly solicit your influence. If sir the affluent may suit their own inclination as to the amount of work they will perform, and the time they will perform it in, and six hours be a fair day's labour for the bank clerk, and even ten hours of work for the artisan and labourer, surely something less than 14 or 15 hours toil may be expected from those whom necessity compels to stand wearily and drearily behind a counter six days, week in week out. I am sir &c
>
> A WHITE SLAVE OF KINGSTON [86]

Not only were young men expected to work long hours, but Kingston in 1866 was very unhealthy.

Cholera had visited Kingston in 1841, and it was agreed that the mayor and five other councillors should consider the sewerage of the borough, although they seem not to have done anything and another cholera outbreak occurred in 1849. If the town had adopted the Public Health Act, 1848, Kingston would have been able to raise finance from the rates to pay for improvements.[87] It didn't do so until 1855, and by then the Surbiton residents backed by Coutts had decided to become arbiters of their own destiny and promoted their own bill the Surbiton Improvement Act, 1855. [88] Kingston was therefore left with lower rates and no idea how to progress.[89]

The situation became even more problematic in 1863 with the arrival of the railway.[90] The Census Enumerators Returns for Kingston in 1861 show a population of over 17,600. Ten years later the population was nearly 27,500. These figures include Surbiton but Richardson's population statistics in Appendix XII reveal that Surbiton was growing at a much slower pace because land release here was controlled to some extent and landlords, such as Coutts, appear deliberately to have chosen not to build in an inflationary market.[91] Much of the increase in residency occurred a short distance from the actual town of

Kingston. The railway line reaching Kingston made the town more accessible and the 1871 census shows residents born in most of the English counties, from Ireland, Scotland and Wales living alongside others born in more than seventy locations outside the British Isles.

Cholera again returned to Kingston in 1866. Sixty-seven residents had died between June 1 and August 31, 1865. During the same period in 1866 the number had risen to ninety-three, more than half the result of a range of highly infectious diseases. During these three months cholera killed seven people, seven died from diarrhoea, two from typhus, one from typhoid, eleven from phthisis (consumption) seventeen from measles, nine from whooping cough, two from bronchitis and three from pneumonia. Two-thirds of those who had died were children. Dr. Price Jones, the medical officer, bravely completed a house to house inspection. In the back lanes he found seventy-seven houses, nine of which were dilapidated. Of these:

> 23 required lime-whiting and cleansing, 44 had open privies, 9 only had water closets, 23 were supplied with water from the Lambeth Waterworks and 18 were without water.
> In the Wanderings, Young's-buildings, Fairfield-road, Thames-street, Canbury Fields, Hope-avenue and Church-street 183 houses were inspected, of which 19 were in a dilapidated state, 36 required cleansing, there were 127 open privies, 13 of which were dilapidated; 17 had trapped water-closets, 17 open pans, 41 houses had water from the Lambeth Waterworks, 8 were without water.
> Fifty-six actions were served, and upwards of that number received verbal instructions to disinfect, cleanse, and otherwise purify their dwelling, privies, and out-houses. All were liberally supplied with chloride of lime, so as to ensure immediate disinfection. The Back-lanes, Horsefair and adjacent street were weekly disinfected with Burnett's Fluid and carbolic acid. The streets and lanes were flushed weekly with water by hose fitted to plugs, and drains and gullies daily disinfected.

During the twenty-five days after August 31, the nineteen further deaths did not include typhus, cholera, diarrhoea, typhoid, smallpox or measles, and people thought that the sanitary measures undertaken had been beneficial. The report stated that the 'Divine Command of wash and be clean' had worked.[92]

The sanitary measures did not provide a long-term solution. Making landlords responsible for keeping property in good-order—or in some cases pulling down the old housing—would have reduced the problem of disease more effectively. Once the town had controlled the outbreak of cholera, Kingston dispensed with the services of the medical officer.[93] Kingston Council had always been slow to tackle problems, and, although the Artizans and Labourers Dwellings Act, 1868 gave the council legal powers to enforce landlords to keep their properties in good order, they did very little. Later during the 1870s and 1880s the Y.M.C.A. were to find it difficult to keep their rooms in Brick Lane in reasonable repair. They were not alone as many of the houses in Kingston at this time were poorly constructed with inadequate sanitation.

An Association in Difficulty; 1867

The fifth anniversary of the Kingston Y.M.C.A. did not take place until October 6, 1867. Mr. F. Gould, by this time a J.P., took the chair, the new vicar of Kingston the Rev. Alfred Williams opened the proceedings with prayer before a crowded audience that contained several churchmen including the Rev. E. Garbett of Christ Church, Surbiton. The Y.M.C.A. was not thriving. Mr. Sawer, the current secretary, told the meeting that their liabilities were £13.13s towards which they only had a balance of £3.11s.

> Last year the affairs of the Society were so low that it was considered expedient to dispense with the Annual Meeting … They met twice a week – on Monday for prayer and on Wednesday evening for biblical discussion or to hear a lecture. The reading room had been closed for some months, as the funds of the association did not permit the extra expense necessarily incurred in the daily supply of papers, lighting, etc. The numbers of members at present on the books was 19 … The association felt their want of success was the lack of influential support from persons of standing in the town – not that many gentlemen in the neighbourhood had not given them great assistance but what they asked for was a more general support...

Before the end of the meeting the mayor Joseph East, to whom the Association owed £10, said that he was willing to forgo the amount.[94]

During the sixth anniversary in November 1868, Mr. Carn read the report in which he said that they had moved to new and less expensive premises in the Temperance Hall in Brick Lane, and, whereas previously the cost had been £26, the current accommodation cost £16.18s per annum. The Association now only owed £5. The reading room again opened every evening from seven till ten, and was supplied with papers and books that could be changed every Tuesday and Friday from eight till ten p.m. The number of members who renewed their subscriptions had been sixty.[95] On December 16, 1868, the members and friends of the Association took tea together at the Temperance Lyceum, and, as the meeting did not commence until eight o'clock, to suit the convenience of young men who were engaged in business, the arrangement resulted in securing a numerous gathering.[96]

The Departure of the Rev. Lawrence Byrnes; 1869

Lawrence Byrnes decided to leave Kingston and move to Clifton in Bristol sometime between the end of 1868 and the beginning of 1869. The *Surrey Comet* on May 8, 1869 detailed the farewell address to the young men in which Byrnes urged them to read Paley's *Evidences*.[97] Later that month, Byrnes and his family left Kingston. Sturney writes that from time to time Byrnes 'returned to preach at his first church.'[98] There is however no further mention of his connection with the Kingston Y.M.C.A.

Why did Lawrence Byrnes leave the area in 1869? His condemnation of the Kingston traders, some of whom could have been members of his congregation, may have been partially to blame for his move to Clifton in Bristol. During his last two years at the Congregational Church, there were hints that some of the members were 'out of sympathy' with his teaching.[99] The *Surrey Comet* dated March 14, 1868, however, contains a notice about a church meeting at which Mr. Byrnes acknowledged the feeling and sympathy prayers in his affliction. At the time of his leaving there is a hint that the move may have been due to the health of his family.[100]

Byrnes did return to Kingston on several occasions to give talks and sermons, but his wife and children remained in Bristol. On September 16, 1871, the *Surrey Comet* reported that he had made a successful ascent of Mont Blanc on August 26, 1871 from Chamoney and that he was 'the 449th person to do so.'[101] Lydia Byrnes died in the early months of 1876 at the age of fifty-one.[102] In 1877 a new church was built on the site of the old Clifton church. It had a large west window in geometric gothic with side lancets and a timber ceiling.[103] On the 1881 census Lawrence Byrnes can be found living with his children, his nineteen-year-old twin sons Lawrence and Henry and his sixteen-year-old daughter Alice, in Linden Lodge, Clifton, Gloucestershire. He continued as the Independent Minister of Pembroke Chapel, until 1890, dying aged eighty on July 4, 1902.[104] Unfortunately the Pembroke Chapel, Clifton was closed in 1930.

The Kingston Y.M.C.A. wasn't the only association with difficulties. The 1860s was a difficult decade as many of the English branches declined. It is uncertain why this decline happened but in 1861 the branches listed in England totalled one hundred and thirty-two. In 1867 only ninety-four remained.[105]

WHAT HAPPENED AFTER 1869

After 1869

Activity after 1869 was intermittent and diverse. There was a lecture in February 1870 on 'St Paul's Missionary Journeys.'[106] At the end of July 1870 Alderman Gould spoke on the 'science' of Phrenology at the lecture hall Bridge Foot.[107] The *Surrey Comet* reported that:

> the walls behind what may be called the platform were hung with numerous diagrams illustrating different constitutional temperaments, as the sanguine, the nervous, the lymphatic and the bilious (an example of the latter type being found in a portrait of Judas in Leonardo da Vinci's "Last Supper") and portraits of divers characters who have flourished in various ages of the world, including those of Tasso, Nero, Pope Alexander, and Melanethon, the friend of the great German Reformer Martin Luther … Arranged upon a table in front of the lecturer were a crowd of plaster casts taken from the heads of men of genius, murderers, and idiots … Mr. Gould … stated that twenty-three years had passed away since he last lectured on phrenology in this town and since then the science had gradually come to be accepted in most quarters … [108]

In October J. Lee, Esq., a Fellow of the Royal Geographic Society, lectured on the Eddystone Lighthouse with Alderman Gould again in the chair. Well executed diagrams were on display, and Miss Ranyard lent a model of the lighthouse in stone. Not many attended the anniversary commemorated in the same month even though the tea was held back until eight o'clock.[109] In January 1871 the Rev. A. McAuslane of London lectured at the Assize Courts on the 'Life and Character of Oliver Cromwell.' The *Surrey Comet* office and various other addresses in the town sold tickets, the front seats selling for 6d, back seats for 3d. and a few reserved at 1s. Mr. Gybbon Spilbury was scheduled to lecture on 'Jerusalem Rediscovered' the following week.[110] The last mention of the Y.M.C.A. before the new activity in 1874 was the celebration of the anniversary in November 1871. This was held in the lecture hall, Bridge Foot. Although the Vicar of Kingston, the Rev. A. Williams, was said to be in the chair, he came in late and apologised as he had been double booked and had another engagement at the Wood Street schools.

However the report was as follows:

> The society has languished of late in consequence of not having received the hearty co-operation it had a right to expect from Christians belonging to the various denominations in the town; while one cause of its present lack of prosperity is attributed to the introduction of secular entertainments, which are all very well in their proper place, but are held to be quite foreign in the spirit and objects of a Christian Association.[111]

This reference was probably to the 'penny readings' mentioned earlier:

> An effort is now being made to resuscitate the society, and place it upon a more scriptural basis—a task which has kindly been undertaken by Mr. F. Gibson, a gentleman who has come to reside in Norbiton, and who takes a great interest in the work of these societies.

The *Surrey Comet* report continued:

> Since many of the audience knew Mr. Gibson so well, the Rev. Williams 'could only say he rejoiced in the good providence of God which had sent Mr. Gibson among them and that he had entered on such an important work as this.'

> Mr. Finlay Gibson, a tutor in classics and mathematics sketched out the principles and objects of a young men's Christian Association. He combated the opinions of those who argued that the basis of such a society as this should be broad enough to allow of the introduction of instruction classes, and innocent amusements, such as sacred concerts, &c., and quoted from a report from Mr. Shipton, the secretary of the Parent society, in order to show the baneful effect of providing secular entertainments in connection with societies of this description ... he had not lived in Kingston long before he discovered there was a great deal of infidelity in the place. Indeed he had never met in any other town with so much outspoken infidelity. One instance of this was given in the case of a boy whom the lecturer observed watching an orchard with the view of stealing some of the fruit. When he reminded the boy that God's eye was upon him, the reply he made was, "Ah, if there is a God." A young man asked his own father if there was a future world, and the father's answer was, "No; it is a pack of lies." ... He believed there was also a great deal of secret infidelity, and he alluded to the case of quite a young lad in the town who had asked him a question which had exercised the minds of many Christians, and had been a favourite argument with infidels. These doubts ought to be removed by having classes for biblical instruction...

The Rev. H. Bayley said:

> they must all have felt deeply impressed with the earnest address which Mr. Gibson had given them. He was very glad this association was revived again, and he hoped the revival would long continue, and become a great blessing to the town.[112]

Finlay Gibson correctly asserted that William Edwyn Shipton opposed secular entertainments. William Shipton was elected Secretary of the London Young Men's Christian Association in 1851. He had joined the Y.M.C.A. and became a volunteer worker in 1849, but he moved up in rank and by 1855 to 1885 managed the conferences held in the European capitals. He was said to be 'a striking and eminently sensible speaker.'[113] He did, however, have strong views on various issues, perhaps because of his early life.[114] He was orphaned at the age of four, and spent his childhood in the London Orphan Asylum at Clapton.[115] In 1859 Shipton wrote that he would be 'glad if the Brethren could see their way clearly to confine themselves entirely to those religious agencies which were peculiarly the work of the Association.' Shipton was not alone in his opposition to educational involvement. Evangelicals doubted education.[116] Their uncertainty rested partly on a perceived threat of science to the basic principles of Christianity. Darwin's theories of evolution frightened many people. Mr. Philpott of the Surbiton Academy, a supporter of the Kingston Y.M.C.A., voiced the concerns that many would have felt in 1861:

> learned objections which most people could not answer, often did much mischief to the mind, and were like horrible dreams, people did not believe them, but yet could not entirely shake off the impression they had made. Young men should arm themselves by an experience of the Truth of the Gospel against all literary or critical objections. He denounced mere secular education from which the Bible should be excluded, and urged that in such a busy age the Church of Christ should be astir.[117]

It is also possible that evangelical Christians failed to promote education during the 1860s because apprentices had so little leisure, and young lives were often cut short by premature death. Time spent on 'winning souls for Christ' appeared to be more important than evening classes.

Many of the young men who joined the Y.M.C.A. were nonetheless interested in improvement, and the library catalogue in the Aldersgate Street Association was, according to Binfield, 'far beyond the strict requirements of the Y.M.C.A.' The members of this branch not only had access to religious books but also biography, history, philosophy and poetry (Keats, Longfellow, Milton and Wordsworth) and much more.[118] For the Y.M.C.A. change came slowly through a variety of channels. In 1864, when the Temperance Hall and Working Men's Institute started in Kingston, the Association had an obvious rival. The *Surrey Comet* stated: 'All persons without restriction' could join the new Institute, the subscription being 1s 6d per annum or 2d. a week. Newspapers such as the *Telegraph, Morning Star, Standard, Illustrated News, Builder, Bee-Hive, News of the*

World, and *Weekly Record* were available, as were games and activities such as chess, drafts, solitaire, dominoes and singing classes.[119] By 1864 the situation in the various associations was also changing. The Leeds Y.M.C.A. had science and art classes.[120]

Changes to the aims and constitution of the New York organisation were also significant. The early associations had only allowed membership to those belonging to an evangelical church, but, following the devastation of the Civil War, the New York Y.M.C.A redefined its constitution. Robert McBurney, who had previously worked as a clerk whilst engaged in evangelistic work in the Methodist Church, joined the New York Y.M.C.A. Together with others he amended the rules in 1864, allowing membership to all young men under the age of forty who were of good moral character and who paid $2 in annual fees. Following these changes but continuing to be involved in young men's spiritual needs, the New York Association also cared about housing, employment and social wellbeing. In 1866 the constitution was revised to read 'The object of this Association shall be the improvement of the spiritual, mental, social and physical condition of young men.' This 'four-fold work,' programme was said to refocus on the 'whole man.' McBurney's ideas, together with those of other key players were to remain influential, and said to be 'widely emulated in other Associations.'[121] By 1871, New York offered courses in vocal music, mathematics, mechanical drawing, natural sciences, bookkeeping, writing, French, German and Spanish.[122]

Following the report in November 1871 when Mr. Finlay Gibson spoke to the young men in the lecture hall, Bridge Foot, there was a talk in December entitled 'True Manliness.' Reference to the Kingston Association then ceased until 1874.[123] In September of that year the *Surrey Comet* reported the following:

THE YOUNG MEN'S CHRISTIAN ASSOCIATION —

The members of this association, who meet at the Gospel Hall, Applemarket, intend holding evening classes during the coming winter.[124]

A NEW BEGINNING

JANUARY 1874 – JANUARY 1880

A New Beginning

The Committee of young men who met in the Gospel Hall in the Kingston Apple Market, on Saturday evening January 10, 1874, appeared to be much more self assured than those who had met under the guidance of the Rev. Lawrence Byrnes and later received a lecture from Mr. Finlay Gibson. There is no evidence that the original Y.M.C.A. started in 1858 had ended, but the *Surrey Comet* of October 1877 reported that a Y.M.C.A. had been started in the Baptist Chapel in 1872. Meetings for Bible study had been held, and in May 1874 a tract distribution society had been formed among the members and thirty-five-thousand tracts and books had been circulated. In 1875 cottage services and outdoor preaching had taken place in Teddington and Hampton Wick.[125] The article implies that although the Rev. Lawrence Byrnes had encouraged the Y.M.C.A. started in 1858 to stand alone, at least some of the members had gravitated to the Brick Lane Baptist Chapel after he had left Kingston, possibly encouraged by Mr. Gibson, who emphasised the spiritual side of the work.

The group who met in the Gospel Hall in 1874 clearly disassociated themselves from this Association. Some of the young men who had wanted to start the new Association may have been members of the original Y.M.C.A. and wanted to return to a society located outside a church and with a reading room. They also wanted to provide evening classes, a common feature in other Y.M.C.A.s, in particular the Aldersgate Street Association.[126] The meetings in 1874 and subsequent meetings of this new Association, the future Kingston Y.M.C.A, give the impression that the course of action followed had been considered very carefully before their first meeting. Funds were available, and the group had prepared what they wanted to achieve in advance.

The Baptist Church continued to house the remains of the 1872 Association, and by 1880 the minister was referring to their group as 'the Y.M.C.A. in connection with the Baptist Chapel.' The minister the Rev. H. Bayley, explained the reasons for the separate existence of the two Associations, both still functioning in 1880 and located at each end of Brick Lane, at an anniversary service of the Baptist Y.M.C.A. Mr. Bayley said that:

> while admitting that unity was strength he was not altogether prepared to support that idea. He believed that while they could find, as they did here, a body of young men prepared to carry out such a programme as that before them, they were in their right place, and in that way would be better able to influence young men than by joining in a larger association, because they knew those with whom they were in the habit of meeting in their ordinary places of worship on Sundays, and they also knew their friends who were likely to assist them in carrying on the work … he thought he could show, if necessary, very good reasons for their separate existence here as a Young Men's Christian Association in connection with this place of worship. The association referred to by the chairman (the other Y.M.C.A. not attached to the Baptist church) had been defunct and resuscitated since this association had been formed. This one had never been defunct, and if they had been amalgamated, the probability is that this Association might have died out.[127]

The 1858 organisation possibly had become defunct and another formed in 1872 in the Baptist Church, later taking the title of the 'Baptist Young Men's Christian Association.' Although the newly formed 1874 Kingston Y.M.C.A. had complications in 1879, it continued despite difficulties. On the other hand, the Rev. H. Bayley may have been alluding to Surbiton Y.M.C.A., an organisation started in 1868 but closed in 1879, and in 1880 the Baptist minister would not have known that this Association reopened in May 1882 and by 1885 had amalgamated with the 1874 Kingston Association. Mr. Bayley did not mention that another reason for his retaining the Y.M.C.A. in the Baptist Church may have related to the decline in church members and worries that joining another organisation would reduce the commitment of those involved in their place of worship. As we shall see later, many other churches probably reacted in the same way.

The meeting in Kingston Apple Market at the beginning of 1874 represented a move towards a fresh-start by certain young men, and may have included some of the Brick Lane Baptists. These young men, some of whom were working in London, would have known what was happening in other Y.M.C.A.s in the city. They mention Aldersgate Street branch in the minutes, and they probably knew what was happening in the New York Association, although it is improbable to suggest that they were aiming to copy their New York counterparts.[128] Nevertheless they were prepared to move away from those who wanted the Association to remain wholly devoted to religious activities.

It is also significant that although a meeting on July 14 resolved that all the ministers of the town and leading men should be requested to act as vice-presidents, on August 11 this new Kingston Association agreed that 'the election of vice-presidents be postponed until some need is felt for them, or some members bring the matter forward.'[129] The young men who joined together in January 1874 obviously did not want outside interference, as they did not consider the matter of a president and vice-presidents until more than two years later on January 31, 1877, three years after the initial meeting.[130]

10. This picture is labelled 'Old Buildings in Apple Market demolished, Kingston.' It is generally agreed however that this is a picture of buildings in what used to be called the 'Horsefair' in Kingston but these buildings would have been similar to those found in Kingston's Apple Market in 1874. (CR)

Among the usual features of the Committee such as the coming and going of the members, religious services and the paying of bills, two events of major importance occurred during the next two years. These events set the character of the Association for the future. The first involved the commencement of evening classes and the second the leasing of Zoar Chapel as the settled meeting place of the Association. Appendix 1, page 216, sets out the minutes of the first meeting, with the three resolutions stated at this meeting on January 10, 1874, standing out as the centre of the new initiative:

Resolution 3:

> that a reading room be opened for the purpose of gathering together the young men of Kingston & neighbourhood, & affording them an opportunity of spending their leisure evening hours with profit & pleasure.

Resolution 4:

> that the room be opened on Thursday next 15th inst. to commence with a cup of tea at 8.15 p.m. (to which special invitations be taken round).

Resolution 9

> that the following notice be placed somewhere in the room:

> This room will be open free to all young men employed in business from 7 o'clock p.m. to 10 o'clock p.m. every evening (Sundays excepted). Books, papers, periodicals etc. will be provided which are not to be taken away from the room. There will be a class for the study of the Scriptures, held every Sunday afternoon between 3.30 p.m. & 4.30 p.m. at which all are earnestly invited to attend.

Mr. Stringer and Mr. Newson were to provide 'all the necessary eatables and drinkables for the tea.'[131]

Kingston had never taken advantage of the Public Libraries Act 1850, and residents did not benefit from a free public library until sometime between 1881 and 1882.[132] Although the books, papers, periodicals were not to be taken away, the Y.M.C.A. room would be open from seven o'clock to ten o'clock every evening 'FREE to all young men employed in business' (Sundays excepted).

The advertisement in the *Surrey Comet*, cost 10/-, and one hundred posters were printed, fifty of these to be placarded in the town and the remainder exhibited in shop windows. On May 20, 1874, a report from the treasurer showed a credit balance of £7.17s 3d remaining in the funds that had been available. Six months later on July 14, 1874, it was proposed and seconded 'that the association be united with the London Association.'[133] In Table 1 shown on page 231, it will be seen that not all those who were present at the initial meetings continued their attendance into the latter part of the year. The mobility of the earlier period continued into the second half of the nineteenth century.

Who were the young men who met in the Gospel Hall in 1874?

Finding the answer to this question has been complicated because committee members were recorded with an initial rather than a full forename and as 1874 fell between census dates, many individuals came and went without being named on the census. We can identify some of those who attended the first committee meetings between January and July 1874 (see Table 1). Mr. Edgar Lindsey Stringer served as treasurer. He lived in Shrewsbury House in The

Crescent in Surbiton with his father, mother, sister, three servants and the coachman. His father was a shipbuilder, and in January 1874 Mr. Stringer was nineteen years of age. The secretary, Mr. Jasper Newson, came into the area and left between census periods. We know about him because Mr. Walter Hill, son of a later secretary of the movement, mentions him in a paper.[134] Birth and christening records indicate that Mr. Newson was twenty-two years old in 1874. Mr. Hill writes that Mr. Jasper Newson 'moved abroad due to ill health.' Mr. Newson was appointed secretary at the first meeting and remained constant in his attendance until September 1876 when his inability to attend committee meetings resulted in his communicating in writing with the Committee. He resigned in July 1877. In the 1874 to 1879 minute book his address is listed as Suffolk Villa, Knights Park, Kingston.

11. Clarence Street—Kingston upon Thames, circa 1905   (CR)

Mr. John Morten who lived in 'Frascati' in St. James Road, Surbiton with his father, mother, sister and two housemaids, was the third committee member. His father Frederick Morten was 'master' of Miller and Morten, a company with fifty-four employees. In 1891 Mr. Morten junior is described on the census as a salesman. In 1874 he would have been twenty-two years old. He attended the first meeting in January 1874 and then left the area but returned and rejoined in December 1881. His sister Mary married William Walter on the 16 January 1879.

(William Walter joined the Kingston Association at the end of 1874 and eventually took the role of association treasurer.) Thomas Francesco Lardelli, who had been born in Brighton, lived in Ewell Road Surbiton in 1871 but had moved to Victoria Road in 1881. He worked at the Stock Exchange as a stockbroker's clerk. In 1874 he was twenty-three years old. Henry Rimer does not appear either on the 1871 or 1881 census, but his profession was entered as solicitor when he married for the second time in 1884 at All Saints Church Kingston to Catherine Ellen Mitchell. In 1874 he would have been thirty-six years old. H. Maxwell, was probably Herbert Maxwell, an eighteen-year-old law publisher. On the 1881 census he lived in Highfield, The Avenue, with his elder brother Arthur W. Maxwell, an insurance clerk who became one of the Surbiton Association secretaries. The identity of W. Maxwell who attended on January 21 is uncertain. Finally Joseph Hobgood (Hapgood) in 1871 was working for Frank Bentall, and living in Clarence Street over the Bentall shop. Clarence Street is shown in Figure 11, but the picture does not include the shop. By 1881 Joseph's address had changed to 48 Denmark Hill, Lambeth, and he was described as a draper. In 1874 he would have been twenty-three years of age.

The addresses of two other young men appear at the back of the 1874 to 1879 minute book. They are W. Wallis, 33 Albert Road, Norbiton, and G. Siggers, 61 Cleveland Road Surbiton, but the minute book does not mention their ages or occupations. Nor does it mention J. Dale, H. Carter and R. Wright, the young men who made up the Y.M.C.A. Committee in 1874. Of those we do know only Mr. Hapgood lived above a shop; the others resided in comfortable homes with excellent prospects, and even Mr. Hapgood had bettered his situation by 1881. Although there appears to be a contrast between this new Committee and the young men who had been nurtured by the Rev. Lawrence Byrnes and later lectured by Mr. Finlay Gibson, some of these young men were undoubtedly part of the original association. The difference was that by 1874 their opinions had matured and they were not in complete harmony with Mr. Finlay Gibson.

New Members and Evening Classes; September 1874

On September 1, 1874, a decision was made to 'reach the young men of Kingston by the formation (if practicable) of Evening Classes', and on this date Frank Newson, brother of Jasper Newson, joined the Association.[135] Later Frank was to play a prominent role. Mr. Hertslet, an Officer of the Metropolitan Board of Works, also joined the Committee about this time but will be considered later.[136] Despite association members not wanting a president or vice-presidents, they agreed that they should invite Captain Cundy to act as chairman.[137]

12. Members of the reading room and classes January 1874—May 1879 minute book   **(YMCA)**

13. Members of the reading room and classes January 1874—May 1879 minute book   **(YMCA)**

14. Members of the reading room and classes January 1874 – May 1879 minute book   **(YMCA)**

In 1871 Captain Cundy was living next door to Edwin Stringer in The Crescent, and by 1874 he was obviously known and liked by the members of the Y.M.C.A. Born in Shoreditch, Captain Cundy had been a glove manufacturer although he had spent some time in the army as he retained the title of captain. (In 1881 he was living in Norbury House, Surbiton.)

Before the start of the evening classes it was decided that the young men were to be invited to a tea on September 24, at a charge of 4d. The 'tea meeting' was to consider the subject of classes, and it was further agreed that fifty posters should be printed and circulated about the town.[138] The classes were started, and the lists of those who became members of the reading room and those who attended classes are to be found at the back of the 1874 to 1879 minute book and are shown in Figures 12, 13 and 14. In December 1874 the Association printed a further one hundred programmes, and this time seventy-two young men arrived for a 'tea meeting' on January 14, 1875.[139]

The classes were again successful, and at a public meeting held on October 1, 1875, the Association decided that the formation of further classes for the winter months should be as follows:

Arithmetic	Tuesday	8 – 9
Reading & Writing	Tuesday	9 – 10
Shorthand	Wednesday	9 – 10
Singing	Friday	9 – 10

(if the master could be arranged for)

The charge for members of the reading room was to be one shilling per quarter and subscription for each class was 6d.[140] Any young man could use the reading room and join the evening classes, but the Committee only admitted those who were evangelical Christians into the membership of the Association. Initially a member proposed a prospective member, and the Aldersgate Street branch 'membership letter' to inquire into suitability was used. The Committee then decided whether they could join. Obtaining answers to the 'membership letters' proved difficult as they required decided evidence of a prospective member's conversion. The Committee therefore changed the procedure to allow new members to be proposed by a current member and accepted after a satisfactory enquiry into suitability.

Zoar Chapel; 1876

By the end of 1875 the premises used by the Kingston Association were clearly insufficient. Given the continuing close relationship with the Baptist Church in Brick Lane, the Association sometimes used the school room belonging to the church, but in April 1876 it decided that they must find more desirable premises 'for the more efficient carrying out of the work of the Association.'[141] They therefore took the opportunity of leasing Zoar Chapel, a building very close to the Congregational Church. *Phillipson's Almanack and Directory 1876* lists Zoar Chapel as the first building in Brick Lane east from Eden Street, whilst the 1880 edition refers to this building as the 'Y.M.C.A.' Sturney calls it 'the old Meeting House,' the name indicating a Quaker connection. Ayliffe in 1913 refers to the premises as 'a building rented by Mr. Warren, of Hampton Court, who for many years conducted religious services there. This building was the first home of the Y.M.C.A. in Kingston, and ultimately came into the possession of Mr. C. Burrows.'[142]

In 1875 Mr. Arthur Edward Fricker, the son of the founder of the Eagle Brewery, was landlord his father Mr. Thomas Hunter Fricker, having died in January 1873. Mr. Arthur Edward Fricker himself died in January 1886.[143] The 1881 census shows Charles Burrows as the proprietor of a grocer's shop at 11 Eden Street. The Y.M.C.A. minutes dated October 28, 1885 state that Charles

Burrows lived next door to the Association rooms and during that year requested to lease their cellar for £5 per annum.[144] When the Y.M.C.A. left their rooms in 1890, Mr. Burrows may have extended his grocer's shop to include that of the former Y.M.C.A. as the side of the rooms were connected to the back of Burrows' shop.

15. The picture shows the United Reformed Church on the right. It has been calculated that Mr. Burrows' shop would have been to the left of the church where there is now the pavement (bottom right). Zoar Chapel and Gilbert House would have been behind the shop, starting approximately where the Richard Mayo Centre now stands. To the left, at the far end of the street, with a cross on the outside of the building, stands the Union Street (Brick Lane) Baptist Church.   (**AG 2012**)

Zoar Chapel was old, shabby and even by nineteenth century standards lacking in basic amenities. The Association had therefore prepared a specification of the repairs to the Chapel and House and annexed it to the Draft Agreement. The landlord agreed to all the requirements except that of the placing of matchboards round the hall. As the Committee did not think this exception important, the agreement was signed. They also agreed to buy from the present leaseholders eight gas burners, four roller blinds and thirty-seven hat hooks for the sum of £4. Mr. Phillipson's offer of fifty windsor chairs for £5 was also accepted.[145] The minutes stated that the money to pay for the furniture for the rooms and library would be forthcoming from the collection at the door following 'a Lecture of an interesting, but strictly Christian character', to be arranged and held with the kind permission of the Rev. A. Williams, in the Wood Street school room.[146]

Compared with the 1866 fundraising activities in New York where 'rental space' was used to finance and support property development, the Kingston Association premises were antiquated.[147] Nevertheless the Kingston Association did use a form of rental space to finance its project. We know from various sources that Zoar Chapel and the house next door (Gilbert House) cost £30 per annum to rent. Gilbert House was a small cottage attached to the Association's premises. Mr. Cooper, a house painter by trade, had become a member of the Association in November 1875 and was allowed to occupy Gilbert House. The cost of his rent, which was paid to the Kingston Association, was set at £10 a year, but the agreement stated that Mr. Cooper had to pay his own rates and taxes if he had any.[148] Some uncertainty concerning the lease of the Association's premises remains, but the minutes mention that the agreement with Mr. Cooper was similar to that of the Association. Mr. Cooper's lease ran for three years (wanting three days) from June 24, 1876.[149] This duration is confirmed when in May 1879 the minutes note that the lease was about to expire and should be continued again, this time for a year from June 24, 1879.[150]

Having Mr. Cooper in the cottage next door paying rent was very useful, particularly since Zoar Chapel did not have toilet facilities. Although he was not given the title of caretaker and part-time handyman, Mr. Cooper acted in this capacity. After the agreement had been signed he was asked to paint the words 'The Kingston Young Men's Christian Association' on 'the outside wall of the building in 6 inch block letters.' In January 1879 when he painted the reading room, the Committee paid him 10/- over his estimate of 14/-. Later that year he was paid 5/- for 'Beating Matting and extra work attending annual meeting', and in September he received a (reduced) charge for the cleaning of the premises, a sum of 13/-.[151] Mr. Cooper also had the texts on the walls reframed, found somebody to repair a large table on the premises, and spent time looking for a lamp to go above the door of the building. He whitewashed, mended the windows, bought bookshelves for the library, and, when he found a suitable lamp, painted the Association's name on it. When the Association wanted to procure a harmonium to improve the singing at the devotional meetings one of the Committee mentioned that Mr. Cooper had a harmonium for sale at a modest price. Unfortunately, an inspection by the secretary, found the harmonium to be unsuitable, and the Association had to buy one for £5. 5s 0d.[152]

The fact that Zoar Chapel was old and shabby did not deter individuals from renting the premises for occasional meetings. As soon as the Y.M.C.A. moved into the premises, Mr. Bayley, the Baptist minister at the other end of Brick Lane, requested that the Sunday School Union be allowed to use a room once a month, on payment of a guinea per annum. The use was agreed on the understanding that the permission could be revoked at any time by a month's notice.[153]

Presidents, Vice-presidents and Frank Hertslet becomes Secretary

The Association reintroduced the subject of the appointment of a president and vice-presidents on January 31, 1877. Two of the eight members of the Committee opposed the proposal, but, as the other six were in favour of the move, Mr. E.P. Williams was asked to be president and nine local vicars and ministers together with Messrs. Charles Walter, Bedford Marsh, Finlay Gibson and Captain Cundy requested to become vice-presidents. Mr. E.P. Williams declined the position of president, but Captain Cundy agreed to replace him.[154] The annual meeting on March 6, 1877, was of particular importance because George Williams came to speak to the Kingston Association. Captain Cundy was in the chair, and a number of local vicars, ministers and Messrs E. Williams, and Walter attended. Mr. Rimer read the report for the year which stated that the members totalled forty with the average attendance at meetings being between eight and ten but occasionally as high as fifteen. Bible classes and devotional meetings ran throughout the year on Thursdays and Sundays.[155]

Although apparently progressing well at the beginning of 1877, after July and during most of 1878 the Association drifted without any real secretarial involvement.[156] On July 4, 1877, Mr. Jasper Newson resigned. He had not attended meetings for more than a year, and his failing health had made continuing on the Committee impossible. The Committee also noted the death of the Rev. A. Williams, the Vicar of All Saints Parish Church, and someone who had shown great concern for the Association.[157] Although a year after his brother resigned, on July 4, 1878, Frank Newson joined the Committee, as did William Parslow in November of that year and were later to become the backbone of the Association, they initially lacked the experience necessary to take a positive role.[158] Various members were asked to act as secretary but felt unable or considered their health would not allow them to fulfil the position. Fortunately in November, by the time Mr. Rimer the only original member of the 1874 Committee had given in his notice, Frank Hertslet had agreed to become the secretary.[159] He formally accepted the position, writing, 'I trust that I may be able to work up the Association and then hand over the secretaryship to some more suitable member.'[160] Mr. Hertslet was thirty years old and living at 1 Eden Place, Eden Street. From this point in time the Association appeared to take on a more purposeful approach, but elements of disharmony, started to appear within their number.

Association Rules and a Ballot; 1878

Mr. Hertslet first had to draft the rules. He reported to the Committee he had 'gone through all the written minutes since 1874 but could not find that any complete set of rules had been settled for the Association. ... He had therefore drafted out some rules based on the first eight rules of the Parent Society.' These had been sent to each member of the Committee for perusal. The rules were agreed on October 3, 1878 and can be found in Appendix II, page 217. After their acceptance two-hundred and fifty-copies were printed.[161] The Association placed a list of the current members in the reading room, with Mr Rutland Saunders accepting the office of librarian.

Mr. Rutland Saunders had been born in 1863 and in 1878 was probably no more than fifteen-years-old. On December 19, 1878, as the new librarian, he presented a 'Draft set of Rules for the reading room and library', which can be found in Appendix III, page 218. Although they were approved, the Committee wanted an addition to Rule 7. This change in the rule is significant. Even although it does not appear in the minutes, the Committee possibly were careful in preventing disruptions to the meetings. The change in the rule reads as follows:

> (7) That the Librarian submit a list of the names of all intending Subscribers, to the Committee of the Young Men's Christian Association for approval, before issuing Attendance Cards, (addition) and that the Committee be empowered to object to Candidates for enrolment as Subscribers, to expel anyone behaving in a disorderly manner, and generally to enforce the Rules.[162]

Mr. Saunders later told the Committee that he considered 'Rule No. 7 might in some cases prove a hindrance to him in obtaining fresh subscribers,' but it was retained by a majority of the Committee.[163]

In October 1879 Mr. Hertslet stated that to comply with the Association Rule No. 6, found in Appendix II, a meeting had been called to elect a new committee, treasurer and secretary. Members agreed that every member of the Association should have the opportunity to vote privately for any nine of the members that he might think most suitable and voting papers had been issued. Out of the twenty-two voting papers sent out eighteen were returned. Mr. Hertslet told the Committee that he had 'opened the papers himself and had not voted, but had carefully added up the votes.' The nine names of the chosen members were presented to the meeting in alphabetical order and can be found in Table 2, page 232.[164]

This ballot and the way Mr. Hertslet conducted it is of interest for several reasons. The 1867 Parliamentary Reform Bill had given the vote to males over twenty-one years of age who were householders and paid rent to the value of £10 per year. Mr. Hertslet had given the vote to all the members of the Y.M.C.A. although at least three and possibly more were under twenty-one years of age. The 1872 Ballot Act had allowed voting to be secret. In the initial ballot for the Y.M.C.A. Committee Mr. Hertslet gives the impression that he conformed to this regulation. It was however, the Committee who chose the secretary and the treasurer. Mr. William Walter was voted in as treasurer, and the Committee asked Mr. Hertslet to be secretary. The latter gladly accepted the office subject to the reservation that he could not attend every meeting.

The next Committee meeting re-elected Mr. Rutland Saunders as librarian, a post he also accepted, but he stated that he could not undertake to attend each evening but would do the best he could.[165] None of those elected to this Committee had been on the first Committee in 1874. Whereas in 1874 the average known ages of the Committee was twenty-five with a span of nineteen to thirty-six years, five years later the average age was thirty-five, with a span of fifteen to sixty-seven years. None of the later Committee worked as drapers or in retail. Frank Newson the brother of Jasper Newson provided the only connection with the earlier Committee.

During the next two years the committee meetings and subsequent discussions revolved around several major concerns, but it was the open air meetings and the evening classes that would cause the most disagreement between committee members. In particular the problem associated with evening classes was the reason that Mr. Hertslet remained as secretary for only a short period following the election he had organised so well in October 1879.

The London City Missionary and the Open Air Mission

In December 1873 a public meeting held in Kingston had decided to invite the London City Missionary to work in the town.[166] The Rev. A. Williams had said during the meeting that the Mission had laboured in Surbiton for nearly 20 years and:

> if the rich of Surbiton would but come down amongst us there is no doubt that great good might be done. We have not the means that our friends on the hill have ... but with willing hearts we can accomplish great things.'

The Rev. A. Williams 'then referred to the state of our back lanes and many other parts of the town where the people were living in a comparative state of heathenism.' Although early Surbiton had a troubled history of speculation, by the 1870s the middle-class residents who sat on the Surbiton Improvement Committee, had eradicated some of the bad conditions and improved the sanitation.[167] In Kingston little had been done to improve the housing of the poor. Between 1861 and 1871 the Census Enumerators' Returns for Kingston upon Thames show a population increasing from approximately 17,600 to 27,480 and in the back lanes and some other areas, many individuals lived in overcrowded filthy conditions.[168] However, the public meeting did not emphasise improving living conditions but eradicating 'heathenism.' It appears that those attending the meeting believed that the eradication of 'heathenism' would result in higher living standards for those living in poverty.

Mr. William Bowskill, the London City Missionary who lived in Gibbon Road, was probably the missionary invited to Kingston following this meeting. By late 1877 he had joined the Y.M.C.A. and had been voted onto the Committee in October 1879.[169] During the summer months, the Open Air Mission had started to hold services in a tent on the Fairfield, and by 1879 these services had become an annual event.[170] One of those involved in the mission was a retired grocer called Mr. J.J. Britton who lived at 3 St. Andrews Road, Surbiton. He had started work for the mission many years before when he lived in Essex, and during 1878 Mr. Britton had been involved in the operation of twelve mission stations and the distribution of fifteen thousand tracts in Kingston.[171] During the summer of 1879 the Y.M.C.A. lent fifty of their chairs to be used in the tent.[172] On the closing of the Mission in October the *Surrey Comet* wrote:

> To Spread Gospel truth in the dark corners of the land.
>
> Such is the object of the Kingston Open-air Mission under whose auspices during the past five weeks special Tent Services have been held on the Fairfield, which were brought to a close on Tuesday evening by a public

meeting. Believing that in Kingston alone there were thousands of people who never entered a place of worship, or even read a chapter of the Bible a number of gentlemen in the neighbourhood about eighteen months ago determined to establish the above mission. ... In various parts of the town and neighbourhood, and as proof of the unsectarian character of the movement, we may mention that at the 42 services which have been held in the tent during the last five weeks, addresses have been delivered by about 100 ministers of various churches, including Church of England, Free Church of England, Congregational, Baptist, Primitive Methodists, Wesleyan Methodists, Presbyterian and by Gospellers. ... On Sunday evenings the number had averaged from 500 to 600, even in wet weather (they) had not fallen below 200.[173]

A description of this tent or the one used in 1883 is found in the *Surrey Comet*:

A large circular marquee capable of holding nearly 600 people, has been erected under the auspices of the Kingston and Surbiton branch of the Open Air Mission, and Mr. J.J. Britton has, as usual, the management of the arrangement. A substantial railed-in platform has been put up at the lower end of the tent, and this is decorated with flowers and foliage plants. There is sufficient room here to accommodate both the speakers and a small choir, as well as the harmonium.[174]

Mr. Sparks, who also sat on the Y.M.C.A. Committee, engaged in the mission work, as did Mr. Rutland Saunders, who by 1879 was sixteen. Mr. Saunders wanted association members to invite strangers to their meetings. The majority of the Committee were against this proposal. After discussion the majority agreed it was inadvisable for a member to give invitations to young men near the Association rooms immediately before or during the Sunday afternoon meeting. Mr. Rutland Saunders asked if the Committee 'would give him permission to use the rooms of the Association on Saturday Evenings ... so that he could follow up his recent work of open air preaching which he had been carrying on through the summer on Saturday Evenings...'[175] This request was not considered advisable, although the meeting decided that some steps should be taken by the Association to preach the Gospel either in the rooms or elsewhere.[176]

Evening Classes and Objections to Debate and Elocution; 1879
Towards the end of 1879 the Association decided to continue the classes for reading, writing, arithmetic, singing and shorthand and to provide a tea to inaugurate them.[177] Mr. Rutland Saunders wanted to have discussion and elocution included with the other classes. After a long debate the motion was carried whilst 'Mr. Hertslet having stated his reasons for so doing, did not vote.' Mr. Hertslett, Mr. Newson and Mr. Parslow having been appointed to be part of a

subcommittee to prepare and organise a programme, came to a meeting on December 1, 1879, with the report as follows:

Monday		Writing & Shorthand	Mr. W. Parslow
Tuesday	7.45 to 9.30	Discussion & Elocution	Mr. F. Newson
Wednesday		Arithmetic	Mr. W. Lea

The meeting was told that singing was not included as no suitable singing master had been found.[178] The time for the writing, shorthand and arithmetic classes was to be left open to allow the teacher to fix the time. Having presented the report to the meeting, Mr. Newson explained that Mr. Hertslet had not signed it as he entirely disapproved of the 'Elocution and Discussion Classes.' Mr. Hertslet did not want discussions to take place without the Committee being aware of what was being discussed. He wanted the secretaries of the elocution and discussion classes to provide a list of all the pieces to be read, recited or discussed and to give this list to the members of the Committee on the last meeting of each month. Mr. Newson and Mr. Saunders opposed this plan, but it passed. As a consequence, both the subjects for discussion and the pieces to be read or recited had to be submitted first to the Committee. Mr. Newson was requested to act as secretary for the elocution and discussion classes. A number of worthy gentlemen were asked to act as chairmen for these sessions. The rules for the discussion class and the elocution class were considered and agreed and can be found in Appendix IV and Appendix V, pages 218 and 219.[179]

On December 22, 1879, at the next committee meeting Mr. Hertslet handed in a report that was to cause consternation among the Committee:

> To the Committee of the Y.M.C.A. 22 Decbr.79. In obedience to the direction of the Committee I have seen Capt. Cundy and he has consented to write to the various Ministers of the Town (asking their cooperation in the work of the Association) if the Committee decide to carry on the work for another 18 months, but he stated, that, he had for some time thought, that it was a doubtful question, whether it was, or was not, advisable to attempt to carry on the work of the Association, in the face of the denominational Associations now working for their own ends in the Town.

Mr Hertslet was suggesting that the Y.M.C.A. should not continue because many of the churches in Kingston had started their own associations, and so there was no need for the Y.M.C.A. This report must have surprised the Committee, but it was moved, seconded and resolved that the report be received, and Mr. Hertslet moved:

that as denominational associations for Young Men have been commenced since <u>The Young Men's Christian Association, Kingston on Thames Branch</u> was started, it is not expedient to continue the Association. And further that the Secretary be instructed to give due notice to the Landlords that the Association will not require the Rooms after June 1880.

After discussion at some length and with a majority of one, the Committee decided to continue the Association in the existing premises upon a yearly tenancy from June 24. At the same meeting the programme with the list of pieces to be recited and the subjects to be discussed was handed in to the meeting. Mr. Hertslet and Mr. William Walter then left the meeting. It was thereafter moved and seconded, 'That any Member of the Elocution Class be allowed to read or recite any Piece from *Bells Standard Elocutional* and *The Modern Speaker and Reciter*, subject to the approval of the Secy: of the Elocution Class.' Mr. Hertslet remained absent from the meeting on January 3, 1880 and sent in his resignation as secretary. A few days later, on January 12, Mr. Sparkes resigned his membership and his seat on the Committee. At the meeting on the January 3, 1880, Frank Newson accepted the office of secretary of the Kingston Association.[180]

SEPARATING THE SECULAR
FROM THE SPIRITUAL

Free Thinking

Mr. Hertslet's objection to discussion groups and elocution lessons appears unusual and possibly absurd from a twenty-first century perspective. During 1858 to 1869 the Rev. Lawrence Byrnes encouraged the young men of the early Y.M.C.A. to discuss a range of topics. By the late 1860s however an awareness of Lyall's geological theories and the significance of Darwinism had filtered into public consciousness adding plausibility to what had become known as 'free thinking.' Mr. Hertslet would not have been the only church member who considered that discussion of evolution should be discouraged, unless attempted in a framework of Christian guidance. Such discussion could lead people to question their faith and belief. Binfield writes that W. J. Stokes of the Dublin branch in 1862 said, 'discussion classes were … most objectionable, as they tended to bring forth the pride and vanity of the human heart, and to divert men's minds from the simplicity of the truth.'[181] In December 1868 the Vicar of Kingston, the Rev. A. Williams, advised the members of the Y.M.C.A. that:

> People were running hither and thither in quest of intellectuality. He was not going to depreciate intellectuality. He believed that if rightly directed it would not be found in opposition to, but rather in agreement with, the Word of God. It was when it was unsanctified that mere intellectuality became a dangerous thing, and led to sceptical notions in matters of religion. … But freedom of thought should not be confounded with what was called "free thinking" which was only another name for infidelity.[182]

When the Vicar of Kingston spoke about 'free thinking' he was referring to individuals such as Jeremy Bentham, Robert Owen and Richard Carlile. All three men were born during the eighteenth century but their ideas have continued to be influential up to the present time. During the nineteenth century they were classified as 'freethinkers', and said to be the inspiration behind the National Secular Society, which was established in 1866.[183] Bentham was a child prodigy who throughout most of his life aimed to test and re-evaluate the usefulness of existing institutions and beliefs.[184] Owen was a partner and manager of a mill in

New Lanark, who educated the children in his factory, shortened working hours and dismissed all religion as false.[185] Carlile criticised the government through his radical newspaper and spent many years in prison.

The problem for the establishment was fear of an uprising. This was particularly so during the 1840s with the emergence of Chartism. The French Revolution in 1789 remained a fearful recollection for those in power.[186] An event in Esher shows that locally some people were worried, in particular those living near the Claremont Estate owned by Prince Leopold of Saxe-Coberg. At a Vestry meeting held on October 20, 1842, twelve 'fit and proper persons' including a waggoner, a labourer and the local publican were sworn in to serve as parochial constables in an attempt to protect the neighbourhood. Fortunately these people were not called upon to act, as an uprising in this quiet backwater did not materialise.[187] Although there was poverty in some areas, Chartism in 1839, 1842 and later 1848 did not affect Kingston, Surbiton and Esher.[188] Yet there appears to have been interest in the movement. When the Chartist Henry Vincent came to lecture to the Y.M.C.A. in January 1864, the Assize Courts were crowded long before the lecture began.[189]

The National Secular Society — Charles Bradlaugh

The beginning of 1869 presented problems for the Y.M.C.A. Not only was the Association soon to say good-bye to the Rev. Lawrence Byrnes, but in January 1869, the National Secular Society started 'A Crusade Against Christianity', holding a series of lectures in the Temperance Lyceum in Brick Lane. The *Surrey Comet* reported that the Y.M.C.A. had created this situation by discussing the question of whether the Noachian Deluge was universal or partial.[190]

Led by Charles Bradlaugh, the National Secular Society was at heart a working class movement, campaigning on a variety of issues but mainly concerned about equality before the law and freedom of belief and expression. It was an amalgamation of a large number of smaller secularist groups, reputed to have been inspired by early 'freethinkers.'[191] The lectures held at the Temperance Lyceum were noisy and heated. Benjamin Looker wrote to the *Surrey Comet* describing events:

> To the Editor, Sir —
> I think it high time that the attention of the authorities and the public should be directed to the manner in which these infidel lectures now in the course of delivery are conducted. A few days since I was earnestly solicited by a most respectable mechanic in the town to attend a lecture for the purpose of assisting his friends and himself to meet the arguments that were put

forward by the lecturer. I accordingly went last evening and arrived a few minutes before the proceedings commenced. I found the room (which will hold about 150 persons) crammed to suffocation almost entirely by the labouring class (a very large proportion being youths) and several females.

The opening remarks of the lecturer were such a blasphemous and untruthful character that the indignation of many in the meeting was naturally aroused, and a sense of much confusion arose, during which some the gas lights were put out. Thinking that under the circumstances it would be well to see if a ready means of escape presented itself, I descended with much difficulty the narrow stairs which lead to the "Lyceum." To my astonishment I found the door which opens inwardly locked, and it was at least five minutes before the key could be obtained from Mr. Smith (who was on the platform) and myself and several others released. Now Sir, in the interest of the working classes, who are for the most part drawn together by certain infidels in the place going the round of the town and soliciting their attendance, I would ask are their lives to be placed in jeopardy as they were last night? Most assuredly had anything like a panic occurred, the result would have been most lamentable. If certain persons think they are doing a good work by crowding a great number of the working classes together, and by every means endeavouring to release them from all obligations to right living which they have hither been taught in the name of common humanity let it be done without risk to their lives.

Yours truly,
Benjamin Looker,
Kingston Hill, February 12, 1869. [192]

Unfortunately the Y.M.C.A. also met in the Temperance Lyceum in Brick Lane at this time. Happily the nineteen members and forty young men who used the reading room were able to move to the Temperance Hall, Bridge Foot after a Mr. W. Elliott agreed to pay the rent of their new location for the next twelve months. This was possibly because he was encouraged to do so by the Vicar of Kingston.[193] The Temperance Hall would have been near Kingston Bridge, with buildings not unlike those in Figure 16.

The *Surrey Comet* on January 23 announced that several readers had sent in letters denying that either the Temperance Society or the Y.M.C.A. were 'in anyway connected with these men who were being brought down here to propagate blasphemous and infamous doctrine.'[194] In Kingston in 1869 bills were circulated announcing that Charles Bradlaugh would deliver two lectures.[195] There is no evidence that Bradlaugh lectured in 1869 in the Temperance Lyceum in Brick Lane. He was at that time being prosecuted for alleged blasphemy and sedition. In 1877 he nearly went to prison as together with Annie Bessant, another nineteenth century activist, he was connected with the publication of a pamphlet on family planning. After being elected Member of Parliament for Northampton in 1880, Bradlaugh campaigned for the legal recognition of non-religious oaths. A man of divisive views, he spoke in Parliament in 1888 about the London match girl's strike, but attacked the Early Closing Bill as arbitrary and capricious.[196] However when he did come to the area in August 1888 his notoriety appears to have abated, and there was little reaction to his visit.[197]

The Evolution and Secularism Debate

It was in the *Surrey Comet* that evolution and secularism found a voice in the Kingston community, and during the 1870s this debate continued. In March 1873 the Rev. G. S. Ingram wrote a paper entitled 'The Unity and Antiquity of Mankind,' in which he argued that the human race had descended from Adam and Eve.[198] Correspondence between the Rev. Ingram and *Surrey Comet* readers continued in the newspaper for some time afterwards.

16. Old Bridge Street c.1890   **(CR)**

In April 1873, S.R. Townsend Mayer founder of the Free and Open Church Association wrote:

> if we reason illogically we bring not only contempt on ourselves, but on the truth we reason for ... no one for a moment supposes the Bible to be – because we know that it is not – a complete history of the world from the

creation to the end of the first century A.D. Are we therefore to shut our eyes to the 'logic of facts'?

After this letter the *Surrey Comet* wrote, 'the correspondence upon this subject must cease ... we have ample evidence however that the letters have been read with deep interest by many of the thousands who peruse the pages...'[199] Letters didn't cease. In May of that year:

> Dr. Brindley having explained the Darwinian theory went on to say that ... if they looked at the simia, or ape tribes, they would find such distinct generic conditions that they could not say man had sprung from them. ... He advised to pay a visit to the Museum of the Royal College of Surgeons at Lincolns Inn.[200]

Three and a half years later in October 1876 obviously concerned about the issues involved, a Church Congress, presided over by the Bishop of Exeter, met at Plymouth Guildhall to discuss 'Unbelief.' During the debate Edward Garbett, the Vicar of Christ Church, Surbiton, who had been appointed Honorary Canon of Winchester the previous year said that:

> the prevalence of physical study and the marvellous discoveries of natural science were the two principal factors moulding the course of thought. Physical science dealing with natural forces and cognizable agents, conversant with sensible phenomena, and working by demonstrable facts, tended to materialize the intellect and to make it sceptical of all forces which were above sensible perception and incapable of measurable experiment...[201]

Canon Garbett was an outstanding theologian who once told the members of the Surbiton Y.M.C.A. that, 'if anyone felt any difficulty with reference to God's Word, if they came to him he would do his best to assist them, and should always feel honoured and happy to do so.'[202]

For the ordinary lay person, and even some academics, the problems associated with evolution and physical science seemed confusing and even frightening. We remember Mr. Philpott's remark, 'learned objections which most people could not answer often did much mischief to the mind, and were like horrible dreams.' Given this situation it is understandable that discussion, particularly among the less informed, may have seemed problematic.[203] In November 1874 Captain Cundy addressed the Surbiton Y.M.C.A and described the Association as valuable because it 'provided the means for fortifying young men against the snares of Satan, and the wiles of Satan's servant.'[204]

Clearly, times were difficult, and Binfield notes that in 1883 rumour had it that Peterborough Y.M.C.A. had turned out its debating society because that branch had passed a motion supporting Bradlaugh's right to sit in Parliament.[205]

Why did Mr. Hertslet not want evening classes to include elocution?

It is impossible to answer this question with confidence although Association minutes and the *Surrey Comet* offer some clues. In 1871 Mr. Finlay Gibson said he did not want evening classes as these were outside the concern of a Christian organization. By 1880 evening classes for English, reading, mathematics and shorthand had become acceptable due to their practical value. In 1867 the Y.M.C.A. started 'penny readings', and these were immediately frowned upon as being unsuitable for a Christian Association, although later they became very popular as entertainment for many of the Kingston inhabitants.[206] Elocution may have been considered frivolous, of no real worth and perhaps something that had a relationship with 'theatrical entertainment.' Indeed 'popular entertainments' were an anathema, not only in the nonconformist churches but also to many in the Anglican community. The Vicar of Kingston in October 1875 expressed his sorrow:

> that some of our magistrates granted a license for theatrical entertainments in the Drill Hall. I affirm then that amusements of this description are wrong because Scripture pointedly condemns foolish talking and jesting (Eph. V. 4) and warns us against such things by solemn consideration that the Holy Spirit is grieved thereby…[207]

Mr. Hertslet continued to sit on the Committee after his resignation as secretary and probably took an active part in advising Mr. Newson after he, Mr. Hertslet, was no longer involved in activities relating to the reading room, library and the evening classes. His second letter of resignation from the Committee in September 1881, more than a year later suggests the rationale behind his dislike of discussion as well as elocution. He states 'that in consequence of the amalgamation of the reading room and library with the Y.M.C.A. i.e. (the secular with the spiritual) he felt compelled to request that his name should be taken off the list of members but that he was willing to assist the spiritual work of the Association as much as he could.'[208] Although no detail exists in the minutes, by September 1881 people clearly expected and discussed change, which did occur during 1882.

Frank Hertslet had joined the Kingston Association at the end of 1874 and took over as secretary when nobody else wanted the role. He served as secretary for only fourteen months but remained a further twenty months on the Committee after resigning from this position. During this time churches in Kingston, began to form associations for the young men in their congregations, and because of this development Hertslet considered the Y.M.C.A. obsolete and attempted to close it. This attempt implies that he may have misunderstood the value of the Y.M.C.A. as a place where young men from all Christian denominations could integrate, but it may have been otherwise, that he considered that integration could result in assenting to a uniformity among the churches, something a dissenter would have found hard to tolerate.

Religious Dissent

The history of Kingston includes a long period of religious dissent. The Rev. Richard Mayo, who became Vicar of All Saints Parish Church in the time of Oliver Cromwell in 1658, with many others, felt unable to accept the 1662 Act of Conformity, which required parish priests to assent to everything in the Book of Common Prayer. He was ejected from the church and with like-minded dissenters, worshipped in secret, a situation that eventually led to the founding of the Kingston Congregational Church. The Kingston Baptist Church in Brick Lane was formed over one hundred years later in 1787 by members who believed that it was necessary to undergo Believers' Baptism. The Brick Lane Baptist Church and the Eden Street Congregational Church became closer during the 1860s, but by the late 1870s this appears less obvious. In 1882, in the year of Mr. Hertslet's second resignation, a dispute arose in the Union Street Baptist Church over the dismissal of the organist at the church. The first members of a new Baptist church, called Bunyan Baptist Church (now rebuilt and renamed John Bunyan Baptist Church), withdrew from the parent group in Brick Lane and identified themselves as 'Open Baptists', building a church in Queen Elizabeth Road, Kingston in 1885.[209] We do not know to which denomination Mr. Hertslet belonged. He was undoubtedly a dissenter, a man of strong principles who believed fervently in his ideals. Had he lived in 1662 he would, no doubt, also have been prepared to worship, like other dissenters, 'in secret places such as Down Hall.'[210]

Mr. Hertslet was born in Soho in London. He was responsible for providing the Association with a firm backbone of rules and regulations and remained an important influence until his resignation in September 1881. He was a qualified solicitor employed by the Metropolitan Board of Works, a man of integrity, and someone who believed in the democratic process. The Metropolis Management Act 1855 had created the Metropolitan Board of Works to deal with major problems such as the overcrowding resulting in slums and sewage problems.[211] In 1889, the London County Council replaced it.[212] At the time of the 1891 census, Mr. Hertslet was living with his wife Harriet and their five children in Islington. His son Lewis Eccles Hertslet, who was born in Kingston in 1877, went to South

Africa as a medical missionary after qualifying as a doctor. His obituary in the South African Medical Journal in May 1949 paints a picture of a man who deliberately sacrificed himself for the good of others.[213]

The new secretary may have initially needed Mr. Hertslet's guidance. Mr. Newson wrote to Mr. Hertslet after the latter had resigned in 1879 and Hertslet returned to the Committee in February 1880, after Mr. Newson had discontinued 'discussion and elocution.'[214] However, Mr. Newson did not try to persuade Mr. Hertslet to stay when he finally resigned in September 1881. The minutes state, 'it was moved by Mr. Newson and seconded by Mr. Buchanan that Mr. Hertslet's name be removed from the list of members.'[215] By this time, Mr. Newson was an established and competent secretary, and the Kingston Y.M.C.A. was ready to embrace the social together with the spiritual.

MR. FRANK NEWSON —

A PERIOD OF LEARNING — JANUARY 1880

Frank Newson

Following Mr. Hertslet's resignation as secretary on December 22, 1879, a meeting on December 29 had to be postponed because there was not a quorum. On January 3, 1880, Messrs. Bowskill, Lea, Newson, Saunders and Parslow could attend, the Committee could function, and Frank Newson was voted in and accepted the role of secretary.[216] The Kingston Y.M.C.A. minutes over the next few months give a vivid account of a young man using his initiative and steadily becoming a more than competent secretary, despite being left to solve difficult problems with very little help.[217]

17. Knights Park Kingston   (**AG 2012**)

Frank Newson, brother of the first secretary, Jasper Newson, was a shipbroker's clerk. He lived in Knights Park, Kingston with his mother Emily, an elder brother Harry who was a barrister at law in practice at London University, and Emma S. Yarold aged twenty-nine, a general servant domestic. Figure 17 shows Knight's Park as it is currently, but most of these houses were built when Frank Newson lived in the road.[218] Born on December 21, 1856, Frank was just twenty-three years of age in January 1880 when he became secretary of Kingston Y.M.C.A. When accepting the role he said that business matters might prevent his being able to remain secretary for long, and he looked to the various members of the Committee and the Association to aid him. Frank Newson remained secretary of Kingston Y.M.C.A. until the arrival of the Association's first paid general secretary in 1885.

During the next few weeks only four members of the Committee gave Frank Newson the help he required, but, during the following months, his tenacity became apparent. He initially elicited help from Mr. Hind Smith, the London Secretary of the Association and later accommodated Mr. Hertslet, bringing him back into the Committee probably in an advisory role. His 'hands-on' approach as he dealt with certain issues must have taught him the most. These issues involved the open air mission, the reading room, library and evening classes. The ongoing saga of Zoar Chapel and Gilbert House continued as matters of concern. What was not discussed but becomes obvious later was the disorder experienced in Association meetings created by young men who were deliberately disruptive and the slow but inevitable movement towards change. Mr. Newson must have realised that his inexperience, together with the depletion of the Committee, created a difficult situation, and, between the meeting on January 3 and the meeting on January 22, the new secretary took the trouble to contact and meet with Mr. Hind Smith, the secretary of the London Association.[219]

The rise of William Hind Smith in the Y.M.C.A. had developed over a number of years. In 1864 he took over the role of the Leeds Association secretary, this Association had become no more than a set of comfortable rooms used for educational classes with a reading room and library. He set about converting the members without discontinuing the classes. He later repeated his success in the Manchester branch of the Association. During his time in Leeds he married Rebekah Wilson who came from a wealthy radical family and worked with young people as well as the British Workman movement, a cause with the aim of establishing alcohol free coffee houses for working men. Supported by his very able wife, Hind Smith 'emerged as the movement's most active provincial leader.' He replaced Shipton, who was not well, as secretary of the London Association during 1878-9. Hind Smith eventually became General and Travelling Secretary after the National Council of Y.M.C.A.s was formed in 1882.[220] The fact that Mr. Newson could secure Mr. Hind Smith's services at such short notice indicates that the new London Association Secretary realised the major difficulties that Kingston faced and that it needed help. He consented to visit the Kingston branch and address the next annual general meeting on January 22, 1880. Mr. Newson had also written to Mr. Hertslet 'in accordance with the tenor of the resolution passed at the last committee meeting.' Whether Mr. Hertslet replied is unknown, but he attended the meetings on January 22.

18. The old house in Oak Lea Passage   (AG 2012)

Mr. Lea could not attend the meeting on January 12, Messrs Hertslet, William Walter and E.P. Williams did not attend, and the meeting accepted Mr. Sparkes resignation. However business continued as usual, with the treasurer handing in, through Mr. Newson, a statement of accounts for the year 1879 with vouchers showing a balance of 8d to be carried forward to 1880, the balance left from the reading room, library and evening classes totalling £2.12s 3d.[221] During this meeting the secretary 'handed in a draft copy of the 1879 annual report for the Committee's inspection.' Thereafter the seventeen-year-old Mr. Saunders, the twenty-one year-old Mr. Parslow, and the twenty-three year-old new secretary discussed and altered the report together with the London City Missionary and eventually agreed unanimously to adopt, print and circulate the result of their labours. As they had received no replies from their circular letters to ministers and others in the neighbourhood, the secretary said that he would go to see the recipients of these letters 'to endeavour to stir them up to take an active interest…' Finally Mr. Parslow was appointed assistant treasurer to assist the treasurer Mr. Walter in the collection of subscriptions. Mr. Parslow later called on Mr. Walter and arranged that he would aim to meet all other expenses if Mr. Walter could collect a sufficient amount to pay the rent. By June 1880 Mr. Parslow had collected £22.1s 2d including a special donation of £5 from Captain Cundy and had disbursed £21.6s 4d leaving a balance of 14s 10d.[222]

Mr. Parslow joined the Y.M.C.A. in January 1876 at the age of eighteen. During his early years he lived in Oak Lea Passage (sometimes referred to as the Bittoms). Figure 18 shows a current view of the passage. The old house in the picture is unlikely to have been Mr. Parslow's home, but he may have passed this house on his way to attend meetings at the Y.M.C.A. The 1871 census shows William Parslow, aged thirteen, living with his father a postman, his mother, and his grandfather, aged seventy-four, who had also been a postman. Mr. William Parslow and Mr. Frank Newson remained the central figures in the Kingston Y.M.C.A. for several years.

Advice from Mr. Hind Smith

Mr. Hertslet and Mr. Walter came to the meetings on January 22, 1880, as did Mr. E.P. Williams.[223] The first meeting was a committee meeting and, as he had promised, Mr. Hind Smith attended. Mr. Newson stated particulars of the work of the Kingston Association, covering details such as the Sunday afternoon meetings, the Thursday evening meetings, the reading room, library and the evening classes. These were all dealt with and criticised by Mr. Hind Smith.

> Mr. Smith, though more accustomed to a Bible Class, no means objected to an address on Sunday afternoons; and specially recommended members to undertake the distribution of Bills &c in the streets and to invite young men into the meeting.
> He approved the alternate Bible Class & Prayer Meeting on Thursday evenings; but should have liked to have seen a Bible Class & Prayer Meeting each once a week. With reference to the Elocution Class and Discussion Meetings he thought that while they might not do much harm they could not do much good and would recommend that the affairs of the Reading Room, Library should be conducted by a separate Committee. A member

having subsequently stated that some members of the Elocution Class had been induced to come to the Sunday Afternoon Meetings, Mr. Smith said 'if that was the case, he would not recommend their discontinuance.'[224]

At eight p.m. the Committee adjourned to attend the annual meeting, the Association room 'being all but full' with seventy attending. After a hymn the chairman, Captain Cundy, started with prayer and called upon the secretary to read the report. The report having been read, Captain Cundy continued to address the meeting, dealing especially with the problems related to denominational associations, in particular those belonging to the Baptist Chapel, which were not mentioned in detail. Thereafter Mr. Hind Smith gave a long and very interesting address during which he criticised the annual report but expressed his satisfaction that notwithstanding the difficulties of the Association, the Committee was still able to mention cases of spiritual blessing.

> He exhorted members to be more active in their work outside the Association and mentioned several cases of spiritual blessing which had resulted from personal dealing with young men and the giving away of Bills in the street. Towards the close of his address he invited Christian Young Men who had not joined the Association to do so, and concluded with a solemn appeal to the unsaved to delay no longer but accept Christ.

At the conclusion of the address Mr. E. P. Williams engaged in prayer, and the meeting ended after the singing of a hymn. A sum of £1 9s 2d was collected in a plate at the door.[225]

Following the annual general meeting, the Committee meetings continued to be sparsely attended. The meeting called originally for January 29 was reconvened for February 2, at which time Messrs Parslow, Saunders, Bowskill, Newson and Lea attended. Mr. Parslow drew attention to the inefficiency of the lamp outside the Association's rooms. He had obtained an estimate from Mr. Offer for a new lamp and, together with fixing, it would cost £2.10s 0d, with the glass extra. The cost would be another £1.13s.0d with coloured glass and embossed letters. The meeting discussed whether to obtain a London estimate, but eventually decided to buy Mr. Offer's lamp and the glass, but leave the embossed letters 'to stand over' for the present.[226] The motion that the Association should spend £1 on books for the Library carried unanimously and it was agreed that they should hold a Tea for the young men at the Association, because 'the evangelistic services did not reach the class of shopmen so much as the rougher class.'[227]

Only the four younger men of the Committee attended a meeting on February 7. They scheduled the 'Tea for Young Men' for Friday, March 5, 1880, and agreed to ask Mr. Shipton to address the meeting. Several of the members of the Association had already started visiting the lodging houses, preaching in the streets, and distributing bills before the gospel meetings, so they agreed to follow Mr. Hind Smith's advice to establish a special branch with Mr. Rutland Saunders in charge.[228] However, they rejected Mr. Hind Smith's proposal for control of the classes to pass out of the hands of the Committee but agreed to discontinue 'discussion and elocution.' [229]

Following this decision Mr. Hertslet returned to the Committee on February 23, 1880, and took the chair whilst Messrs Parslow, Saunders and Newson were appointed to draw up a quarterly programme.[230] While Mr. Bowskill, Mr. Hertslet, and occasionally Mr. Walters came to the meetings, Messrs Newson, Parslow, Saunders and to a lesser extent Mr. Lea performed the majority of the work. Unfortunately Mr. Rutland Saunders resigned in August of that year.

AFTER THE RESIGNATION OF
MR. RUTLAND SAUNDERS
1880 – 1882

Open Air Branch

Initially the open air branch under the guidance of Mr. Saunders progressed favourably as there were generally between forty and fifty listeners, but no mention of where the meetings took place. The work at the lodging houses was also encouraging, with congregations occasionally amounting to fifty people in the winter at each of the six lodging houses regularly visited. The workers were welcomed and great attention paid. Mr. Saunders said he had 'confidence that the result of the meetings would be the conversion of souls.' He criticised the Y.M.C.A. membership, however, saying, 'although the work of trying to induce young men to come to the Sunday afternoon meetings still continued, as the members did not persevere … the work could not report any increase, but rather the reverse.'[231] On August 27, 1880, Mr. Saunders handed in a letter resigning his post as manager of the open air branch, saying that:

> Since the Association had taken up the work it had neither materially assisted it either by its actions or by its words and that he thought in consequence it would be better to separate it and that it would be to the benefit of the work to do so.

The discussion that took place during the Committee meeting was somewhat vehement, and, although the Committee accepted the letter, they could not accept its statements. Mr. Saunders resigned on September 10, 1880.[232] Mr. Newson was therefore left with a vacancy to fill.

Mr. W. T. Lea took over the position of leader or manager of the open air branch on Saturday nights whilst Mr. Newson took over as leader or manager of the work of preaching on Sunday evenings at the lodging houses and of the bill distribution before the Sunday afternoon meetings.[233] A statistical review of the work put before the Committee later showed that between August 28 and December 1880, seventeen open air meetings had taken place at twenty different locations with forty members speaking. In all twenty workers had taken part with an average of nine at each meeting, fifteen being the highest and four the lowest. On average, those attending meetings ranged between fifty to seventy-five people. There were six denominations involved, and the work was successful although there was a great want of 'an efficient staff of speakers.' Invitations to young men to attend Sunday afternoon services at the Y.M.C.A. rooms were sent regularly, and the numbers attending the meetings had considerably increased.[234]

In June 1881 a third band of workers had started visiting the lodging houses. Although the minutes are silent concerning why this problem had occurred in June, it is probable that this group only worked in the summer months and having returned to start their services, they claimed that they had precedence over the Y.M.C.A. because they had been servicing these areas for several years. After a meeting of the three bands arrangements were made as follows:

(1) It was arranged that Mr. Bayley (it is assumed that Mr. Bayley was the Rev. H. Bayley the minister of the Brick Lane Baptist Church) & his friends (having shewn (sic) that they had conducted meetings for the last three or four years at Williams' Lodging Houses & also latterly at Oban's & that they had also held Open Air Meetings outside between the two Lodging Houses) should alone hold Meetings in these two Lodging Houses and this Open Air Station the other five Lodging Houses viz Turners, Days, the Public House Lodging House and the two Germans be left absolutely to the Association and the band of Friend's Mission Workers conjointly.

(2) That the Public House Lodging House being closed in the afternoon, the Association conduct the meeting there every Sunday & also in turn at one of the three following, viz Days, the small German & the large German, & that the Friends (Quakers) conduct the Meetings in the other two. Turner's was understood to be left to the Association, as indeed had been the case for some time past.[235]

Although this situation appears complicated, no disagreements occurred, and the three bands of workers adjusted to these arrangements.

Reading Room, Library and Evening Classes
Following Mr. Saunders' resignation to take up the work of the open air branch, Mr. Parslow had agreed to act as librarian. In June his report on the library showed that on his appointment he had received a balance of £2.13s.3d from Mr. Saunders and that the members of the reading room had paid subscriptions of 10/9d making a gross total of £3. 4s 0d. The Association had spent £2. 12s. 3d on new books for the library and a new tablecloth for the reading room leaving a balance of 11/9d. The small attendance at the reading room occurred because the

members preferred to take the books home. Since the Association had taken over the library, members had borrowed eighteen books, and Miss Ranyard had contributed ten fresh books and he had bought the poetical works of Cowper, Longfellow and Hood. He felt that some of the larger books should be allowed to remain out for longer than a fortnight and that young men wishing to join half way through the quarter should be allowed to do so for 6d instead of a shilling. The report was adopted, the suggestions postponed, but agreed later.[236]

Following the voting in of the new Committee, found in Table 4, several classes were proposed, these included reading, writing, arithmetic, shorthand, singing, elocution and debating. However the Association resolved not to include the last two due to objections by some of the members, and singing was also 'laid aside for lack of a teacher.' The managers of the various classes were to be as follows:

Writing and Shorthand	Mr. Wm H. Parslow
Arithmetic	Mr. A. Gaydon
Reading	Mr. S. Herbert Fry

The charge for joining the reading room was 1/- per quarter, together with one class 1/6d and 6d for each additional class. Subscriptions were to be paid to the managers of the classes, and they had to hand them over to the librarian. The secretary approached Captain Cundy, who agreed that the classes should start with a Tea 'on the condition that he was not to be supposed to give another in March of next year.' The Tea was arranged for Tuesday, November 9 and the secretary instructed to make all the necessary arrangements.[237] The new rules for the reading room appear in Appendix VI .[238] On September 30, the voting for the new Committee was carried out on the same plan as the previous year. Thirty-two voting papers were sent out and thirty returned. Mr. Newson was elected secretary, Mr. William Walter, treasurer and Mr. Parslow re-elected both assistant treasurer and librarian.

The meeting agreed to appoint Messrs Lea, Parslow and Newson to take charge of the management of the meetings and authorised them to issue a programme as usual for the ensuing quarter. Mr. Bowskill continued to come to Committee meetings and Mr. Hertslet continued to act in an advisory capacity, but the majority of the work of the Association rested now in the hands of three young men, Messrs Newson, Parslow, and Lea, particularly the first two. The shorthand class had twenty members, and the others had about twelve to fifteen. Two people had given books to the library, and evening lectures would be given in the reading room. Various speakers were considered for lectures, a Mr. Griffiths' offered to deliver a lecture on the 'Illustrations, Allusions and Metaphors of the Bible' and a Mr. Fitzgerald on 'Ritualism or Infidelity.' The Committee decided that a lecture by a Mr. Price on 'How to Get On in the World' was more appropriate.[239] In January the receipts for the year were shown to be £8. 16s 1d and payments had been made of £7. 10s 11d. The number of subscribers to the reading room and library was twenty-three, and sixty-five of the books had been borrowed. Forty-two pupils were attending the classes, with some of them going to more than one class.[240]

Mainly about Rutland Saunders and S. Herbert Fry
Mr. Rutland Saunders had proposed Mr. S. Herbert Fry for membership on March 18, 1880, and Mr. Fry had taken the vacant seat on the Committee just under a month later on April 13, 1880. (Although he was only on the Y.M.C.A. Committee a short time, he remained a member for some time afterwards and is of interest for several reasons.) Mr. S. Herbert Fry was born into the famous Quaker family that included the founder of Fry's chocolate company whose wife was the famous prison reformer Elizabeth Fry. Samuel Herbert was born in Brighton in 1860 but came to live in Kingston soon after as his father Samuel Fry opened a photographic studio in 9 Surbiton Park Terrace. In 1872 the *Surrey Comet* ran this report:

> Improvements in Photography:
> Among the most recent improvements in the photographic art is a process patented by Mr. H. Vander Weyde of New York and Mr. Sarony of Scarborough. Mr. S. Fry of Surbiton Park-terrace has purchased the exclusive right to work the patent in Surbiton and Kingston. The process comprises an entirely novel method of finishing pictures, and the results produced are very beautiful as quite a fresh method is employed of producing background and drapery effects upon large vignette pictures. The patentees have undertaken to protect those who hold licenses from any attempt by unauthorised persons to produce similar pictures.[241]

Samuel Fry, S. Herbert's father, regularly corresponded with George Eastman, and the company Samuel Fry & Co. Ltd. promoted a special brand of dry plates called the 'Kingston Special', which by 1883 were supplied to photographers in America. Samuel Herbert managed his father's photographic company, later becoming a member of the (Royal) Photographic Society.[242]

In 1881 Samuel Herbert was living in Grove Crescent with his father, Samuel, his mother Jessie, his brother Cecil Courtney and his sixteen year old sister Beatrice Jessey. He was in charge of the Y.M.C.A. reading class during the latter part of 1880. Sometime after April 1881 he married Edith Emma Smith in Croydon, and by 1891 he was living in 'Homeside' in Minerva Road with Edith and his two children eight-year-old Jessey Edith and five-year-old Arthur Bertie Edmund. However, the Frys are of interest for another reason. On May 25, 1882, *The Times* announced the marriage of Miss Beatrice Jessey Fry to Mr. Rutland Saunders at St. Botolph's Bishopsgate.[243] Rutland Saunders left the Association in September 1880, but was destined to have further dealings with the Committee.

THE BAD BEHAVIOUR OF YOUNG MEN
1880 – 1882

Mr. Hind Smith's Advice

Mr. Hind Smith came again to the Committee meetings, including the annual meeting on January 15, 1881, to criticise the work of the Association and offer suggestions as to its future conduct. He said that:

> he had examined the Report for 1880 and considered it favourable and satisfactory, that it appeared to him that the work of the Association was doing took the right form and that he was glad to see that the Association put "right things" first, while not neglecting evening classes and other things for the mental good of the young men. He exhorted the members to remember that they were workers together with Christ, and to trust fully in Christ whether they saw results or not.[244]

At this point the Association considered the question of the bad behaviour of young men who were disruptive at meetings. The minutes had mentioned nothing about this issue until 1881. The fear of a disturbance may have caused Mr. Hertslet to oppose bringing in young men off the street in the summer of 1879. Mr. Hind Smith at the annual meeting in 1880 had encouraged this action, and it is possible the problem had started at this time. The *Surrey Comet* often commented on the unruly behaviour of young men. When the Rev. Lawrence Byrnes first came to Kingston, he said that he considered 'the mass of young men in the town … were ungodly young men.'[245] Finlay Gibson had also said in 1871, 'he had not lived in Kingston long before he discovered there was a great deal of infidelity in the place. Indeed he had never met in any other town with so much outspoken infidelity.'

Within the Victorian psyche, 'infidelity' and being 'ungodly' inevitably resulted in unruly and at times immoral behaviour. The current view is that being a non-believer does not automatically produce disruptive and degenerate behaviour. What does lead to disorder are large numbers of young men and young women living outside parental guidance with leisure time unfilled by meaningful activity. This is compounded when a location has numerous beer-shops and taverns. In Kingston there were many beer shops and taverns and between 1851 and 1881 the population had increased considerably.

In 1851 the Kingston census shows over 12,300 people living in the area, but by 1881 the figure had increased to nearly 36,300. Many reasons account for this increase, but the coming of the railway to Kingston in 1863, the removal of the toll on Kingston Bridge during the early 1870s and Kingston's proximity to London undoubtedly proved major factors, as did the building of large houses and an accompanying demand for domestic staff. Between 1851 to 1881 the numbers of young men, in the locality between fourteen and twenty-five increased almost threefold.

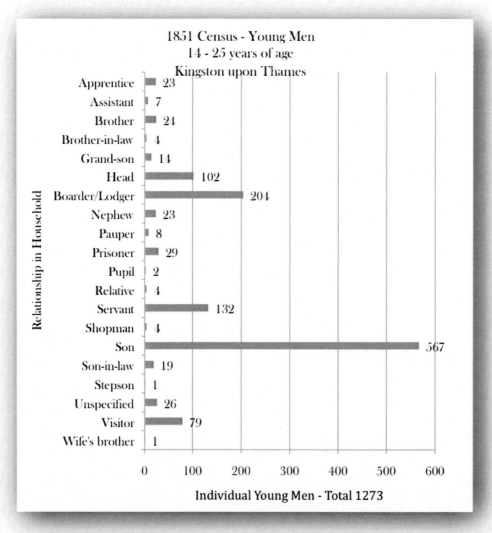

19. Calculated from 1951 Census   (AG)

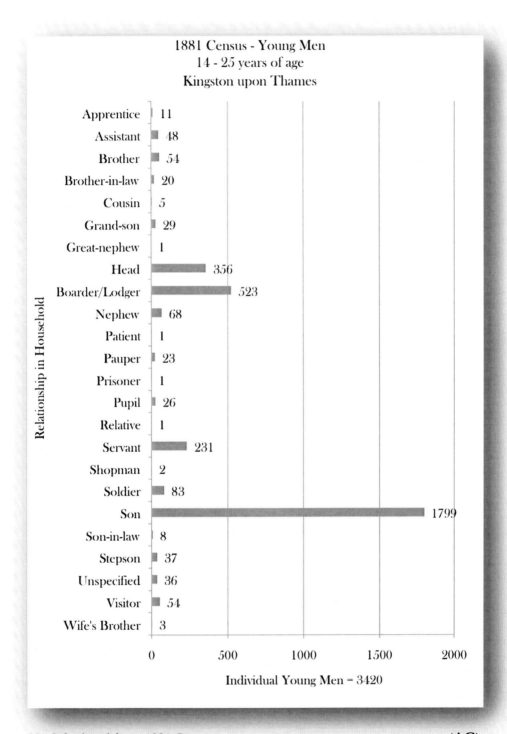

1881 Census - Young Men
14 - 25 years of age
Kingston upon Thames

Relationship in Household	Individual Young Men = 3420
Apprentice	11
Assistant	48
Brother	54
Brother-in-law	20
Cousin	5
Grand-son	29
Great-nephew	1
Head	356
Boarder/Lodger	523
Nephew	68
Patient	1
Pauper	23
Prisoner	1
Pupil	26
Relative	1
Servant	231
Shopman	2
Soldier	83
Son	1799
Son-in-law	8
Stepson	37
Unspecified	36
Visitor	54
Wife's Brother	3

20. Calculated from 1881 Census   **(AG)**

A breakdown of the relationship of these young men to the heads of their household can also be found in Figures 19 and 20. Whereas in 1851 the apprentices, assistants, boarders, lodgers and servants, living away from their families totalled 366 in 1881 they numbered 813.

In September 1880, at about the same time as the young men of the Association were experiencing their difficulties, Mr. E. H. Fricker, a J.P., informed the *Surrey Comet* of a situation that was taking place only a short distance from Zoar Chapel. Mr. Fricker said that he had drawn:

> the attention of Inspector Croucher to what he termed a great nuisance in the High-street chiefly on Sunday evenings. Gangs of young men, he said, assembled on the footpath between the Ram Inn and Harris's foundry and by their language and conduct made themselves very offensive, not only to foot-passengers, who were frequently compelled to step into the road to pass them, but also to the residents of that locality. One or two instances had come to his knowledge of young women being rudely seized and kissed, and he trusted that the police would take steps to protect the public from such insults.[246]

The same gang of young men may have upset the Association meetings. It is unlikely that churches faced similar problems as newspapers would have reported this. Zoar Chapel may not have been considered a church, however, and, being run by young men for young men, a disruptive element may have found amusement in upsetting the meetings. Nobody had called the police, which may have encouraged those involved in the disturbance. Even within the membership some young men, in particular associate members, acted inappropriately. No one disclosed exactly what one of these young men had done, but the culprit requested to speak to the Committee and at a meeting with them, expressed his contrition for his conduct, stating that keeping loose company had had something to do with it. Because of his regret he was allowed to stay.[247]

At the Committee meeting on January 15 1881 Mr. Hind Smith was asked as to the best mode of dealing with badly behaved young men, particularly those who disturbed meetings he said that:

> the question was one of considerable difficulty but that he was inclined to think that on the whole it was better to ensure order and quietness by, if necessary ejecting the ringleaders, and even to call in the services of the police if occasion so required. He also stated that he considered that the Week Evening Bible Class should be conducted with a view to the profit of members rather than of unconverted young men, who should not however be overlooked by them. He suggested that a 'Strangers' Meeting might with profit be commenced.[248]

At the annual meeting that followed, Captain Cundy praised the patience shown by the members in dealing with these difficult situations.[249]

Plans for the Future

Doubtless Mr. Hind Smith and Mr. Newson had conversation regarding the future of the Kingston Association before the 1881 annual meeting. In his address to the Meeting Mr. Hind Smith said:

> He would remind those present that this Association was part and parcel of the General Young Men's Christian Association and not distinct by itself.[250] He then passed on to speak of the great extension of the Association's work in London, the opening of the East Central Rooms, the extension of the old premises at Aldersgate Street the great blessing that had attended their efforts & above all of the purchase of Exeter Hall for the sum of £25,000 by five gentlemen for the use of the Young Men's Christian Association. The Hall was to be opened on the 29th March when he hoped to see the Kingston members present. He congratulated the Kingston Association on having kept the primary object of the spiritual good of young men first in view after exhorting members to live up to their profession concluded by an earnest appeal to the unsaved to accept Christ.[251]

Why did Mr. Hind Smith remark that the Kingston Association was 'not distinct by itself'? To answer that question, we need to consider what happened the following year. In March 1882 Mr. Newson reported to the Committee that he had received and accepted an invitation from the secretary of the Wimbledon branch to attend a meeting of the various branches of the Association in the district. Mr. Hind Smith presided over the first meeting, which the minutes referred to as the South West District Quarterly Meeting, but later as the South West District (Union of Branches). The other branches in the group in May 1882 were Barnes, Fulham, Twickenham and Wimbledon.[252] William Hind Smith, together with another provincial leader, had developed a system of provincial 'divisions' in the movement. Whilst branches could remain independent except in terms of membership, this development would act as a support network.[253]

Mr. Hertslet attended his last Committee meeting on July 29, 1881. The minutes do not mention this change, but he must have known that it was inevitable. At the annual meeting held on February 3, 1882, it was decided to revise the rules. Whereas Rule 2 had read:

> That the object of the Association be the improvement of the spiritual and mental condition of young men.

Rule 2 now read:

> That the object of the Association be the improvement of the **spiritual, social and mental condition of young men.**

It was also agreed that there should be a new Rule 14:

> That young men over 15 years of age of good moral character be admitted as Associates on payment of a fixed subscription entitling them to all the privileges of membership except the right of voting at meetings.

The door was therefore open to all young men, as long as they acted appropriately, to become associate members, but not all young men found acting appropriately easy. The associate member who had been allowed to stay after apologising for acting badly resigned in June 1882, leaving his membership card torn in half and a message saying that he had done with the Association. In June 1882 a decision was made to form a Kingston Y.M.C.A. Cricket Club, a decision that undoubtedly encouraged a number of young men into associate membership. [254]

ZOAR CHAPEL AND GILBERT HOUSE

Zoar Chapel and Gilbert House

We have already mentioned the problems associated to Zoar Chapel and Gilbert House. The Kingston Association leased Zoar Chapel in 1876 together with Gilbert House, the premises next door. The cost to the Y.M.C.A. was £30 per annum, but the agreement also included letting Gilbert House to the Cooper family for a sum of £10 per annum, with the Association using some of Gilbert House facilities, including the W.C. The accommodation therefore only cost the Y.M.C.A. £20 per annum. When the Association took over the premises, the chimney was smoking and had to be swept at a cost of two shillings. The sweeping did not solve the problem, and the Association paid James Offer, a gas fitter and smith, who also lived in Brick Lane, eight shillings to repair the chimney. The smoking chimney remained a problem even after it had been heightened at a cost of 16/-.

Although other Y.M.C.A.s must have experienced similar circumstances, some met in almost luxurious surroundings. In America by the 1870s, the Y.M.C.A.s were affluent. When he visited the Kingston branch and spoke at its annual meeting in March 1877, George Williams would have compared the premises with those he had seen in Philadelphia, particularly as Mr. Rimer during the reading of the annual report stated that 'the year had been a trying one in many respects … they hope, however, that as the new premises are suitable to their wants, the Kingston branch may in time become one of the most flourishing in the Kingdom.' The minutes reported that Mr. Williams gave 'an interesting account of his visit with a deputation to the Philadelphia Exhibition last year, and described the power and numbers of the Y.M.C.A. in the U.S.'[255]

The contrast between the Kingston branch and those in New York would have been enormous. In 1867 the New York Y.M.C.A. board bought a plot of land for $142,000 dollars and constructed a five story building which opened in 1869. *Harper's Weekly* described it as 'entitled to be designated the handsomest clubhouse in the city.' This structure on the corner of 23rd Street was designed by the architect James Renwick, Jr., who also built Grace Episcopal Church and St.

Patrick's Cathedral in Madison Avenue. Its features, which other Y.M.C.A. buildings copied, included a central lobby with rooms radiating off so that the secretary could keep an eye on all the activities taking place. The New York Association paid the mortgage by letting out the ground floor to stores and the upper stories as office space. By 1884 New York had eight branches of the Y.M.C.A., all of which were prosperous.[256]

The London Association at the time of the 1851 Great Exhibition met in 7 Gresham Street. Later the Association used the Aldersgate Street branch, the building with an exceptionally good library. During the 1880s, the Y.M.C.A. acquired the lease of Exeter Hall in the Strand, a meeting place with a room built to contain four thousand people and where the Anti-Corn Law League and anti-slavery meetings had previously been held. In many of the major cities, such as Manchester, Glasgow and Birmingham, the Y.M.C.A. provided very worthy buildings for the use of their members.[257]

Despite the derelict state of the Kingston building and the smoking chimney, the Association rented out the rooms to other groups, with the initiative coming from those who wanted to rent. This was either because most buildings in the location of Kingston were in a similar state of disrepair or rents in better-quality buildings too expensive. Over time a variety of individuals and organisations made requests to use the premises. In particular in July 1880 there was a request to use the rooms as an infant school.[258]

Zoar Chapel a Primary School; 1880

The Rev. Albert Stewart W. Young M.A. replaced the Rev. A. Williams as the vicar of All Saints Church after the latter's death. Mr. Young had been *in situ* only a few weeks when his congregation found that their young vicar was prepared to involve himself in a variety of good causes. On August 4, 1877, he preached his first sermon at the Parish Church. Six weeks later his sermon on the Indian famine so moved his parishioners that the collection totalled £59. 2s. 6d.[259] By 1878 he had tackled the problems of the infant school children in Kingston whose accommodation, he stated, was 'in a dangerous state of dilapidation.' A letter to the *Surrey Comet* questioned Mr. Young's involvement stating that:

> He reminds us that the present infant schoolroom was intended to be temporary only, but that 20 years have passed, and it has not been replaced by another building, and is now 'in an almost dangerous state of dilapidation...the vicar urges that the building of this infant school is a project in which "the whole parish should feel a real concern and apply themselves to in an energetic and self-denying spirit."

The writer said, 'the whole parish' had not been concerned because the infant school was a Church of England school, and continued:

> The inevitable School Board will come even in Tory and backward Kingston, and then I venture to predict, one of its acts will be to "take over" the schoolroom the Vicar wishes to build – supposing that he succeeds – because there is lacking the zeal and liberality required for its support.
>
> A Friend to National Education.[260]

Although we cannot doubt the Rev. Albert Young's wish to improve the school accommodation used by the infants in the parish, the letter shows that the 1870 and 1880 Education Acts may have provided another reason. The 1870 Act allowed voluntary schools to continue unchanged, but, in those areas where they were needed 'school boards' were to be set up. These were elected bodies funded out of local rates, and, unlike voluntary schools, the teaching of religion in schools with school boards was to be 'non-denominational.' By 1880 as many schools had been set up by school boards, it seemed possible to make school attendance compulsory for children up to the age of ten, although children could still continue their education up to the age of thirteen on a voluntary basis.[261] The new infant school had not been built, and to avoid its being taken over by a school board the Rev. Albert Young had approached the Y.M.C.A.

> The Secretary handed in a letter from Mr. Young inquiring if the School committee could have the use of the Rooms for about 6 months as a temporary Infant School and if so at what rate. After some consideration it was deemed advisable that the children should be admitted provided satisfactory terms could be arranged. Mrs. Cooper was called in to the Committee and stated that she would be willing to undertake the extra trouble and cleaning for an additional payment of 3/6 per week (which was to include the cost of a charwoman to scrub the place out once every week) but that she did not approve of the children passing though her house to the Water Closet. It was pointed out also that considerable damage would be done to the paper wainscoting of the larger room, and it was agreed that a sum of 3/6 per week should be charged to cover this item. Also that it would be expedient to stipulate that Mr. Young should provide his own wood and coal for firing to be kept in a separate box. It was agreed that the net rent should be charged at the rate of 8/- per week. It was therefore moved by Mr. Hertslet seconded by Mr. Newson & carried "That Mr. Young's application for the use of the Association Rooms as a temporary Infant School be consented to subject to his making all arrangements with respect to W.C. accommodation, and that the rent per week be 15/- to include gas and cleaning, that all coal and wood be supplied at Mr. Young's expense and the same be kept in a separate box, and that any damage beyond fair wear and tear be paid for.[262]

Mr. Hertslet was involved in these negotiations, although there is no indication that he had any connection with the outcome a week later. On August 6, 1880, the secretary handed in a letter from Mr. Young, stating that 'the Baptist School Room had been engaged by him as a temporary Infant School, and that the Association's Rooms would not therefore be required.' The *Surrey Comet* on September 4 wrote the following:

> A Christian Example
>
> In these days of sectarian strife and bitterness it is quite refreshing to record the following act of kindness on the part of the Rev. H. Bayley, pastor of the Brick-lane Baptist Chapel. The infant school in Wood-street having been demolished, and it being necessary to find a temporary home for the children during the period which must elapse before the new school is erected the Vicar of Kingston applied to Mr. Bayley for the use of the Baptist school-room for that purpose and the request, we are pleased to say, was most readily granted. Deeds are better than words. The Vicar of Kingston, happily, has always shown a kindly disposition towards the Dissenting denominations of the town...[263]

If the Rev. Albert Young had intended to retain this particular school as a voluntary Anglican school, he had initially asked the help of the interdenominational Y.M.C.A. and eventually accepted the assistance of the Baptists in Brick Lane to achieve this end.

Mr. Cooper's Tenancy

Mr. Cooper suddenly, at the end of 1880, decided to offer up possession of Gilbert House to the Association. In a letter he wrote that, if this offer was not acceptable, he would sublet the rooms to other parties. He offered to continue to clean the premises until a substitute could be found. Later Mr. Cooper said that he had written the letter after undue pressure when worried by business matters.

'Business matters' alone may not have prompted him to write the letter. It may also have been family matters, because Eliza Cooper was expecting baby Mabel, and she already had Joseph who had been born in 1877. The letter from Mr. Cooper was dated November 29, 1880, and was handed in after the agenda for the Committee had been prepared. The secretary reported that 'there was felt to be a need for another room as an additional classroom and that a right of way from the reading room direct into the street was also much needed.' The Committee considered that this would be a good time to acquire the extra space. They discussed this idea and concluded that ideally what they needed was:

The kitchen of the cottage adjoining the Rooms together with the right of way from the Reading Room through the Cottage to the street and the use of the W.C. be acquired if possible…

Mr. Cooper was to be thanked for his offer to clean the rooms and that he be asked to give up his agreement in exchange for the duplicate in the possession of the Association.[264]

Mr. Cooper said that he couldn't find his copy of the agreement.[265] He told Mr. Parslow that he regretted having signed the letter and wished to recall it, and that the loss of the house would be highly detrimental to his painting business. It also would inconvenience him in carrying on his work of 'text posting.' Mr. Parslow thought that the Committee should not have acted so quickly as the letter was not put onto the Agenda and Mr. Cooper should 'in consideration of his being connected with the Association be treated somewhat indulgently in the matter…'

A long discussion ensued in which Mr. Hertslet and the Secretary both denied that any undue pressure had been brought to bear on Mr. Cooper to induce him to sign the letter and the Secretary detailed the history of the various negotiations with Mr. Cooper showing that the step he had taken with regard to the cottage was with his own free will and consent: he also pointed out that although notice of the letter having been received was not inserted on the Agenda paper six members of the Committee had been informed of its receipt prior to the date of the Committee Meeting … With regard to showing Mr. Cooper as much consideration as was possible consistent with the interests of the Association there was no difference of opinion on this point.

Mr. Cooper was then called in and reiterated the arguments advanced by Mr. Parslow on his behalf. He stated that he regretted having signed the letter and wished to continue tenant of the cottage. His attention was drawn to the fact that the agreement for the tenancy of the cottage contained no clause to the effect that he could not be ejected on due notice being given, but that there was a clause which rendered him liable to pay his proportion of rates and taxes levied on the building. After a long conversation, during which Mr. Cooper's views were elicited about a continuance of the tenancy, he withdrew.

Eventually Mr. Cooper agreed to give the Association certain rights in return for waiving their claim to the rates and taxes that were due from him and that he could continue with the tenancy up to September 29, 1881 as before, but with the following provisos:

That the Association have a right of way along the passage leading from Brick Lane through the cottage into the Reading Room

That the Association be granted the use of the room adjoining the Reading Room on any evening when it may be required.

That young men attending the Reading Room and classes and members of the Association be allowed to use the W.C. belonging to the cottage.

That the rent to be paid by Mr. Cooper to the Association be at the rate of Ten pounds per annum payable on the usual quarterdays. [266]

On December 28, 1880, Mr. Newson reported to the Committee that:

As Mr. Cooper was still unable to find his agreement he had got him to sign across the duplicate that the agreement was cancelled and had also signed the duplicate on behalf of the Association to the same effect. Mr. Parslow had witnessed both signatures.

Later Mr. Parslow wanted to increase Mr. Cooper's payment for cleaning the Association rooms, but the Committee refused, as they thought Mr. Cooper was paid sufficiently well.[267]

Although the minutes omitted to record the fact, Mr. Cooper and his family did move away from Gilbert House and let the rooms to a tenant up to the end of the lease on September 29, 1881. On the 1881 census taken on April 3, Joseph and Eliza Cooper were living in Browns Yard, Fairfield Road, Kingston with their four year old son Joseph, baby Mabel and Caroline Patter, a general servant. Mr. Cooper was cleaning the rooms up to September 29, when the lease expired. After this date a Mrs. Turner accepted an offer to 'attend to and clean the rooms' and the Committee allowed her to live rent-free. Mrs. Newson, the secretary's mother, who had known Mrs. Turner for a considerable time, said that she had informed her of the nature of the duties she would be expected to perform. Mrs. Newson also promised to see that the rooms were properly kept.[268] Thereafter Mrs. Turner was referred to as 'the housekeeper.'

The Militia in Kingston; 1881

Despite the poor quality of the rooms and the lack of facilities, the Committee continued to receive requests from outside bodies to use the premises. Mr. Parslow reported that he had given orders for the gas to be laid on in the kitchen and passage of the cottage, but he regretted that the work had not been done. It was arranged to have one pendent only in the kitchen.[269] In April 1881:

A letter was handed in from Mrs. Julia Luck asking for the use of the Rooms for a Reading Room for the militia during their stay in the town. The

Secretary reported that he had seen Mrs. Luck and that she was very desirous to obtain the use of the Room and would endeavour to arrange matters so as not to interfere with the Association's work.[270]

Kingston had always had a military presence because the town was situated on the Thames close to Hampton Court, and the road between Portsmouth and London was a route of strategic importance. In 1642 the soldiers of Charles I stayed in the town while the king lived in Hampton Court Palace. A few years later Parliamentarian soldiers were stationed in Kingston, and in 1647 Sir Thomas Fairfax lodged in the Crane Inn in the market place. A year later Lord Francis Villiers was killed on the outskirts of Kingston, presumably on a lane named Villiers Path that runs between Lambert's Road and Surbiton Hill Road.[271] In 1782 county titles were introduced for Infantry Regiments to encourage the enlisting of recruits.[272] The Militia Barracks were situated on the south side of Fairfield Road between Eden Street and Fairfield West. The Childers Reforms, undertaken by the Secretary of State for War in 1881, Hugh Childers, resulted in the East Surrey Regiment being formed out of an amalgamation of the 31st (Huntingdonshire) Regiment of Foot and the 70th (Surrey) Regiment of Foot. In April 1873, eight years before their merger, the 31st and 70th were linked together into 47 Sub-District Brigade and were trained in Kingston.[273]

The minute book does not give a description of what was required to relax the militia between periods of training. Two letters dated in May 1876, one from the vicar of St. Paul's Church in Kingston, the Rev. Arthur Cornford, and another from a Lucy P. S. Ovens of Knights Park, reveal the requirements. Lucy P. S. Ovens wrote that

> the old Schoolroom in Wood Street is open for their use every evening, and writing materials, books, papers, draughts and dominoes are provided. A piano is hired, and singing goes on at intervals, the evening being concluded by reading some verses from the Bible, prayer and hymns. The attendance varies from 100 to nearly 300 from both regiments of militia. The number of men now in Kingston removed for the time from their homes and employments makes such a place of resort most necessary, and the only shelter from the evils of drink and of the streets…The reader employed to visit the tents and hospital daily, as well as to be present on the room every evening, must be paid. The hire of the room amounts to nine shillings every week. Contributions earnestly solicited…

The Rev. A. Cornford wrote that

> in order that we may benefit them during their stay amongst us, which will be extended to several weeks, two rooms have been opened every evening (except Sunday) for their use, where they may find innocent recreation. The

opportunity of writing letters and reading the papers is also afforded them, while those who like can engage in something more directly profitable, such as reading the Holy Scripture and Prayer. The "Army Scripture Readers" and "Soldiers' Friendly Society" have sent down a reader to assist in this work, but there are heavy expenses connected with it...[274]

21. St. Paul's Church Kingston   (CR)

Five years later in April 1881, the Y.M.C.A. Committee agreed to help Mrs. Luck, who had taken over the organisation of recreation facilities for the Militia that year. They arranged to 'let the large room only of the Association to her on the following terms & conditions':

> That on Tuesday & Thursday evenings the meetings for the Militia be closed at 8.15 & that the men be all cleared out by 8.30 p.m.

> That Mrs. Luck shall make good any damage or breakage.

> That she also appoint a competent person, who shall be present at all times & shall be responsible for the maintenance of proper order.

> That she arrange to have the matting removed every Monday, the Room thoroughly cleaned out every Saturday night the matting replaced and everything put in usual order for the Sunday Meetings.[275]

The Committee had every right to be cautious as there could be incidents regarding the behaviour of the militia when they were in Kingston. In July 1881 two privates in the 1st Royal Surrey Militia came before Mr. E.H. Fricker J.P., charged with disorderly conduct and refusing to quit the British Oak Inn when requested to do so and of assaulting the sons of the landlord.[276] The secretary was left to arrange with Mrs. Luck for payment of 10/- per week if possible (to include gas) but that he shall in no case accept less than 7/6 per week.[277]

Repairs and Upkeep of the Premises; 1881

Although there is no indication that there were problems relating to repairs to the building before the summer of 1881, in July of that year the secretary reported to the Committee that he had written to the landlord, Mr. Fricker, twice urging him to do repairs to the building but had received no reply to either letter. At a meeting on July 29, it was agreed:

> that the Secretary write to Mr. Fricker again drawing his attention to the state of the building and to the fact the rent to Midsummer is not yet paid; and further to inform him that the Committee would not feel justified in parting with the rent (which is raised by subscriptions) until the repairs are executed [278]

As no reply had been received from the landlord by August 29, the secretary spoke to Captain Cundy to try to induce him to communicate with the landlord.[279] On September 13, 1881, nothing had been settled:

> Mr. Parslow reported that he had on that day seen the Landlord, but that the interview was most unsatisfactory and that he could hold out no hopes of his executing the repairs demanded. It was therefore agreed 'that the Secretary write to Mr. Fricker stating that unless he executed the necessary repairs immediately the Committee will call the attention of the Sanitary Inspectors to the state of the building.' [280]

Not until December 2, 1881 did the Committee received a letter from Mr. Willmott, the brewery manager of the Eagle Brewery on behalf of Mr. Fricker when he said that he would be willing to allow £5 towards repairing and cleansing the Association rooms.[281] In February 1882 both the lack of conveniences on the premises, and the damp state of the outside walls of the premises were mentioned.[282] In March Mr. W. Brown gave an estimate for the construction and fitting of a urinal in the W.C. for the sum of 15/- and the Committee decided to repair the W.C. with money from the landlord. Mr. Parslow reported that Mr. Fricker intended to put some air bricks in the cellar to try to cure the dampness of the walls.[283]

Zoar Chapel would not have been the only building needing renovation. Most early buildings had poor foundations, porous bricks, thin external brickwork, unseasoned timber, and chimneys incorrectly flued. Building construction depended on a builder's own honesty and competence.[284] A report by Edwin Chadwick in 1842 had resulted in the Public Health Act of 1848, but this act served as no more than a 'Form of Bye-laws', national guidelines to be applied locally. Most local authorities chose not to set up local boards of health under the Act due to the cost of appointing officials, Kingston being one such authority. Only when the Artisans and Labourers Dwelling Act (Torrens Act) 1868 empowered local authorities to compel owners to demolish or repair insanitary dwellings were tenants, in theory, able to keep their properties in a habitable state. In practice, compliance with the 1868 Act was not always used, as some landlords were part of the elite in the locality and able to sidestep involvement in costly renovation.

The problems relating to Zoar Chapel were ongoing. The smoking chimney has already been mentioned, as has the lack of toilet facilities and the damp. In April 1882 Mr. Brown had erected an urinal, but had not repaired the W.C.[285] On October 18, 1882, the rooms were thoroughly cleaned, matting taken up curtains down, floors scrubbed, and the chimneys swept. The pump belonging to the cottage had become useless and had to be repaired. Mr. Shelley the plumber charged 5s 6d, and the money deducted from the next payment of the rent.[286] In July 1883 the copper was also found unfit for use because Mr. Cooper had kept some paint or whitewash in it and it also had to be 'thoroughly cleansed.' The Committee first decided that they should draw Mr. Cooper's attention to the state in which it had been left, but, as the cost to clean it was only 1s 2d, they dropped the matter. As there was no proper lid the secretary was instructed to procure one. Mr. Cooper would not have been available to remedy the state of the copper. On July 13, 1883, he, his wife and family left for Australia, having previously been given a letter of introduction from the Kingston Association to the Brisbane Y.M.C.A.[287]

In the same month Mr. Newson wrote to Mr. Fricker about the skylight roof of the scullery, but as usual his letter was ignored. Mr. Newson said that the state of the roof and the skylight demanded immediate attention. The Committee procured an estimate and forwarded it to the landlord, giving him notice that unless he saw to the repairs in a week the Committee would arrange for the work to be done and deduct the cost from the rent.[288] Mr. J. Young's estimate was £1. 8/-. The Committee considered it satisfactory, and did as they had threatened. In August Mr. Edmund Hunter Fricker called to enquire about the repairs to the scullery. The minutes state that 'he was informed that the repairs were completed and left word that in future cases he would see to the repairs in place of his brother Mr. A.E. Fricker.' (This is incorrect as Mr. E.H. Fricker was the brother of Mr. T. H. Fricker, the original owner of the Eagle Brewery who had died in 1873 and the uncle of the current owner Mr. Arthur Fricker.)[289] There is no reason to doubt that the visit was made and Mr. E.H. Fricker's statement was correct. Mr. Edmund Hunter Fricker was sixty-three years of age in 1883, a magistrate and a timber merchant employing seven men.[290]

In February 1884 Mrs. Turner was too ill to undertake her duties and had to engage help at 3/6d per week. The Committee agreed that she should have an allowance of this amount for six weeks to pay for the substitute, the allowance continuing beyond the six weeks as Mrs. Turner remained unable to undertake some of her duties.[291] In May the subject arose again, and the allowance continued until June.[292] By September 1885 Mrs. Turner asked to be relieved from her responsibilities due to her illness. The minutes refer to the dilapidated condition of the living rooms at the Y.M.C.A. premises in Kingston but not to the fate of Mrs. Turner and her children.

Requests to use the Premises; 1881 – 1882

Surprisingly, requests to use the rooms continued although the sanitary arrangements in the premises remained extremely limited. On November 4, 1881, Miss Ranyard requested their use to hold a midday prayer meeting at a cost of 1/6d per week.[293] In April 1882 Mr. Hugo of Great Swan Alley, London, wanted to rent one of them for language classes. The price would be 1/- for one hour in the morning and 6d for each additional hour and 6d additional for firing per day when required. In June a Mr. Morel applied to use one of the rooms one or two nights a week for holding French classes on the same terms as Mr. Hugo. It was agreed but for male pupils only.[294] In September 1882 the Hampton Wick Junior Cricket Club were allowed the use the rooms for 1/- per meeting plus 6d extra for a fire if one should be required.[295] When requested to pay, they 'disclaimed all responsibility for using the premises when the Club was known as "Alpha C.C." The secretary also claimed the charge was excessive. Eventually it was decided to let the matter drop to avoid unpleasantness.[296]

In October 1882 Miss Walker, who had helped prepare teas, wanted to practice occasionally on the harmonium during the daytime, and the Association agreed that she could do so whenever she felt inclined and that a key should be procured for the harmonium. In December 1882 a Mr. Wheeler wanted to practice the harmonium on Friday afternoons. As he was not connected with the Association, he was charged 1/- on each occasion.[297] In March 1883 the Blue

Ribbon Mission wanted the rooms placed at their disposal for daily prayer meetings. To accommodate the Mission the normal week night meetings would be postponed during the progress of the event and there would be no charge, except that the Mission was requested to compensate the housekeeper for the extra trouble occasioned by the meetings.[298] In May 1883 Mr. J.J. Britton also asked for the use of the rooms to hold occasional meetings with the Religious Agencies of which he was secretary. This request was agreed on payment of 1/- per night to cover cost of gas and attendance.[299] In June 1883 Mr. Robert Buchanan applied to use the rooms on June 8, when he proposed to hold a lecture on 'Bees' in aid of the Cottage Hospital at Surbiton. He was charged 2/6d.[300]

In consequence of the social meetings happening once a quarter instead of once a year as formerly, estimates were procured for the supply of china and spoons, and four dozen cups and saucers, nine large plates, three milk jugs, three sugar basins, two tea pots, one coffee pot, four dozen plates (small), and four dozen spoons were bought. The crockery cost £1. 17s 2d. The four comet burners and globes complete for the hall were bought for 8/-.[301] Mr. Coote had applied to use the rooms on July 27, to hold a tea and meetings for the policemen of the district. As Mr. Coote had on two occasions come down to Kingston to give addresses without charging out of pocket expenses, he was granted the use of the rooms free but he was to pay for any further services from Mrs. Turner. Miss Edmondstone was allowed to use the rooms from two-thirty to eight-forty-five p.m. for a meeting on October 20, in connection with the Special Mission to policemen, at a charge of 2/6 plus housekeeper services extra if required. The secretary reported that he had received an application from the secretary of the Home for Little Boys, in Farningham, for help with the arrangement of the meeting to be held at the Leopold Hall on October 25, 1883. Arrangements were made for the boys to sleep at the Association rooms.[302]

The only refusal by the Y.M.C.A. to allow a group to use their premises was made in March 1882. Mr. Blandy had applied for the use of the large room for one evening each week to allow his group to hold a devotional meeting, singing-practice &c. The minutes state that special circumstances were connected with the application that would cause serious trouble should it be granted. The secretary wrote to Mr. Blandy, regretting that the Committee could not let the rooms for any denominational purpose. This group was made up of the men and women who had vacated the Brick Lane Baptist Church and who, in March 1882, established Bunyan Baptist Church where opening services were held in the new building on January 7, 1885.[303] The *Surrey Comet* dated November 19, 1881 gives some detail of the circumstances behind the 'absenteeism of between thirty and forty members' of the Baptist Church and of a meeting held in the Wesleyan schools in St. James Road soon after. The meeting had been called to express their sympathy with Mr. Tarry, who had been dismissed from the role of organist after eight years' service. The officers of the church had made this decision rather than the church members who had appointed Mr. Tarry. This act was considered 'illegal' by those who had left the church.[304] Mr. Charles Blandy was a thirty-nine-year-old groom and gardener who lived in 5 Alex Cottages, Mill Street, whilst Mr. John Tarry, the organist, was a thirty-nine-year-old bootmaker who lived in Blenheim House in Brook Street. Mr. Blandy had been the secretary of the Y.M.C.A. at the Brick Lane Baptist Chapel when this Y.M.C.A. had met for their anniversary in October 1880, the occasion being mentioned previously in the chapter, 'A New Beginning.'

THE VICAR OF KINGSTON

AND THE EARLY CLOSING MOVEMENT

JUNE 1881 – JUNE 1882

Early Closing on Wednesdays

An event took place in Kingston on June 21, 1881, the Vicar of All Saints Church, the Rev. A.S.W. Young M.A. became associated with the Early Closing Movement. Not only the young men, but the Y.M.C.A.'s founder George Williams had always supported the movement. Mr. Young described how he had become involved at a meeting held on the first anniversary of this event. He said:

> he was surprised one evening, while sitting in his study, by a deputation who came to ask him if he would use any influence he might possess to procure one day in each week for early closing. That request, in itself most reasonable, as it appeared to him, was entirely in accord and harmony with the thoughts that had been in his own mind upon the subject, although it did not appear to him in what way he could be of any use ... Sometimes he wanted to see young men in the town, about joining confirmation classes and for other purposes, and they said they could not come to see him until after a late hour, and this prevented their coming at all, because he would have been obliged to keep them out so late ... He felt that it was a serious thing that young people should be confined so late, and precluded from enjoying the fresh air and scenery so necessary for their health, and which all other classes of society were able to get. But it occurred at once to his mind that it might be a delicate matter for him to interfere in, as he would be coming between two classes of society. Still, he felt that if there was one person who, more than any other, might venture on such an officious step, as some might think it, it was the clergyman of the parish ... who from the position he occupied, formed as it were, a centre of society in the parish, and was a kind of fulcrum, so to speak, of society generally, around which all might turn and work in harmony...

Mr. Young had issued an invitation to all the tradesmen in the town and neighbourhood to come and talk 'in a friendly way,' and about thirty of the principal shopkeepers met him in the schools in Wood Street.[305] The neighbourhood was canvassed with two gentlemen to every street and the result

22. All Saint's Church, Market Place, Kingston upon Thames   (**AG** 2012)

was made known in the local press with a list of those who agreed to the principal of early closing on one day of the week. Thereafter early closing by a number of the shops became a feature in and around the town.

At a meeting exactly one year after the date, tradesmen, including Mr East, and several workplace assistants met to affirm their support for the continuance of closing early on one day of the week. During the meeting the Kingston branch of the Amalgamated Society of Carpenters and Joiners received thanks for the practical interest and support manifested in their letter to the local press. The meeting also praised and thanked the vicar:

> for his invaluable advice, his strenuous efforts, his letters to the Press, and for the great influence he has so beneficially exercised, and asks his acceptance of this cabinet and address from the assistants in all trades, as a small token of their appreciation of his labours...

The address was as follows:

> This testimonial, together with a cabinet, is presented to the Rev. A. S. W. Young M.A., vicar of Kingston-on-Thames, by the assistants in the various houses of business in Kingston, Surbiton, and Norbiton, in grateful recognition of his kind and unwearied exertions in promoting the movement for a general suspension of business in the above district at 5 o'clock on Wednesdays.
> The first anniversary of the early closing movement, June 21, 1882.

It is reported that the Vicar said:

> I am sure I do not know what in the world to say in answer to this great surprise which you have thought fit to spring upon me tonight. I have been confounded. I had no idea this sort of thing was in preparation ...What I have done has been a most pleasant and agreeable work to me; and it has been so very little – simply to write a few letters to the Press...and I am very glad indeed that before thanking me, you have not forgotten to offer your thanks to them, (the employers) for they deserve them more than I do, as the matter has touched them really and closely; and the fact that they have so generously made the concession shows that they have real sympathy and interest in your welfare.[306]

The problem persisted. In October 1886 a draper wrote to the *Surrey Comet* 'while customers will come it is not wise (in a financial point of view) to close the shutters,' and he appealed to the mechanics and the working community at large to procure shorter hours.[307] In May 1887, presumably writing about closure on a Wednesday evening, the *Surrey Comet* published a letter from a tradesman:

> Dear Sir – Walking at 6.30 this evening from the Promenade through High-street, Market-place, Thames, Clarence, and Church-streets I counted 29

shops open, exclusive of butchers, fishmongers, confectioners and tobacconists. Now, sir, is this fair to those who give the holiday to their assistants? … No doubt many would close if they were asked, but since the movement was started nothing has been done to place it on a firm footing, and many now remain open who formerly closed at 5 o'clock...[308]

The vicar's involvement did not end here. In 1890 Mr. Young, together with the mayor, Councillor James East, Mr. Cowdery, the Y.M.C.A. secretary and others, made a further attempt to promote early closing on a Wednesday in Kingston. As we shall see later, in 1890 their activities appear to have been more successful.

Although the early closing of the shops was piecemeal for some employees even by 1887, life was occasionally very pleasurable. In August of that year one of the breweries treated their entire workforce to a trip up river on two steam launches to a meadow 'kindly lent for the day by Lady Aylesford.' Here they enjoyed a sumptuous lunch, indulged in team sports and a short game of cricket. After a four-hour return journey the workforce arrived back at ten p.m.[309] Although many still continued to work long hours, leisure time for others was increasing, expectations were rising, and Kingston Y.M.C.A., possibly under the guidance of Mr. Hind Smith, was about to revise its rules to include 'social' objectives.

'SOCIAL TO BE ADDED AFTER SPIRITUAL':
RULES, SUBCOMMITTEES AND DISCUSSION
1881 – 1884

A Period of Change

The general meeting of the members of the Kingston upon Thames branch of the Y.M.C.A., held at their rooms in Brick Lane, Kingston on Thursday evening September 29, 1881, at 8.30 p.m, gave no outward sign of the changes destined to take place following the meeting. Captain Cundy took the chair and after a hymn had been sung, he led the meeting in prayer and then called upon the secretary, Mr. Newson, to state the results of the voting. Twenty-five papers had been returned, and it was put to the meeting, 'that the above nine members do act as the Committee of the Association for the twelve months ending 30 September 1882.' The Committee can be found in Table 4, Page 234, (the September date was changed later to June 30, 1882). Mr. Newson was voted in again as secretary, Mr. Buchanan, assistant secretary, Mr. Walter, treasurer and Mr. Parslow, assistant treasurer. As Mr. Lea was leaving the Association he received a *Crudens Concordance*.[310] In December 1881 Mr. John S. Morten, who lived in Frascati, St. James Road, Surbiton, rejoined the Association. He was one of those who came to the first meeting when he was twenty-two years old, and was therefore one of the founding members of the reformed 1874 Y.M.C.A.[311]

On February 3, 1882, the rules were revised, the most significant being the change in Rule 2, placing 'social' with 'spiritual' and 'mental' and Rule 14, allowing young men of good character to be admitted as Associates.[312] A revision of the rules appears in Appendix VII, page 220. Thereafter Mr. Newson also restructured the branch, probably under the guidance of Mr. Hind Smith, giving a wider number of members responsibility for the organisation of their Association with subcommittees appointed to regulate and organise the different departments. The subcommittees were classified as finance, religious meetings, open air, social and intellectual, visiting and cricket club.[313]

In March 1882 Mr. Newson reported to the Committee that he had received and accepted an invitation from the secretary of the Wimbledon branch to attend a meeting of the various branches of the Association in the district.[314] These branch quarterly meetings were connected with the National Council of Y.M.C.A.s formed in 1882 to coordinate the activities of the local associations in England, Wales and Ireland with headquarters located in Exeter Hall.[315]

Branch Quarterly Meetings 1882—1884; 'South West Suburban District (Union of Branches)'

March 1882 — June 1882

The invitation to the first meeting came from the secretary of the Wimbledon branch inviting the treasurer, secretary and another member of the branch to attend. Mr. Newson and Mr. Parslow attended and reported to the Committee on April 3, 1882. The other branches represented were Barnes, Fulham, Twickenham and Wimbledon, and the meeting was presided over by Mr. Hind Smith. Mr. G.H. Lee had been given the position of travelling secretary for what became known as the 'South West Suburban District (Union of Branches)', and he had arranged for the various branches to meet for the first time at the Wimbledon Association on April 28, 1882.[316] (We shall meet Mr. G.H. Lee later as he had formerly been a member of the Surbiton Y.M.C.A.)

The meeting adopted the following resolutions, which were later brought before the Committee of the Kingston Association for confirmation:

(1) That the basis of union of branches of this District be that adopted at Paris 1855. *The Young Men's Christian Associations seek to unite those young men who, regarding Jesus Christ as their God and Saviour according to the Holy Scriptures, desire to be His disciples in their doctrine and in their life, and to associate their efforts for the extension of His Kingdom amongst young men.*

(2) That the right of voting at business meetings electing delegates &c be not given to Associates and that all the management of the affairs of the Association be vested in the hands of the members as now & hitherto.

(3) That the Secretary at least one other member of the Committee of each Branch of the Union attend the quarterly meeting of representatives of branches of Y.M.C.A. in this district.

(4) That it is advisable that meetings of the Sunday School Teachers in the various Districts be convened for the purpose of conferring with them as to the best means of dealing with the older scholars about to leave their schools.

The Kingston branch confirmed and adopted these four resolutions.[317] In June the secretary reported that he had received a circular from the National Committee with regard to the Conference of the British Association in Glasgow in September. No delegate from the Kingston branch was available to go.[318]

July 1882–June 1883

At the Fulham meeting on July 21, 1882, Mr. W.E. Shipton was elected chairman and Captain Cundy offered two prizes of £2 each (in books) for the two best essays on 'Union with Christ.' A list of the members from each branch went to the district secretary, and all alterations were to be advised quarterly. On October 20, when the meeting was held in Kingston, the chief business focused on the selection of representatives for the S.W. Suburban District at the Conference to be held at Birmingham.[319]

In April 1883 the secretary handed in a copy of the draft constitution proposed at the quarterly district meeting in January for the adoption by the district committee. After careful consideration of the draft, the Committee made small changes to the wording and decided that

> the Subscription for each Association be a definite fixed sum, which shall not in any case exceed the rate of sixpence per member to be paid on entry of the Branch into the District Union in and thereafter in advance.[320]

The minutes did not include a copy of this draft. In May 1883 Mr. Lee wrote to the Kingston branch, asking if they could render assistance at the South London Mission of Messrs. Moody and Sankey, but the meeting considered Kingston was 'too far off' to allow an active part. [321]

July 1883–June 1884

The secretary reported that he and Mr. Parslow had attended the quarterly district conference held on July 20, 1883, in Wimbledon. The chief business of the meeting was a discussion of the rules, which the Kingston branch adopted and then authorised the treasurer to pay the minimum subscription of 5/- per annum. The branch did not send any delegates to the Liverpool Conference in September.[322] In February the meeting was held in Croydon.[323] In April 1884 a circular letter from the district secretary drew attention to the International Conference in Berlin. No delegates were expected to go from the Kingston branch.[324]   On May 5, 1884, the chief business of the meeting involved the admission of Egham and Streatham to the Union of Branches, and Mr. Shipton would go to Berlin at his own cost. The next quarterly meeting would be held at the Kingston rooms on July 18, 1884, and the secretary was to be instructed to provide tea for the delegates.[325]

Kingston Y.M.C.A. Subcommittees; 1882 – 1884

The Kingston Subcommittees were formed out of the members. The cricket club committee began in June 1882, with members expected to pay an annual subscription of 2/6d. By July 1882 the rules had been prepared and agreed, but the number of subscribers only totalled fourteen and comparatively few turned up to practice. (The Initial Rules are to be found in Appendix VIII, page 220.) The cost of equipment had totalled £2.12s.10d., including £1 donated by Captain Cundy. By July 1883 the club had twenty members and a field had been hired at a cost of £10 to enable the cricket club to practice. In June 1884 the club was more active and had begun to keep 'things' at the lodge in Richmond Park Road opposite the Mid Surrey Cricket Ground. (A new set of rules were prepared in April 1884 and are to be found in Appendix X, page 222.) The religious meetings and the visiting committee were less active, dealing with numbers and the attendance at the meetings whilst the open air committee was concerned about the work of preaching both in the Mission Tent on the Fairfield and in the surrounding district.[326] (The Rules of the open air branch are to be found in Appendix IX, pages 221 and 222.) The finance committee dealt mainly with subscriptions and the payment of bills. The social and intellectual committee were very active dealing with the reading room and classes. Musical entertainment became a feature of quarterly meetings, and, as the Association had bought china and spoons, they could easily prepare refreshments. These meetings developed into social events.[327]Mr. Philip Salisbury was requested to take charge of the singing, making all arrangements in conjunction with the social and intellectual subcommittee, and the Association thanked Miss Salisbury for her assistance.[328]

The Membership Problem

Despite all the changes and the advice given by Mr. Hind Smith, the membership remained small. Numbers had increased, but when compared with the number of young men in the Kingston area, this was insignificant. In 1879 the Association had a membership of twenty-two; at the close of 1880 it had increased to thirty-five. Although about one-hundred young men came to partake of a social tea paid for by Captain Cundy in October 1881, the membership was only fifty in 1882 and fifty-four in 1884.[329] This fact was in part due to the mobility of the young men, and the minutes referred continuously to the departure of members

and the arrival of others. Nevertheless other factors were involved. Captain
Cundy, speaking at the annual meeting in February 1883, may have appreciated
what these were. He said:

> Although the association was so small in numbers, they must not suppose
> that it represented the entire Christian youths of Kingston, because there
> were other associations in the town connected with the various chapels and
> nonconformist churches, but he begged leave to say that he thought it a very
> great pity that this association, which was purely unsectarian should have
> its hands weakened and its representative character destroyed by these
> other associations, which were denominational.[330]

YOUNG MEN'S CHRISTIAN ASSOCIATION

Resolution

setting forth the relation of Young Men's Christian
Associations to Christian Churches, adopted by the English
National Council of Y.M.C.A.'s May 7th, 1886

Inasmuch as the increasing publicity resulting from the growth of
Young Men's Christian Associations and the extension of their
work renders it desirable that the relation in which these
Associations stand to the Churches, should be clearly defined
and understood:-

It is hereby resolved and affirmed that:-

"The Young Men's Christian Associations recognize 'the
Churches of God which * * are in Christ Jesus' as existing by
Divine appointment for the maintenance of the institutions of
public worship, and for the ministry of the word of God, and
earnestly disavow any intention or desire to enter upon functions
proper to the Churches. The Associations seek to be, and desire
to be regarded as helpers to the Churches in effort and service
directed to wards a class of persons not easily reached by
ordinary Church agencies and consider it to be alike their
privilege and their duty to lead young men into the fellowship of
the Churches and under the influence of the Christian ministry."

23. A copy of the Resolution found on page 196 of the
minutes dated August 9, 1886.   **(YMCA)**

Unfortunately Mr. Bayley did not attend this meeting, but his remarks in October 1880, which have already been considered, give an insight into his thoughts on the subject. At the heart of the problem, however, was the reduction in church members. Certain churches did not encourage their young men to join another organisation even if the organisation was interdenominational.[331] This situation had become sufficiently problematic to result in a resolution being produced by the English National Council of Y.M.C.A.s in May 1886. A copy of the resolution, was attached to a page in the May 1885 – December 1887 minute book.[332] By adding 'social' to the aims of the Association and including Rule 14 allowing young men of good character to be admitted as associates the Association hoped to reach out to those individuals who remained unconnected to the churches.

Yet to reach out, the Y.M.C.A. needed a core of Christian young men to encourage and inform those previously unconnected with the Christian faith. The fact that members in the Association came from a variety of churches and spoke to one another about their different interpretations of the scriptures, remained a difficulty into the 1890s. In September 1882, speaking about the Y.M.C.A. members as a whole, Mr. Shipton had said, 'They met simply to tell what Christ had done for sinners, and ask them to repent and turn to Him. They should not discuss questions of church policy…'[333] For some this exclusion seems to have been impossible. In October 1883 one of the members resigned not only his seat on the Committee but also his membership in consequence of undisclosed 'doctrinal differences.' [334] This problem persisted beyond 1886 into the period after the move to Warwick Lodge although many who left continued to support the movement with annual donations.

The Subject of Change

The importance of changing the Association to attract new members continued to be a major issue. After selecting a new Committee in June 1884, shown in Table 7, page 237, Mr. William Walter and Mr. Frank Newson were re-elected treasurer and secretary for the coming year. A long discussion about the changes needed to attract new members followed. It was agreed that the present premises were unsuitable and 'that it is advisable to change the rooms for the better.' There was also 'universal condemnation of the mode of conducting some of the meetings.' The question was asked:

> What further steps can be taken to make the Association attractive to the young men of the neighbourhood?

Mr. Charles Knapp, aged 16 years at this time, compared the social advantages afforded by the Kingston Institute with those afforded by the Association and advocated the establishment at the YMCA of the following ideas:

Lectures
Debating Society
Bagatelle Chess and Draught Clubs
A Gymnasium
Cricket Club to be continued
Football Club
Swimming and Rowing Club

Mr. Knapp concluded with the following motion:

That the present condition of the Association is not such as tends to make it attractive to the young men of the town and the members wish to express a desire that the Committee selected to serve in the ensuing year will do their utmost to add to the amusements (both social and intellectual) in every way that will give additional interest to the Association and more inducement to others to join.

Mr. Parslow moved and Mr. Hodges seconded the motion:

That when the above resolution is referred to the Committee the matter of Bagatelle Club shall not be ventilated.

The resolution was lost, Mr. Knapp however, intimated his willingness not to press the subject of a bagatelle club at present.[335] Nevertheless at a later meeting he suggested botany and natural history classes and a museum filled with specimens supplied by members.[336]

In this way in 1884 the Kingston Association tried to increase its numbers. Success came slowly, and only after an amalgamation with Surbiton, a move to Warwick Lodge and the competence of a very talented general secretary in 1893 did numbers increase substantially. Moreover the years between 1884 and 1893 were beset by numerous complications.

24. Canon Edward Garbett, Vicar of Christ Church, Surbiton Hill, 1863-1877.

(CCS)

THE REV. EDWARD GARBETT

CHRIST CHURCH SURBITON

1863 – 1877

Surbiton

Very little is known about Surbiton before 1800, and some suggest that the area was no more than a sparsely occupied part of south west Kingston included in documentation with other areas as an appendage of the town.[337] When describing the location in 1835, Ayliffe mentions Aspin's Farms, indicating that before 1800 there was farming on or near the Common. What is known is that the Elmer's Estate, a cluster of homesteads at the bottom of the Surbiton hill including the Waggon and Horses public house, and the acreage owned by the Jemmett family, predated the 1800s and Surbiton was involved briefly in national events in 1648.[338] During a skirmish between Royalist and Parliamentary troops, the younger brother of the Duke of Buckingham, Lord Francis Villiers was mortally wounded.[339] After this brief interlude of notoriety Surbiton returned to obscurity with land around the Common remaining uncultivated and covered in 'furze.'[340]

This situation changed in 1808 when an Act of Parliament authorised the release of the common and wastelands in the area.[341] At first the pace was slow, and when Mr. William Walter, Kingston's borough treasurer, decided to build on Surbiton Hill in 1826, no other residence looked westward nearer than Maple Farm. Later, when the first passenger train ran through the location on May 21, 1838, the pace of change began to move more quickly.[342] A new town started to emerge and when Thomas Pooley failed to address the difficulties associated with building his estate and Coutts and Drummonds — the bankers — took over, an increase in the population was inevitable.[343] In 1845 the parish of St. Mark's was formed out of the parish of Kingston. By the early 1860s the number of Surbiton residents had reached about 5,690 and certain evangelical families, including those of Mr. J.A. Strachan, Mr. George Cavell, and Mr. Charles Walter, had begun to attend prayer and devotional meetings in a house in Ewell Road.[344]

On fine Sunday mornings this group with their families would walk out to worship in Hook. A committee was formed, and in 1861 it was decided that due to the population increase another church should be built.[345]

25. Christ Church, Surbiton   (AG 2012)

The Rev. Edward Garbett

The vicar who was appointed to the incumbency of the new church, the Rev. Edward Garbett, was born in Hereford in December 1817 and was the sixth son of the Rev. James Garbett, 'custos and prebendary' of Hereford Cathedral.[346] Educated at the Cathedral School he progressed, at nineteen years of age to Brasenose College, Oxford, receiving a B.A. in 1841 and an M.A. in 1847. In 1842 he became curate at St. George's in Birmingham, and in 1854 perpetual curate of St. Bartholomew's in Gray's Inn Road. Apart from writing books, editing and writing articles for newspapers, in 1860 he accepted the Boyle Lectureship, and in 1861 became a select preacher at Oxford. After accepting the living in Surbiton, in 1863, he was appointed Bampton Lecturer at Oxford in 1867. It was said of him, during this period 'there were few subjects of ecclesiastical importance upon which he did not write with force and discernment.'[347]

The Boyle Lectures were named after Robert Boyle, a natural philosopher born in the seventeenth century who became convinced that the new experimental science gave insights into Christianity as revealed in the Scriptures.[348] Printed in 1690, *The Christian Virtuoso; Shewing that by being addicted to Experimental Philosophy, a Man is rather Assisted, than Indisposed, to be a good Christian* was Boyle's last book.[349] In his will Boyle left a codicil to be enacted after his death, providing for a series of lectures to protect Christianity against atheists. The first lecture took place the year after his death in 1692.[350] Garbett's lecture in 1861 was entitled 'The Bible and its Critics: an enquiry into the objective reality of revealed truths.'[351]

The Bampton Lectures were founded by the bequest of John Bampton, Canon of Salisbury, who also bequeathed funds for the annual preaching of divinity lectures. The lectures started in 1780, and a portion of the Extract of the Last Will and Testament of Bampton shows the qualification needed to be chosen to complete this task:

> I direct and appoint, that no person shall be qualified to preach the Divinity Lecture Sermons, unless he hath taken the degree of Master of Arts at least, in one of the two Universities of Oxford or Cambridge; and that the same person shall never preach the Divinity Lecture Sermons twice.[352]

The Rev. Edward Garbett's lectures in 1867 were called 'Dogmatic Faith, an inquiry into the relation subsisting between revelation and dogma.'[353] The Vicar of Christ Church on Surbiton hill was thereby able to provide intellectual assurance for those troubled by the Darwinian theory of evolution. He was widely esteemed not only by those around him but also by others who were not members of the Anglican church. In 1872 at the fifth annual meeting of the Surbiton Y.M.C.A. the Rev. J. Portrey, a Wesleyan minister, said that he congratulated himself on being present on the occasion under the presidency of the Rev. E. Garbett:

> Some years ago it was his privilege to read the Bampton Lectures written by that gentleman, and he was as much in love with the spirit of the writer as with the subject of the book. Little did he think he should ever have the honour of standing on the same platform with the author of that volume. He would also mention that the work, 'God's Word Written,' by the same author, was adopted as a text book at the Wesleyan Training College at Richmond, and he was therefore thankful to the assembly for the association that had been formed between him and them that night. They might congratulate themselves on having met on a basis broad enough to admit all Christian men and there was no need for a broader one.[354]

The Pressure of Deep Domestic Affliction

Like many families before and during the nineteenth century, the Rev. Edward Garbett was beset by 'the pressure of deep domestic affliction.'[355] In 1867, the year in which he wrote the Bampton Lectures, his twelve-year-old daughter Elizabeth died, and, before he left Surbiton, two of his sons had also died. At the Y.M.C.A. annual meeting in 1869, he spoke of 'the shadow over the sunshine' that another member Mr. Lee had suffered:

> ... for it had pleased God to take away one of his darling children after a long and painful sickness. He was sure all their hearts went with their brother Lee, especially those among them who had painfully drunk the cup of affliction, and whose affections had been drawn upwards more and more by the removal of many dear pledges which had passed into the upper world.[356]

26. Surbiton Cottage Hospital circa 1900   (CR)

Although Surbiton was considered a more healthy area than Kingston and therefore housed many of the rich during the nineteenth century, infection resulting in death remained a common occurrence. The mortality rate in the area during the mid 1860s was twice as high as it was in the 1880s. Surbiton's death rate statistics, supplied by R.W.C. Richardson who sat on the Surbiton Improvement Committee, appear in Appendix XII, page 224. It is not possible to be completely accurate, as Richardson's population figures are estimated and the deaths are the number at five-year intervals. It is also unlikely that Richardson included babies who lived for a short time after birth but died soon afterwards. Nevertheless these statistics show the marked improvement between the mid century period and 1885. In 1865 more than two people died in every hundred each year whilst in 1885 the mortality rate had reduced to fewer than one person in every hundred. The improvement in health in the Surbiton area was mainly due to the work of the fifteen Improvement Commissioners who were motivated by the necessity to improve their own amenities. These residents supervised the transformation of the area from a mainly agrarian community into one where sewage disposal, running water, street repairs, lighting, cleaning and refuse collection were normal.[357] In October 1870 Surbiton Cottage Hospital, shown in Figure 26, opened to receive patients. Richardson does not give very much information concerning the mortality rate before 1877, but by including Extracts from the Medical Officer of Health's Reports from 1880 when diphtheria hit Surbiton, he reveals the efforts made to find the cause and deal with a situation that could have decimated the locality. Nevertheless the deaths of the young were not uncommon even towards the end of the century. Dr Coleman's Report is to be found in Appendix XIII, page 225.

In what used to be the North Chapel (Prayer Room), the East Window, seen in Figure 27, is dedicated to the memory of 'the children of the congregation' who died during the 1860s. These children not only included Elizabeth Garbett, who left this world on April 21, 1867, but also Alexander Duncan Owtram, aged ten years, who passed away on June 25, 1867 and Louis Walters Horne, aged six months, and his six year old sister Beatrice, who both died the next year.

The 1870s was also a sad time for the church congregation and in particular for Edward Garbett whose son William Humphrey Garbett, aged twenty-four, died in November 1874 and is remembered with his brother Frederick Lewis Garbett in a window with the inscription, 'We have found the Messiah.' It is uncertain how William Humphrey died, but Frederick Lewis drowned in the wreck of the S.S. Javed on January 16, 1876. On June 27, 1874, the ward of Archibald Scott, Robina Gordon Stewart, also died. Robina was fourteen years of age, and a plaque dedicated to her memory was placed among the others on the walls of what used to be the North Aisle. Archibald Scott lived in Gordon Villa, South Bank and was General Manager and later a director of the London and South Western Railway.

27. Stained Glass Window in Memory of Children of the Congregation.

These were: Elizabeth Garbett, aged twelve years, who died April 21, 1867; Alexander Duncan Owtram, aged ten years, who died June 25, 1867; Louis Walters Horne, six months and his sister Beatrice six years, who died 1868. Lower compartments: presentation of Christ in the temple; the raising of Jairus's daughter; innocents around the throne of grace; children praising Christ in the temple; the nativity; Christ blessing little children; and Christ with the doctors in the temple.

Upper compartments: Christ as the good Shepherd; Christ in majesty; Christ as the Sower. Executed by Lavers & Westlake.   **(CCS) (AG)**

In 1875 Edward Garbett became Honorary Canon of Winchester, and in 1877 he and his family accepted the living of Barcombe in Lewes, leaving Surbiton in December of that year. By 1878 the death rate appeared to be declining, but a few months after his arrival in Surbiton, the new vicar, the Rev. James Bardsley, also lost a child.[358] Although the mortality rate in Surbiton was lower than the average in England and Wales (see Appendix XIV, page 226), the deaths of young children were relatively common, even in the homes of the affluent.

28. Stained Glass Window in Memory of Canon Edward Garbett. Executed by Lavers & Westlake.   (CCS) (AG)

It is difficult to comprehend how our nineteenth century contemporaries found the emotional strength to deal with this ever-present 'shadow over the sunshine.' Not everybody did; Charles Darwin was deeply affected by the death of his daughter Annie who died of tuberculosis at the age of ten in 1851.[359] Canon Garbett gives every indication that he managed to cope with the loss of his children during his time in Surbiton. He encouraged the young men of the Y.M.C.A. to 'take the Bible as their guide, wherein they would find the secret of human happiness, the strength to meet death, and the happiness awaiting them in the other world, where pleasures would never cease, and life would know no ending.'[360]

SURBITON Y.M.C.A. – THE EARLY PERIOD
JULY 1868 – OCTOBER 1879

Beginning of the Y.M.C.A. in Surbiton

It was generally accepted that it wasn't the Rev. Edward Garbett who formed the Surbiton Y.M.C.A. The movement started in Surbiton because a few young men working in the area found it difficult getting to Kingston in time for the meetings. This problem is understandable given that the distance between Christ Church and the market place in Kingston was more than two miles. The roads in the 1860s made journeys on foot precarious, particularly during the bad weather. Not only going to the meetings proved hard, but so too did coming home from meetings ending at 9.30 p.m. when most young men would have had to get up very early in the morning. As we shall see later, one of the young men, Mr. Lee, had moved to Wimbledon, and the line between Kingston and Wimbledon only opened in 1869. Before this date a train from Surbiton station would have been the only method of return. It was not at the insistence of the Rev. Edward Garbett that the Surbiton Association was started but by the request and perseverance of certain young men.

Nevertheless, from the time he arrived in Surbiton the Rev. Edward Garbett showed an interest in the Association. In October 1864 he apologised for not coming when the Kingston Association met in the Assize Courts for their third annual meeting saying, 'he would have come but for an indisposition and hoped after a time to give a lecture for the Association.'[361] Three years later in October 1867, when he did attend the annual meeting of the Kingston Association in the Assize Courts, he moved a resolution 'that the meeting, considering the objects of the association, expresses its full sympathy therewith and pledges itself to hearty co-operation and support.'[362]

Two Anomalies

Two anomalies relating to the early years of the Y.M.C.A. in Surbiton remain. The first is the uncertainty about when the Association started. The second concerns where the young men initially met. The fact that the Association was started by two young men may explain some of the confusion. In a report dated Saturday, November 27, 1869, the *Surrey Comet* clearly affirmed that the Surbiton Association had been formed in July 1868.[363] A year earlier a report dated October 17, 1868, and possibly the earliest report we have of the Surbiton Association, stated that approximately twelve months had elapsed since they had first met together in the old School Room in Ewell Road. What appears likely is that the early meetings had been sporadic but more regular after July 1868. The booklet produced after the fifth annual meeting reported that the London Society had received the Surbiton Association into union in 1869. It is not unusual to find the start of an association shrouded by time. Clive Binfield points to a similar problem relating to the first Y.M.C.A.: 'most sources of information date from years after the event and depend on reminiscence.'[364]

29. The Old Chapel, Ewell Road, Surbiton also called Surbiton Hill Hall, and regarded as a Mission Room.   **(AG 2002)**

Apart from the *Surrey Comet* the only information relating to the early period of Surbiton Y.M.C.A. appears in one annual report, a pamphlet dated 1871–1872. We must therefore rely on the reporting of the nineteenth-century shorthand writers in the pages of the local newspaper for the details of the early years of the

Surbiton movement, but here we find further confusion. D.G. Smith, writing in the book *100 Years: The Story of the Parish of Christ Church, Surbiton Hill, 1863 – 1963* about the Halls and other Church Premises, states:

> In 1865 as the day school in Ewell Road had grown, it was decided to acquire the Britannia Road site and to erect permanent school buildings there. In 1876 the old Wesleyan Chapel in Ewell Road (now the dental laboratory) was rented for other organisations including the Y.M.C.A.[365]

By 1868 any Y.M.C.A. meeting in Christ Church Schools should have been on the Britannia Road site not in Alpha Road. However on October 17, 1868, the *Surrey Comet* reporter writes that the Association's annual meeting 'was held in the Alpha Road Schools on Thursday evening, about 50 first taking tea together.'[366] The next year he placed the annual meeting at the Christ Church schools, in Britannia Road. For the annual meeting in 1870 again they supposedly met at the Alpha Road Schools site. It would seem likely that the reporter who wrote the report in 1868 and 1870 mistook Alpha for Britannia Road as one road flows into the other, which is an assumption that the Rev. E. Garbett's remark from the chair at the October 1868 meeting reinforces:

> ... he felt great pleasure in meeting them again this evening. It had pleased God that they should meet in this new schoolroom which He in his infinite grace had given to them; and for that they had great cause for deep gratitude.[367]

The new schoolroom would have been in Britannia Road, and the Y.M.C.A. probably used this facility until 1876.

The change appears to have occurred in October 1876. The only remaining minute book of the Surbiton Association notes that the meeting was held in the Mission Room with one of the initial discussions being the cost, which was £7. 10/- per annum. The use of the room continued until November 1878 and is almost certainly the building in the Ewell Road shown in Figure 29. However the final meetings of the Surbiton Association held in May and October 1879 took place in Highfield, in The Avenue, the home of Arthur Maxwell.

When the Surbiton Association reopened in May 1882, the first meeting took place in the Mission Room, but meetings held immediately after took place in the homes of the Committee. Later, as we will see in August 1882, the Association found a permanent address, taking over Mr. Poole's greengrocer shop, back parlour and passage. This coincidence has obviously added to the confusion as the address of the shop was 2 Alpha Road.

The Rev. Edward Garbett — President of the Surbiton Y.M.C.A.

Not only is it obvious that the Rev. Edward Garbett was by 1868 at the heart of the Surbiton Association, but we can also catch a glimpse of the humanity behind the scholarship. At the annual meeting held in October, after prayer, he gave a short address, saying that:

> He wished they should sometimes give pleasant evening entertainments, and he thought it was a very rational thing to do. Their object in meeting together was to help each other by mutual sympathy. Meeting together now and then was a great thing to cheer their hearts, and it would help them to strengthen and encourage each other. It was now the fashion in many parts of the world, both by educated men, and he was sorry to say ministers of the Gospel, to decry against the truths of the Gospel: and when a person spoke of the truths of the Bible and of the goodness of God, he was pooh-poohed. … Not one solitary untruth had ever been proved in the Word of God; but there had been corroborative proofs in its favour of the most marvellous kind, by discoveries on ancient monuments and elsewhere; and gave them his word for it that no error had ever been proved against the Bible. If any one felt any difficulty with reference to God's Word, if they came to him he would do his best to assist them, and should always feel honoured and happy to do so.

At this meeting the secretary Mr. King said that he was very sorry he was not able to place a glowing report of the society but although it was not flourishing regarding the number of members, it was in a satisfactory state. We learn also that the young men met on a Thursday from eight to half past nine. He thanked the Rev. Edward Garbett for allowing them to hold their meetings in the schoolroom.[368] We learn later that this was lent to them free of charge.[369] At the annual meeting in November 1869, it was stated that the devotional meetings took place on the first and third Thursdays these had been varied by addresses by Christian ministers and friends, and on the last Thursday of the month there was a class presided over by Mr. Charles E. Norton who lived in Cadogan Road and was a clerk to colonial merchants. A Bible class was started on Sunday afternoons, the first being devoted to prayer and praise, the second and fourth to Bible studies, the third to an address by a Christian friend. Every year the annual meeting took place in November, and every quarter there was an open meeting for friends and family.

Mr. Shipton was present at this meeting and was invited to speak. He was very pleased that Surbiton had a Y.M.C.A. He spoke:

> of the conviction that was deepening in his own mind that in a suburban district like this, to which an increased number of residents of London are resorting from year to year the real battle of religion will have to be fought.

London is getting deserted; the churches are empty; and the Nonconformist churches, once so strong are migrating to the suburbs; and in all religious activity the tendency is to get outside London. He felt very thankful that a society had been originated here; that there was a similar one at Kingston, and another at Teddington; and he hoped ere long London would be completely surrounded by these associations.[370]

Surbiton Y.M.C.A. Activities

The Surbiton Association was somewhat different from the Kingston branch even during the early years. There was no mention of a library, nor a reading room and the speakers were mainly churchmen. The secretary of the Teddington branch association Mr. Jones, said that the programme of events at Surbiton had made their branch determined to adopt a higher tone of religious thought by the exclusion of all topics of a merely secular interest from their discussions.[371]

One of the main activities of the Association was encouraging young men to write essays with prizes for the best efforts. All the subjects of study were of a religious nature. Prizes were distributed at quarterly meetings. The *Surrey Comet* reported one of these meetings that took place on February 15, 1873 at Christ Church Schools. Tea was served at half past seven to the seventy-six people who attended. These included several notable individuals from the area who took an interest in the Association. The results of the essay competition were announced after speeches. The title of the essay had been 'The Eternity of Future Punishment and the Eternity of Future Glory.' Nine essays had been sent in. The first prize, the Rev. Garbett's work entitled *God's Word Written,* was awarded to Mr. Passey and the second Bishop Beveridge's *Private Thoughts on Religion* was presented to Mr. G.H. Lee. The latter decided to forego the prize in favour of Mr. Sharp, who was third.[372] The following quarter Mr. Lee was one of the adjudicators of the essays, and these comments show that essay writing was a form of teaching for some whose education had been less advanced than others:

> Three essays had been sent in, all very creditable to the writers. Having described the leading ideas developed in them, Mr. Lee went on to say with reference to the adjudication that Mr. Dickinson and himself had had frequent conferences together, and it was only after a great deal of consideration that they came to their decision. The essay to which they awarded the first prize seemed to show in style as well as matter more care, thought and research on the part of the writer than was the case with either of the other two. The essay for which the second prize was awarded bore the mark of careful composition, but it ended very abruptly. It might with advantage have been much more amplified and a little more method in the arrangement would have improved it. The remaining essay bore the impress of much thought, but it did not bring out the lessons from the life of

Solomon (the subject of the essay) so vividly as did the others. There was a great deal of what was called "padding" in it—matter that would have fitted almost any religious subject. It reflected very great credit on the writer, however, and Mr. Lee hoped to see him take a prize next time. [373]

For some, essay writing served as a means of improving literary skills as well as being a religious activity. Although there is no mention of a reference library or a reading room, the young men would have needed to read a selection of books to enable them to write their essays.

The Fifth Report of the Surbiton Y.M.C.A. 1871—1872

This sixteen page pamphlet gives an invaluable glimpse of the Association not seen in the *Surrey Comet*. Mr. Garbett was president; there were 19 vice-presidents, and these included Captain Cundy, and Charles Walter (probably the uncle of William Walter, treasurer of the Kingston branch). There was also a Mr. George Lee senior, a vice-president who lived in Penrhyn Road, aged sixty-two in 1871. The census shows that he was a clerk '1st class civil service.'

The 1871 to 1872 Committee are to be found in Table 8, page 238. Mr. George H. Lee was the chairman of the Committee and probably the son of Mr. George Lee. He was also almost certainly the George H. Lee who in 1881 lived in Glenmore House, Worple Road, in Wimbledon. By 1871 he would have been 35 years of age. In 1881 census ten years later he is listed as 'Accountant Official Trustee Department of Exchange Comm.' and therefore he most likely worked in London. The line from Wimbledon to Kingston opened in January 1869, and attending a branch in Surbiton before this date would have been his only option once he moved from Penrhyn Road to Wimbledon. This fact would explain why he, in particular, wanted to have a branch of the Association in Surbiton.

Mr. John King, a gardener and the Surbiton secretary of the movement, had his address—4 Paragon Place, Surbiton—printed next to his name on the Fifth annual report pamphlet in 1871. He had to give up the secretary's position in May 1873 through the pressure of other engagements. In 1891 the census shows that John King, his wife Elizabeth and three grown up children were all helping in their 'Fruiterer (Green)' business situated in 3 Paragon Terrace, Berrylands Road. At a quarterly meeting Mr. G.H. Lee said that as chairman:

He knew better than any one how greatly the association was indebted to Mr. King, who had been connected with the association since its establishment in 1868. He was possessed of good plain common sense, and a high moral character, so that no one could say of him that he was otherwise than a Christian. The association owed much to him, and some of the members now wished to show him, by a small present, that they esteemed him as a man, and for the work's sake. Mr. Lee concluded by heartily expressing the good wishes of the association to Mr. King.

Capt. Cundy then amid loud applause, after some remarks endorsing what Mr. G.H. Lee had said, formally presented to Mr. King a complete set of Maunders' Treasury, and a handsomely bound copy of Milton's and Young's poems.[374]

Two meetings stand out as being exceptional in the life of the Surbiton Association. The first took place October 1872 and was the occasion when Mr. G.H. Lee gave a talk about his visit to Amsterdam to represent the Association at the Y.M.C.A. Conference. (Appendix XI, pages 223 and 224.) The other occurred in May 1874 at a quarterly meeting, to which George Williams had been invited, and which will be discussed in the next Chapter.

The Y.M.C.A. in Surbiton; October 1876 – October 1879

The minute book of the Surbiton Association found with the Kingston minute books begins on October 26, 1876. The Committee meeting took place in the Mission Room with the Rev. Canon Garbett in the Chair and the Messrs. Lee, Cavell, Dale, Friend, King, Lillywhite, Lake and the secretary also present. Few of the Committee were 'young' men. George Cavell, a stockbroker who lived in 'Grantham' in the Ewell Road, was fifty-nine years old. Mr. Dale would have been sixty-five, Mr. Lake forty-six, Mr. Lee thirty-eight and Mr. Lillywhite, a gardener twenty-six. Meetings would be held on Tuesdays, the quarterly social meetings, where prizes were awarded for essays would continue, and Bible classes would meet on Sunday afternoons.[375]

The next Committee meeting occurred in the Mission Room on January 2, 1877, with Mr. George H. Lee in the chair. The meeting reported that some young boys had come into the social meeting without invitation, and it was decided that they would not be admitted again as they had been disruptive.[376] At the annual meeting in December 1876 it had been announced that the Association was in a satisfactory condition. The total number of members admitted to the branch was ninety-two, this figure being probably the figure of those admitted since 1868, as the secretary reported that the general attendance was not as large as the Committee would wish. On average ten members were present both on Thursdays and at the Sunday meetings. The meeting agreed to prepare a short report with a balance sheet and list of subscribers and to print copies and send them to those involved with the Association. The following report dated February 1877 gives details of the activities:

Dear Sir or Madam: I have much pleasure in transmitting herewith the List of Subscribers and Balance Sheet for the year ending 29 September 1876. Also a list of arrangements for the months of March, April and May 1877.

These lists were not included in the minutes.

The Committee desire to see the Association increasingly useful in the neighbourhood and they earnestly request the sympathy and co-operation of all interested in the spiritual welfare of men.

The Committee trust that you will continue to support the Association and you would greatly oblige by forwarding your subscription to the Treasurer or myself, on or before the 1st June next, or if preferred Mr. Lillywhite, (one of the Committee) who has kindly consented to act as collector will call upon you after that date.

The total number who have been admitted to the privileges of the Association through this Branch is 92. The Meetings are free to all men and are now held in the Mission Room for which an inclusive rent is payable and the Committee trust that the necessary funds will be provided to enable them to meet this increased expenditure.

The Committee prepare and freely distribute every month a list of their quarterly arrangements. Besides the Bi-weekly meetings the President (Rev. Canon Garbett) is now again holding on the 2nd and 4th Tuesday Evenings in the month, classes for instruction in the Fundamental Doctrines of Christianity to which all men of every class are invited. Meetings for children and young people are arranged for the 3rd Tuesday evenings. During the year ended 29th September 1876 besides the Annual Meeting there were held 34 Devotional Meetings, 40 Bible Classes, 21 Meetings when special addresses were delivered, 4 Social Meetings and 4 Members Quarterly Meetings. Gospel addresses to men were also delivered on the five Tuesday Evenings in May 1876 by Evangelists specially invited with good results.

The Committee have received much encouraging testimony and they trust that during the present year a large number of men may be brought through the agency of the Association into the Redeemer's Kingdom.
I am &c.[377]

Subsequent meetings discussed various methods to encourage new members. The April Meeting suggested that the Y.M.C.A. should form a band. The May meeting, considered the suggestion together with one that there should be special services for unconverted young men.

What was Forgiven and what was not Forgiven

Two noteworthy situations occurred during 1877 and 1878. The first occurred sometime between the meeting on February 6, and that of April 10, of that year.

One of the younger members and the Committee on April 10, 1877, had had a disagreement, and the meeting decided to try to achieve a peaceful settlement and to report the outcome at the next meeting of the Committee. Mr. Poole reported that he had seen the young member who had apologised for what had happened and for any wrong expressions he had used and who was willing to resume his place as before. After some discussion the meeting decided that the secretary write to him to say that the Committee had not accepted his resignation, that his letter would be destroyed and that he would be cordially welcomed as a member of the Association and Committee. [378]

The second situation started on June 12, 1877. The Committee accepted a new member into the Association and received him onto the Committee on July 24. In January 1878 the new member sent a letter to the Committee expressing his regret that owing to ill health he had to give up work for the present and would therefore be unable to fulfil his remaining engagements in the current programme. The Committee replied expressing its sympathy and thanking him for the valuable service he had rendered to the Association. At a meeting held on March 25, 1878, the chairman of the Committee said that a reverend gentleman 'had called on him about a fortnight back and made some grievous statement against the character of this member.' After consulting with the president and vice-president the Committee decided to write the following letter:

> Dear Sir, A Statement has been made by the ... of a character gravely affecting your position as a member of the "Surbiton Young Men's Christian Association." With a view to ascertain the truth we ask your attendance on Friday next at 7 o'clock at the residence of Mr. Cunning (Athol House, Maple Road, Surbiton) for the purpose of meeting ... the undersigned.
>
> G. Cavell (Pres.) Geo. Cunning (Vice P.) G.H. Lee (Chairman of Committee of Surbiton Y.M.C.A.)

The member admitted 'an adulterous connection and issue there from,' but said the connection had now ceased. What was meant by 'issue there from,' is uncertain. The Committee asked him to send in his resignation to the Surbiton Y.M.C.A., and he was 'strongly advised to leave the neighbourhood.' He promised to send his resignation to Mr. G.H. Lee but made no promise to leave Surbiton as he had debts 'precluding his departure honourably.' The chairman read the letter received from the member:

> Dear Sir, As circumstances of a painful nature have arisen in connection with my social relationship, I am compelled to resign all connection with the 'Surbiton Y.M.C.A.'

Will you therefore kindly present and urge acceptance of the same and thereby oblige,
Yours very respect^y. [379]

Neither the man who admitted the adulterous connection nor the reverend gentleman appear on the Kingston census, and it seems as if both had been in residence outside Kingston but had left by 1881. The affair did not end there because some of the members appreciated that one of their number was living in the household of the member who had committed adultery, and at the meeting on May 30, 1878, the chairman of the Committee said that:

> He thought it would have a bad influence on a young man living in an immoral house. After some discussion on the subject it was proposed … seconded … and carried 'that the Pres. (G. Cavell), Vice P. (G. Cunning) and Chairman of the Committee (G.H. Lee) have an interview with [the young member] showing him the necessity there was that he as a member of the Y.M.C.A. should give up living with someone who was an adulterer.[380]

The next meeting took place five months later in October 1878 without any mention of the incident. A further meeting happened in November of that year and in May 1879, and then a final meeting occurred in October 1879 when the Surbiton Association closed. The Association reopened later, however, but the meeting marked the end of the early Surbiton Y.M.C.A. that had started in 1868.

Why did the Association Fail in 1879?

The minutes clearly point to one specific reason why the Association did not flourish. In November 1878 at the meeting before the final Committee meeting members sent a letter to the subscribers with details of the balance for the year September 1878:

> It has always been felt by the Committee that the interdenominational character of the Association was of value in influencing young men, it has therefore been carried on upon this basis for the past 12 years. Your Committee however regret to find that the many congregational and denominational agencies which are at work in Surbiton absorb the labours of the members in other directions and that in consequence the meagre attendance at the various meetings is such as to lead your committee to the conclusion that it is wise for the present to suspend holding the usual meetings as heretofore on Thursday evenings.[381]

Captain Cundy also mentioned this reason at the Kingston annual meeting February 1883.[382] It appears that the churches in both Kingston and Surbiton were encouraging young men to stay within the orbit of their denominations rather than join with others in the interdenominational Y.M.C.A. The formation of clubs and groups in the various denominations was a feature not only in Kingston but also in Surbiton.

Why then did Kingston Y.M.C.A. continue to function and Surbiton did not? The answer must lie in the personalities behind the decisions. The Kingston Committee was elected by the members, with four of the Committee being between sixteen to twenty-two years of age, and not adverse to bypassing senior authority. A further reason was that Mr. Newson, the new secretary of the Kingston Association, contacted Mr. Hind Smith and thereafter the branch had the continued support of the parent body. In Surbiton an apparently unelected Committee comprised of men of mature years unanimously agreed to end the Association. Mr. Lee, a founder member, seems to have been moving towards involvement with the Wimbledon branch rather than that of Surbiton, as the Wimbledon Y.M.C.A, opened on October 6, 1875.[383] By 1882 Mr. Lee was acting as a travelling secretary for what was to became known as the 'South West Suburban District (Union of Branches).' Finally the removal of Canon Garbett away from Surbiton could also have been a contributing factor.

In 1878 the Surbiton Association decided to continue with the Sunday afternoon meetings, but in May 1879 it also suspended these meetings until October when they would be reconsidered. In October the meetings remained suspended, and the Association decided that the secretary call together the Committee the first convenient evening of the new year. This did not happen, and it was not until May 1882 that a meeting did take place, and by this time the secretary, Mr. G.H. Lee, was otherwise engaged.[384]

THE 'TEMPERANCE' DEBATE

MODERATION v TOTAL ABSTINENCE

Temperance in Kingston and Surbiton

When the Rev. Lawrence Byrnes came to Kingston in 1851, he is reputed to have found that there were no fewer than eighty-two taverns and public houses in Kingston and Surbiton compared with the small number of churches. Despite this comparison he made no move to close down these breweries or public houses.[385] Beer remained an important part of the working man's diet, as during much of the nineteenth century water was not safe to drink. The early temperance movement was less a reaction to beer than a response to the spread of spirits—in particular gin—during the eighteenth century. Wine and fermented grape juice had connections with the church as a central part of the sacrament of Holy Communion. In the early Christian church alcohol taken in moderation was pleasurable and, in certain circumstances, a sacred experience. The word 'temperance' may have come to signify 'total abstinence' but originally it implied moderation.[386]

During Byrnes' ministry brewers were the most ardent supporters of the early Kingston Young Men's Christian Association. The brewer William Hodgson, mayor of Kingston in 1861, gave the Association a large Bible. Mr. Joseph East found premises for the young men when they left the Congregational Church, and reduced the debt by £10 when their finances were in deficit. Byrnes referred to Joseph East as his friend the mayor. Joseph East held this office twice, in 1865 and 1866. The maltster William Wadbrook also gave a donation of 10/- to the Y.M.C.A. in 1864. Unlike shopkeepers in the retail trade, the brewers were reputed to look after their staff, giving them occasional holidays and treats. Up to 1870 Kingston appears to have had no problem accepting that drinking alcoholic beverages in moderation was normal behaviour. In areas of the town where there was poverty and a 'state of heathenism', which undoubtedly included drunkenness and violence, it was believed that the London City Missionary and the Open Air Mission would improve these circumstances by changing lives for the better.[387]

In other localities situations were different. Mr. De Fraine, who came to lecture in March 1863, was employed by the National Temperance League and on occasions lectured on the beneficial effects of being a total abstainer. When he came to Kingston, his subject was 'How to get on in the World,' rather than abstinence. When the Chartist Henry Vincent arrived in the area, he was also associated with teetotal Chartism but his topic was 'The philosophy of true manliness.' He may have mentioned the importance of sobriety but he did not emphasize 'total abstinence.' In Kingston most of the establishment were maltsters and brewers and much of the economy centred round this industry. The subject of abstinence appears not to have been a major theme before the 1880s.

Surbiton, however, had formed a Temperance Society in 1866, and by 1870 meetings were being held in Christ Church schools with the Rev. Edward Garbett, president and Mr. G.H. Lee, treasurer. A meeting in November 1871 appears to be the fourth anniversary of this movement, and one-hundred and seventeen 'pledges' were on the books. It was also announced that Mr. Thomas Fewkes, who had 'for upwards of 30 years been an earnest and energetic worker, had died.'[388] In Leeds the problems of alcoholism were so great that the Baptist minister Rev. Jabez Tunnicliffe started a movement in 1847. The movement called 'The Band of Hope' encouraged children and those whose lives had been ruined by an overindulgence in 'strong drink' to change their ways. New members were expected to sign 'the pledge' promising that they would refrain from drinking 'strong drink' in the future. There were rallies, marches, demonstrations and taverns built where only coffee was served.[389]

William Hind Smith in 1864 had started his career in the Y.M.C.A. movement in Leeds as Association secretary. His wife Rebekah Wilson was involved in the British Workman Movement, with the aim to establish 'tavern' coffee houses. The plan was to create a place, other than public houses, in which working class men could socialise. Jabez Tunnifcliffe was a firm supporter of the Y.M.C.A., and Hind Smith claimed that he had enrolled fifteen hundred young men in Leeds as teetotallers.[390] Whereas Shipton had not considered it part of the Y.M.C.A.'s work 'to provide any man with amusements', he also believed that total abstinence should be left to the conscience of the individual, and therefore outside the remit of the Association.[391] Hind Smith, on the other hand, considered that total abstinence should be an important aspect of the Y.M.C.A. work. Binfield writes that, although George Williams had signed the temperance pledge in his youth and remained committed, temperance wasn't at the forefront of the Y.M.C.A. movement until after Hind Smith became the London Secretary.[392]

An interesting situation occurred in Surbiton at a quarterly meeting in May 1874 to which George Williams had been invited. The guest list also included Captain Cundy; the Rev. G. W. McCree, Secretary of the United Kingdom Band of Hope Union; and the Rev. Dawson Burns M.A., another leading temperance reformer. After tea the Rev. J. F. Osborne announced a hymn which was followed by a prayer by the Rev. Edward Garbett. Mr. Williams then took the chair and spoke at some length about the object of the Association, which was:

> to bring young men together under the influence of the Gospel and to teach them the true principles of Christian life…Many instances of the power of prayer and praying perseveringly had come under his notice…they must make use of simple means and not let opportunities slip by of speaking to their companions who were living without Christ.

Mr. Williams then called upon Mr. Lee, who addressed the meeting:

> I am known to be a teetotaller to most of you; for twenty years I have had a strong conviction and belief that drink is not necessary, and does a vast deal of harm amongst young men – and indeed amongst all class of the community at large. There are many other beverages that we might imbibe, if we cared to do so when Christian friends associate together; but strong drink is absolutely unnecessary for the purposes of social intercourse. Last quarter I desired to know what the "Word" said about "Wine", so I proposed that that should be the subject of an essay; but I am sorry to admit that only two essayists have written about it. I shall now call upon those two gentlemen to receive the prizes for their essays. The first prize was given to one of 18 years abstinence.

At this point the chairman said that temperance was 'not the great object of this Association, but only a branch apart…' There were loud remarks of 'Hear, hear.' The Rev. Dawson Burns rose to speak and was loudly cheered. He said that:

> the question of the temperance movement was of vital importance to this and other societies. While public houses were spreading their branches far and wide, and sapping and mining all the good in the land, they must not be like the ostrich which buries its head in the sands, vainly hoping to escape capture by its pursuers; but they must look up and try to uproot so dire an evil… Once get strong drink in the ascendancy and we should become a nation of savages – we should know no more than the savage of today with his "fire-water." … It was neither physically, morally, nor intellectually necessary; it ate up everything, undermined the system, and generated untold miseries. They should discourage it as much as possible – indeed, it was their duty as Christians to do so.

After the Rev. Dawson Burns sat down, the chairman said that he had been taken by surprise. Captain Cundy said the same, 'he did not expect to hear a temperance lecture, but anticipated some account of the working of the association.' (Hear, hear) The chairman next called upon the Rev. W. McCree who said, 'My friend (Mr. Burns) and myself came here with the intention of speaking on the temperance movement, and I leave it with you whether you will hear me or not.' A motion whether Mr. Mc Cree should speak was carried unanimously:

> Mr. McCree remarked that he had been for 25 years labouring, preaching, and going from house to house in St. Giles's and the Seven Dials. He had explored all London and 18 times had been with murderers in their cells at Newgate – in fact he thought he was the Livingstone of London. He now produced a map made ten years ago on which was a large number of red spots – in all 10,000 – each red spot denoting a public house. He held that it was the duty of every Christian association to shut them up by signing the pledge, and then gave a … description of the horrors attending what he called "the plague spot" of London, observing that within an area of one square mile and that is the poorest locality, £400,000 was spent yearly on drink, whilst on ragged schools for boys and girls and education generally no more than £10,200 was spent in the same area.[393]

Captain Cundy here said:

> As a member of the association he ought to have been made aware of the temperance tone of the evening's proceedings before coming. He differed from the speakers in their views of temperance, for he was in favour of using the gifts of God moderately, and not abusing them. (Hear, hear.)

> Mr. Lee said he was responsible for the presence of Messrs. Burns and McCree, and was careful in naming them upon the cards of invitation sent to the members; so that it was fully anticipated they would speak on this subject. (Hear, hear.)

The chairman interposed and after further conversation and a vote of thanks to the chairman, the meeting closed in the usual way. It was thus that the subject of 'temperance' came to the Y.M.C.A. in the Kingston/Surbiton area.[394]

The Blue Ribbon Temperance Movement in Kingston; April 1883

About this time the Blue Ribbon Temperance Movement emerged in the north-east of the United States. By 1880 it had spread to Canada and England. An Irish Catholic immigrant called Francis Murphy, who had become a hotel-keeper in the state of Maine and sold liquor, thereby violating the law, was imprisoned. In prison, sometime during 1870, he converted to Christianity and vowed never to drink again. After visiting America and hearing Murphy speak, a William Noble brought the movement to England in 1877. W.J. Palmer, a wealthy supporter, purchased London's Huxton Hall, and Noble established a permanent mission that aimed to promote temperance among the poor of London. A reformed drunkard, Richard T. Booth launched a nationwide campaign that lasted for five years.[395]

In April 1883 the Blue Ribbon Mission came to Kingston, holding their meetings in the Drill Hall. By this time there was an enthusiasm in the ranks of Kingston Y.M.C.A. for the Mission, for on March 2, 1883, members agreed:

> that the Secretary write to the Secretary of the Blue Ribbon Mission stating that the Rooms of the Association would be placed at their disposal for the Daily Prayer Meeting; also that the usual weeknight Meetings would be postponed during the progress of the Mission so that there might be no hindrance to the members helping fully in the work; and further that the Association Rooms would be placed at the disposal of the Blue Ribbon Mission for Committee Meetings or other purposes... It was further understood that no charge would be made for the use of the Rooms, but that the Blue Ribbon Mission should recompense the housekeeper for the extra trouble occasioned by the meetings.[396]

The Blue Ribbon Mission in Kingston lasted seventeen days, with the speeches taking up the centre pages of the *Surrey Comet* on the 21 and 28 April 1883. Every morning during these seventeen days, prayer meetings took place at the rooms of the Y.M.C.A. in Kingston and Surbiton.

On the opening day the Rev. A. Cornford, the vicar of St. Paul's Church, Kingston Hill, took the chair. The several speakers and dignitaries present included Captain Cundy in his capacity as president of the Kingston Y.M.C.A. The chairman stated that he had received various apologies including one from the mayor, who had another official engagement; the vicar of Kingston; the Baptist minister Mr. George Wright, who had a severe cold; and the Rev. George Robinson, minister of the Wesleyan Church, who had had a bereavement. The chairman also said that:

> although Mr. Gould, a friend of all good things which tended to benefit the town, was unable to be there just then he did not quite despair of seeing him before the close of the meeting. The chairman went on to explain that when he was asked to take the presidency of the Mission he wrote a strong letter asking one of the secretaries to find someone else, but no one else could be got, and so, rather than be an obstructive in the house of temperance, he had come to the front.[397]

The Rev. A. Cornford, who had previously helped in finding accommodation for the militia in 1876, had been one of the originators in 1865 of the Kingston Provident Dispensary. He would have had some contact with individuals suffering from alcoholism, and was still on the Committee in 1886.[398]

Major Evered Poole conducted the Mission. Each day the Mission had several speakers, and on the fifth day one of these speakers was Mrs. Poole. Her speech is of interest for several reasons. It indicates why the Mission had been given the name of Blue Ribbon and explains the tone of the meeting. It also prompted the writing of several letters to the *Surrey Comet*. Mrs. Poole's oration included the following:

> There were 24 millions of people in England who never entered a place of worship, and there were 185,000 licensed houses for the sale of strong drink, which was just five to one of the number of places of worship, by which the Devil gets five chances to one against us ... During the last ten years they had had harvests that had almost ruined the country and the reason was simply that God did not intend the thousands of bushels of grain raised off the land to be cast into vats. ...

Mrs. Poole then returned to her original text about the woman with the issue of blood who thought that she would be made whole if she could but touch the hem of Christ's garment. She said that:

> she believed most earnestly and solemnly that Christ wore upon the border of His garment a ribbon of blue, and that the woman touched the blue and was healed. The nation is now holding out its hand to touch the hem of Christ's garment so that it may be healed.[399]

The oration attracted a letter in the *Surrey Comet* from an Arthur Rees who lived in Mornington Road, Gloucester Gate. He made the following point:

> Surely the extravagance of fanaticism can no further go. Such language appears to me to be little short of blasphemous. The apostolic injunction to bishops and deacons not to be "given to[o] much wine" clearly sanction a moderate use of stimulants. [400]

In the *Surrey Comet* a week later Mrs. Poole's husband replied, 'Who is Mr. Rees? His audacity is only equalled by his impudence.' A Mr. Charles Davies in his letter explained:

> by the law of Moses, every Jew was commanded to wear upon the borders of his tallith or outer garment a 'ribbon of blue' at each corner thereof. Is Mr. Rees ignorant of this fact?...When your correspondent say that the apostolic injunction to bishops and deacons not to be given to[o] much wine 'clearly sanctions a moderate use of stimulants' he simply begs the question: and much confusion on this subject would be avoided if people would remember that there are two classes of wines referred to in the Scriptures; the fermented – upon which doubtless Noah got drunk; the unfermented or

natural wine – which was beyond doubt the wine produced by the miracle at Canaan and which was no more intoxicating then than it is now.[401]

Mr. Walter East the Brewer, the son of Mr. Joseph East, wrote:

> I have waded through the reports of the mixture of indecency, nonsense, intemperate talk, and perversion of Scripture recently talked by Blue Ribbon leaders, with an endeavour to find a single true reason why a man might be justified in donning a blue ribbon. I have taken all the trouble without success. I have never read such a mass of utter rubblish in my life.[402]

In October 1883, at a Meeting of the Blue Ribbon Gospel Temperance Union, Mr. J. W. Horsley M.A., Chaplain of Clerkenwell prison, brought the argument back to the question of why the problems associated with alcoholic liquor needed to be addressed. Quoting from official statistics, which had, he said, been published on the previous day, he stated:

> the figures showed that the "drunk and disorderly" cases in England numbered 189,000 in 1882 compared with 174,000 in the previous year, and in London alone there had been an increase of 2,000 in the number of such cases during the same period, ... In Manchester the drunk and disorderly cases had increased from 8045 five years ago to 9409 last year. ... At the lowest computation 50,000 people were annually drinking themselves to death in England, and urged that we should not leave the burden of redressing the evil to others but that we should act in the same spirit that our grandmothers did when they deprived themselves of the luxury of sugar in their tea in order to provide funds to assist in emancipating the slaves...[403]

In November 1884 at the Christ Church Surbiton Temperance Society a visiting speaker, the Rev. H. G. Spring, the vicar of Christ Church Battersea, said:

> he had painful illustrations in his own parish of the terrible evil they had met to combat. Some people thought the evil comparatively small and wondered why so much fuss was made about it; but if they only had his experience and went as he had to frequently go into the houses of the intemperate, they would speedily take a very different view of the question.[404]

The Blue Ribbon Mission in Kingston was a major event in the lives of a large number of Kingston residents. There is, however, no indication that many who had signed the pledge kept their promise. There is also no further mention of the Temperance movement in the Y.M.C.A. minutes after the completion of the Crusade in 1883. It is obvious that at the time of the Crusade, some of the young men were in tune with the aims and ambitions of the Mission and would have signed the pledge and kept their promise. It seems likely that others would have signed and later lost their enthusiasm or not signed at all. It appears likely that Captain Cundy would not have signed the pledge, given his attitude in 1874, and attended the initial meeting merely as a representative of the Association.

Was the effect of the Blue Ribbon Crusade short lived? The Christ Church Temperance Society invited Mr. Hind Smith to speak in February 1884. A group called the Kingston Total Abstinence Society and a Kingston Blue Ribbon Union both met in the Albany Hall. St Paul's and St John's Church both had a Temperance Society. In addition a Band of Hope was started in 1885 when the Bunyan Baptist Church moved into their new premises in Queen Elizabeth Road. This movement continued to function at the church beyond the end of the century, continuing throughout the Second World War into the 1950s. Therefore although the movement was short lived, its influence remained in the area well into the twentieth century.[405]

AN OPENING AND AN AMALGAMATION

SURBITON Y.M.C.A.

MAY 1882 – APRIL 1885

Surbiton Reopened

Mr. George H. Lee did not attend the opening of the Surbiton branch. By April 3, 1882, he was a member of Wimbledon Y.M.C.A. and acting as travelling secretary for the South West Suburban District (Union of Branches). This role involved arranging for the various branches to meet at different locations and at three monthly intervals.[406] Two weeks after a meeting at Wimbledon, it was decided to restart the Surbiton branch. There were twenty-five men at an evening meeting held on Friday, May 12, 1882, in the Mission Room in Ewell Road. George Cavel took the chair; Mr. Buchanan, who had previously sat on the Kingston Committee, was present, as was Mr. J.L. Morten, who had been at the original meeting of the Kingston branch in 1874. After a prayer, the chairman, together with Mr. Maxwell and Mr. Morten, reminded the meeting why the old Association had been suspended and the reason for their coming together. The meeting then agreed that the Surbiton branch should be restarted and the president and committee chosen. The new committee is shown in Table 9, page 239.[407] The meeting further agreed that a letter should be sent to the clergy of the district, that this letter would include the 'Paris Basis,' and ask for their support and co-operation as vice-presidents. It would also request that young men in the varying churches should be encouraged to join the Y.M.C.A.[408]

The initial idea was that the Y.M.C.A. should find a suitable room or a piece of ground to build on, but soon after the original meeting, Mr. Poole of Alpha Road offered his shop back parlour and passage for use by the Association. The meeting decided that the agreement with Mr. Poole should be:

> for a term of 7, 14 or 21 years subject to the approval of the committee, (the present one laid before the meeting being for 5 years only).

The builders Messrs Scase, Sinkworth, Tetford and Macdonald were invited to give estimates. Mr. Morten had made enquiries as to the price of linoleum and found it varied from 2/- to 3/- per yard, and the meeting decided that the latter would answer the purposes of the Association best. It also decided to provide cane bottomed chairs rather than forms.[409] After the estimates from the builders had been received, Mr. Scase's estimate of £86.18s.3d was accepted and Mr. McDonald's quote of £112.10s 0d was rejected. As the list of promises to give donations had reached £100. 12/-, Mr. Poole signed a rough agreement whilst a proper agreement was in the process of being legally drawn up. In July the letter drafted by the Committee to send to employers of young men in the neighbourhood read as follows:

> Highfield,
> The Avenue
> Surbiton Hill   July 1882
> Dear Sir
>
> A branch of the Y.M.C.A. having just been restarted in Surbiton, we take the liberty on behalf of the Committee of urging you to lay its claims and privileges before any young men whom you employ. Its objects are:
>
> to invite all Christian young men for the purposes of mutual edification and Christian labour & to draw within its influence the careless & godless of the neighbourhood. The basis of the Association is totally interdenominational & the social rank & position of its members are immaterial.
>
> Will you please use your best endeavour to persuade any such young men as come under the first description to enrol themselves as members of the Association & any who come under the latter to consider the need and advantages of godliness & Christian service. The work of such an Association is great & the benefits are both numerous & practical. We are further desired to ask if you yourself would like to join the Association by giving practical aid thereto, to help forward the cause of God amongst the many young men in this neighbourhood.
>
> The Committee have secured possession of No. 2 Alpha Road (formerly in possession of Mr. Poole, Greengrocer) which after alteration will be opened about the end of August due notice of which you will receive.
>
> Sincerely trusting that you will be able to assist the cause in both of these matters suggested,
>
> We are dear Sir,
> Yours faithfully, Arthur W. Maxwell, Thos D.M. McDonald
> Hon. Secs. Basis of Union Paris August 1855.[410]

Finally the Rules were agreed and are to be found in Appendix XV, page 227.

The Rev. J.W. Bardsley (who had replaced Canon Garbett at Christ Church,) the Revs. H. Askwith; W. Baster; W. Jones; and G. Robinson, Dean and Archdeacon Philpot, accepted the positions of vice-presidents. The secretaries were then directed to write to 'other gentlemen within the location asking them to act as vice-presidents making it clear that a vice-president becomes a member and is expected to take an active part in the Association.' Some replied accepting the role of vice-president. Others declined while some merely wanted to be members. Captain Cundy replied on July 11, 1882, regretting that he would be unable to attend the general meeting and saying that he would like to see just one branch of the Y.M.C.A. for Kingston and Surbiton, as he felt that the neighbourhood could not support the two. He wrote:

> Our Kingston Branch is very small but full of vitality weakened through ... secretaries of 'Friends" "Brethren" "Baptists" and other Christian denominations at different times. Just as the old Surbiton Branch was fatally weakened some time since – your revised Surbiton Branch will be but a Church of England Society mainly formed of 'Christ Church' Christians – Vice-presidents ...

> You have merely two classes 1st young men (Gentlemen) – who are engaged in London during the day and who have their homes here and who would not be attracted by such intellectual and spiritual ... as you would offer them and 2nd your working men – gardeners – labourers and such like who would not consort with the first class and who would require very elementary teaching...

> You will gather I am not sanguine of your success – I shall be glad to find I am wrong – and if I am I will atone for it by giving a donation.

> I am my dear sir — faithfully
> Yours James Cundy [411]

Captain Cundy's argument is somewhat obscure, but he seems to think the Surbiton branch would not be successful.

It was arranged that the opening meeting should be fixed for Thursday evening August 31, 1882. Mr. Cavell was to preside and Mr. Hind Smith to be invited. A programme was drawn up for Thursday evenings from September to December inclusive, the meetings were to be held from eight-thirty p.m. to nine-thirty p.m. and the room would be open for the use of members every evening (Sunday excepted) from seven-thirty p.m. to nine-thirty p.m. when a member of the Committee would be in attendance. It was also noted at this meeting by the secretary that a South West District Union had been formed out of the Suburban Associations in that district and that he and the chairman had attended both meetings, one at Wimbledon and the other at Fulham.[412]

The Progress of the New Surbiton Branch

In the next few weeks, various meetings, now held in 2 Alpha Road, discussed extra additions to the facilities. They agreed that a lending library should be formed, along with a reference library, that a Bible class should be held from three p.m. to four p.m. every Sunday afternoon and that chess and drafts should be introduced into the room. An interchange also occurred between Kingston and Surbiton during the Week of Prayer. Miss Poole, who cleaned the room, would be paid £5 per annum, and the Ladies Temperance Prayer Union would use the Room for their fortnightly meetings free of charge. The following should be brought before the next general meeting:

> That these Rules may be altered only by vote of two-thirds of the members present at the Annual Meeting, subject to confirmation by a like majority at the next quarterly or Special General Meeting.[413]

The next meeting on November 30, 1882, mentioned that Mr. Maxwell was leaving the neighbourhood and Mr. Walker the treasurer had agreed to take this position with Mr. Jeffcott, the sixty-five-year-old deputy chancery paymaster, agreeing to assume Mr. Walker's position as treasurer. The gross expenditure to date had been £143.12s.11d, the exact amount received from gifts and donations. The meeting also noted that the lowest amount of the cost to run the Association would be £40 per annum and therefore, although 1/- was the nominal subscription, more was expected in the shape of donations. The rule mentioned at the last meeting was carried unanimously.[414]

The January meeting discussed arrangements for the quarterly meeting of members and tea on March 1, the tea to be defrayed out of the Association funds. Mr. Rushworth suggested that they might make the Association more useful by bringing it 'more to the notice of shop keepers and others by a personal canvas and a Committee Meeting was called to discuss this.'[415] The next meeting agreed that, every member at the quarterly meeting on March 1 who could spare the time should be asked to choose a district in which he could call on the shopkeepers at least every quarter to ask them to bring the Association to the notice of their employees.[416]

The quarterly meeting took place in March, and the discussion covered a range of subjects, including the decisions to use Moody and Sankey hymn books and for the librarian to prepare a list for members. Mr. Northcroft promised to lithograph it cheaply. Mr. Morten stated that the Kingston Association was looking for members to join its cricket club but anyone who joined was answerable for his own subscriptions as the Surbiton branch could not incur extra expenses. Those who were willing to help in canvassing the Surbiton shops were asked to give in their names at the end of the meeting. Finally the meeting asked every member to assist in the open air work on Sunday evenings.[417]

Open Air Work; 1883

Open air work started on Sunday, May 20, 1883, at 8 o'clock at Red Lion Lane in Tolworth. Various ministers were to be seen or written to.   Future places of meeting or speakers would be posted up in the Association Room, and the speaker for the Sunday evening would have charge of the arrangements.   The secretary was instructed to obtain a few copies of the cheap edition of Moody and Sankey hymns for distribution at these meetings. In June 1883 the secretary mentioned:

> open air work had been commenced in the Red Lion Lane but they were unable at present to hold services in more than one place as the number of helpers was small. Mr. Cavall thought there was plenty of work to be done in the Lane and also agreed that the Association was hardly strong enough to divide, as it was he thought the singing was rather weak but that doubtless would improve. The Chairman strongly advocated Open Air work and urged every member to help and hoped that there would be some means of carrying the good work on in a cottage when the evenings were too dark to permit outdoor work.[418]

The date of the annual general meeting was set at September 27, 1883, when it was agreed that ladies should be allowed to attend, but there were no minutes written for that meeting.[419] However the report ending September 30, 1884, states that:

> The Association had proposed carrying on Evangelistic services during the Sunday evenings of the winter months in a room built in Red Lion Lane, under the auspices of the congregation of St. Matthew's but being unable to obtain the use of the room these meetings fell through.[420]

Other Matters; 1884

In January 1884 an emphasis was placed on a forthcoming essay competition entitled 'Justification—What is it? Where is it? Whose is it?' This had been suggested by Mr. Morten and a prize donated by Mr. Ranyard. The Association was to ask Dean Bagot, Rev. W. Baster and Rev. Bellman to act as judges. In May 1884 Mr. McDonald told the Association that he was shortly 'starting for Canada' and could no longer be secretary. In August the Association thanked Miss Edmonton for the kind use of her harmonium at the services and reported that it had collected money for Mr. Cooper who was laid up and whose family were in 'somewhat straightened circumstances.' In October arrangements were made for the annual meeting to be held in the Mission Room. The Kingston branch had invited Surbiton to join with them on the Wednesday evening during the week for Special Prayer in November. Unfortunately several members had complained that the chairs were very uncomfortable because they were fastened too close together, directions were given for them to be unfastened.[421]

The Membership Question--Was the Membership Small?

The new Association addressed the subject of membership on October 12, 1883. It did not mention declining numbers, but the secretary Mr. Walker said that he and Charles Rushworth had met together to map out Surbiton and made an arrangement for visits to the occupants of Alpha Road, Berrylands Road, Ewell Road, Victoria Road, Brighton Road, Maple Road and Surbiton Park Terrace. Apart from the residents, the visitations would include the Coffee Tavern in Ewell Road, the London and County bank, Messrs Bull & Son, Messrs Ind. Coope & Co., the London & Provincial bank, and the Coffee Tavern in Brighton Road.[422] We can assume that these visitations took place, but the November minutes do not mention them, and subsequent minutes record only seven additional members, with the addresses of some of these new members appearing in the minutes but not on the census.[423] Although those who took part in the visitations probably made great endeavour, it seems unlikely that they succeeded.

There appears however to be little evidence that Surbiton's membership was lower than that of Kingston. The report for the year dated September 30, 1884 mentions that the average attendance at meetings had been sixteen although the Association had a membership of sixty-six.[424] There is however no indication that the membership totals had gone down by this date.[425] A paper tucked in the pages of the Surbiton minute book shows attendance during October 1884 and April 2, 1885 ranging from seven to twenty-six with an average attendance in 1885 of nearly thirteen. If these are compared with the average attendance record of the Kingston branch during January and July 1884, Kingston had an average of just over two at the morning prayer meetings, eighteen at Sunday afternoon meetings, between seven and eight at Tuesday evening prayer meetings, and thirteen at the Thursday evening meetings. The attendance in Surbiton therefore did not differ much from that of Kingston. Certainly the churches did not encourage young men to join an interdenominational Association but there is reason to believe that the Surbiton Association encouraged members from all age groups. They clearly stated in 1884 that they were 'glad to welcome our elder friends,' and two of the members who have been found both in the minutes and the census were Mr. W. Agutter, a retired mercantile clerk, who would have been seventy-six in 1883, and a Mr. J.M. Peates, a gardener who lived in Victoria Road, Surbiton aged eighty-three.[426]

Why did Kingston continue and Surbiton fail?

The Kingston Association would have floundered without Mr. Newson and Mr. Parslow, members who continued over a long period to provide dedicated continuity. The Surbiton branch had lost their key workers after Mr. John King retired and Mr. G. H. Lee departed to Wimbledon. Although there is a sparseness of information in the minutes, the main reason why the Surbiton Association amalgamated with the Kingston branch within three years of opening is clear, and was undoubtedly a growing appreciation of the importance of having a paid professional in charge of organising Association activities.[427] At the end of 1884 only half the subscriptions for the previous year had been collected. In December Mr. Morten took over the post of treasurer. Mr. Walker, who had taken over the post of secretary, said that he would be glad to be relieved from this position as he felt the Association was 'suffering through his want of attention.'[428] By April 1885 some of the members still owed their subscription—having had notice twice that the money was due—and Mr. Morten asked the Committee to 'authorise him to write to these members to the intent that if the Fee was not paid by a given date … it would be considered they no longer desired to be members of the Association.' This request was unanimously agreed.[429]

On April 28, 1885, a special meeting of members was called 'to consider a proposition of the Kingston branch to amalgamate the two Associations.' As the minutes of the Kingston branch are missing between September 1884 and May 1885, the details are uncertain, but the nature of the special meeting suggests that the Kingston members had offered assistance and suggested amalgamation. Captain Cundy may have been involved, as his former letter to the Surbiton branch on July 11, 1882, shows that he would have encouraged this situation.[430] The discussion and the outcome of the meeting held on April 28, 1885 shows that the Surbiton Association were not interested in a new building but in having a paid secretary: 'this position would be of great advantage.' Mr. Cavell took the chair and, after a long discussion, the meeting agreed that the Committees of both Associations should arrange the matter. The meeting then closed with prayer, and in May 1885 an amalgamation resulted in the Association becoming known as the 'Kingston and Surbiton Young Men's Christian Association.'[431]

The Committee contemplated the closure of the Surbiton rooms on April 30,

1885, but meetings in 2 Alpha Road were held for at least seven years following the amalgamation.[432] The increase in expenditure due to running Warwick Lodge was a major factor in the final closure, although the departure of certain members from the Association in 1892 also played some part. The doors to 2 Alpha Road closed sometime between 1892 and 1893.

A PAID SECRETARY

MAY 1885 – AUGUST 1887

A Secretary's Fund and Appointing a Paid Secretary

Between July and September 1884, the Association looked for suitable new premises, but the minute book ending on September 8, shows they were no further forward. The minutes were started in a new book on May 9, 1885, when the Kingston and Surbiton Committee held their first meeting in the Kingston rooms. By this time the decision to employ a general secretary, with the emphasis on collecting sufficient funds to make this ambition a reality had temporarily replaced the desire for new premises. The agreement was that the current secretaries of both the former Kingston and Surbiton branches would remain in their original roles until the choice had been made. Circular letters were to be sent to the members, stating the purposes of the salaried secretary and asking for subscriptions towards the funds. [433]

Mr. J.S. Morten agreed to act as honorary general secretary *pro-tem* to look after the details of the appointment. A fund in the form of promises to ensure that there would be sufficient money to pay the secretary's salary had already been started by May 16, 1885. These promises were expected to cover three years. By the end of the month the subscriptions totalled £106, nearly all of which had been promised for three years, but Mr. Morten wanted to obtain a guarantee for the whole amount before engaging the new secretary.[434] In the meantime sixteen or seventeen letters had been written to district secretaries, in England, Scotland and Ireland to ask for their help to recommend 'any really competent man' for the post, and several replies named suitable candidates. Mr. Hills had been mentioned by Mr. Hind Smith: Mr. Gray by Mr. Southwell (Cardiff); Mr. Stooke by Mr. Jameson (Bristol); Mr. Lapsley by Mr. Oatts (Glasgow); Mr. D. Gardner by Mr. Oatts (Glasgow); Mr. I.F. Sutherland by Mr. Newett (Winchester); Mr. E.W. Stringer by himself. The Committee may have got in touch with two of those recommended as it reported that Mr. Hills and Mr. Lapsley had declined. The Committee thereafter resolved not to take any definite steps to engage a secretary until after the election of the new Committee.[435]

Amalgamation and a New Committee

With the amalgamation, it was decided that a general committee consisting of fourteen members and a chairman would administer the affairs of the Kingston and Surbiton Y.M.C.A. Six of the members were to come from Kingston and six from Surbiton, but there was to be only one programme.[436]

At the annual general meeting Mr. Morten announced that about one hundred and twenty voting papers had been sent out and seventy-one returned with fifteen members having received the most votes.[437] After discussion the Rules were agreed. (See Appendix XVII, page 229.) Mr. Northcroft, the oldest Committee member, signified his willingness to be the chairman of the Committee, and the meeting decided that they should recognise the third Wednesday in each month as Committee meeting night.[438] The adoption of a membership card for the Kingston and Surbiton district was also agreed, but it was decided to put this into action later.[439]

Prospective Secretaries

On July 4, 1885, Mr. Morten made a full report about the correspondence that had passed between him and the applicants for the post of secretary. The two that had been interviewed were as follows:

> Mr. Stooke – Mr. Morten said that he had gone down to Bristol to see him, was very favourably impressed with him, but Mr. Stooke had stated that he would require not less than £150 per annum or £120 with suitable house accommodation. Mr. Hind Smith commented later that he had had Mr. Stooke in view for another appointment. He considered that if he came to Kingston he would probably not remain long before he was called to a post elsewhere.

> Mr. E. W. Stringer – Enquiries proving satisfactory Mr. Morten had determined to go down to Brighton to see him, as a result of the visit he thought Mr. Stringer a very suitable person and recommended him to the consideration of the Committee. It was noted that Mr. Stringer would require a Salary of £120 per annum. After a long and careful consideration the committee agreed that Mr. Stringer should be employed as General Secretary for a term of six months with three months notice on either side at the expiry of that period and that his salary should be £120 per annum.[440]

Terms and Conditions of Mr. Stringer's Employment

By this time the secretary's fund must have reached £120 because, at a meeting on July 15, 1885, Mr. Morten reported that he had written to Mr. Stringer offering him the post of general secretary on the terms formulated by the Committee and that Mr. Stringer had replied to Mr. Morten's letter accepting the post on these terms, and that he would be able to come on July 27. Mr. Stringer had worked for his father, a Brighton grocer, before his new employment, and in 1885 was 26 years of age. Before his arrival the Committee suggested the best means of utilising Mr. Stringer's services:

> it was desirable that he should be present at all the meetings of the Association.

> he should endeavour to look up young men in the day time and be present at the Rooms in the evening to receive them.

> it was desirable that Mr. Stringer should be present at the Surbiton Rooms on Thursdays and at the Kingston Room on the other evenings and Sundays.

> the question of residence was immaterial and should be left to Mr. Stringer's own personal convenience.

Further details were to be left until they could be discussed with Mr. Stringer, and included holiday entitlement of four days at Christmas between 24 and 28 of December and a fortnight's leave in July.[441]

A special social meeting to give a hearty welcome to the new general secretary was arranged for Wednesday, July 29, at the Kingston rooms. A tea at 7.45 p.m. would be provided and a notice to every member would secure full attendance.[442] Unfortunately Mr. Stringer's welcome meeting had to be delayed because the new secretary was unwell but on August 12, 1885, the *Surrey Comet* reported 'a most successful event was held' with between fifty and sixty members and friends attending the meeting to greet the new secretary.[443] Initially Mr. Stringer lodged in 7 King Charles Crescent in Surbiton but later moved to Springfield in Caversham Road.[444] During his time he must have experienced some inconvenience because, although many of the houses on one side of Caversham Road had been completed, in 1885 the construction of the houses on the other side were incomplete and not finished until after he left the area two years later.[445]

By twenty-first century standards Mr. Stringer's duties appear to be excessive. Although it was agreed that Mr. J. S. Morten would take the role of treasurer for the secretary's salary fund; Messrs W. Charles and W. H. Parslow, joint treasurers for the general expenses; and Mr. Frank Newson, treasurer for the Kingston Building Fund, it was also proposed that the present three honorary secretaries, one at Kingston, two at Surbiton retire after the conclusion of the July/September quarter to leave the whole of the secretarial work to Mr. Stringer, who would also be expected to be ex-officio member of all the subcommittees.[446]

He had to visit young men personally during the day time and leave a record of his visits with the Kingston young men at Union Street and of those living in Surbiton at Alpha Road. Once he had acquired his lodgings in Kingston, his walk to work would be short, his headquarters and office being situated at the Kingston rooms. In Kingston he was expected to be in attendance every morning (Sundays excepted) from ten to mid-day and on Tuesday, Wednesday and Friday evenings after seven p.m. He was expected to be in attendance at the Surbiton rooms, on Monday, Thursday and Saturday evenings after seven p.m.

The return trip from Surbiton would not have been easy. Although the two mile route between Kingston and Surbiton had improved since the mid 1860s, on occasions, particularly during the winter months, the route would have been treacherous. If Mr. Stringer had to walk back to his lodgings from Surbiton after dark, he would have found it difficult, particularly if he chose the most direct route that of Clay Hill and Oil Mill Lane (Villiers Avenue and Villiers Road). However, as he was the son and formerly the employee of a grocer he may have owned a bicycle. By 1885 the term 'safety bicycle' was used for bicycles that were an alternative to the 'penny-farthing.' The easiest route on a bicycle into Kingston would have been by way of the Ewell Road.[447] In any case, the route home during late evenings in the mid 1880s would have been fraught with complications due to inadequate lighting, uneven surfaces, and inclement weather.

Association Activities

Mr. Stringer's first Committee meeting took place on August 19, 1885, during which he was elected a member of the Association. He conducted himself well, suggesting that the library books should have a label on the outside and the time allowed for them to be lent out printed on it. The meeting agreed that the Committee should contact different seaside homes connected with the Y.M.C.A. and ask them to send their best prospectus to be framed; that they should bind the *Illustrated London News* and the *Life of the Prince Consort,* and that they should repaint the notice boards of both Associations. Mr. Stringer reported that he had attended meetings of two of the subcommittees and presented brief reports of several young men upon whom he had already waited and then reported on the religious meetings subcommittee.[448]

The general committee and the subcommittees continued during the following months and covered numerous topics. The social and intellectual subcommittee agreed that they should be called the Y.M.C.A. literary and debating society, with fortnightly meetings at the Kingston rooms, and that they should continue to receive the *Evening Standard* newspaper. Shorthand classes would take place every Wednesday evening from seven to eight p.m. at Kingston and every Saturday from seven-thirty to eight-thirty p.m. at Surbiton. Singing practice should also take place for three quarters of an hour every Tuesday from eight-fifteen to nine p.m. in the Kingston rooms.[449]

Later in March 1886 the Committee decided that the Kingston rooms would open at ten a.m. and close at ten-thirty p.m. and they would take the *Daily Telegraph* and continue the debating society into the next quarter. They further agreed that the Surbiton Bible class should start at three instead of at three-thirty p.m. on a Sunday and that the Surbiton Evangelistic Service should be discontinued due to the Church Army having started operations at Surbiton Hill. They agreed that the secretary write to the *Surrey Comet* and the *Kingston and Surbiton News* intimating that they would gladly receive *The Graphic, Pictorial World,* and *Sunday at Home* if any kind friends would like to present them to the Association. They also agreed that there should not be a Good Friday breakfast and that there should be a letterbox at the Kingston rooms.[450] On November 9, the football club was started and in December the goal posts and cross bars were bought for 17/6d.[451]

As the copy of *Moses and Geology* that had been offered as an essay prize by Mr. Ranyard had never been awarded, they decided to announce at the forthcoming social meeting an essay competition, entitled 'The best methods of influencing young men by the Y.M.C.A. in this district.' The essays were restricted to a minimum of eight-hundred and a maximum of one thousand words.[452] However, during the next few months, the topic that took up a considerable amount of committee time involved the defective accommodation rented by the Association in Kingston and an offer to rent the cellars.

Defective Accommodation — Renting out the Cellars

During the first month of his appointment, Mr. Stringer was requested to call and see Mr. Willmott and to write to Mr. Fricker respecting the defective drainage at the Kingston rooms. Mr. Willmott, the manager of the Eagle brewery on the High Street later called with another man only to say that they were unable to find anything the matter with the drainage and considered that other factors caused the noxious odours. It was agreed however that the housekeeper's rooms in particular were in a dilapidated condition.[453] The secretary also reported that Mr. Brewer, who lived next door, had complained that smoke from the Y.M.C.A. rooms was a nuisance, and that this must be due to a defective chimney. Mr.

Newson enquired about the chimney, and the secretary was asked to look into the matter. It was found that the chimney was not defective but that some of the rooms were not connected to the flue. Mr. Newson stated that perhaps the evil might be remedied and expense obviated by using gas and undertook to look into the matter.

The secretary reported that Mr. Burrows the grocer, who lived in the house next door to the Y.M.C.A, had offered to rent the cellars under the Kingston rooms for £5 per annum, and that he would make an entrance from his own premises so as not to interfere with the Association. As Mr. Burrows lived in Eden Street, he probably did not live next door, rather the back of his shop backed on to the side of the Association's premises, see Figure 15, page 45. Mr. Burrows' shop would probably be on the extreme right of the picture facing into Eden Street, whilst the Y.M.C.A. site faced into Union Street (previously called Brick Lane). Mr. Burrows said that he would yield possession if the Committee agreed to his proposition and required him to do so at three months' notice. The Association questioned if they had the power to sublet, but if they did, they unanimously resolved that they should allow Mr. Burrows the use of the cellars at the rental he had suggested. They therefore requested Mr. Parslow to draw up an agreement to that effect.[454]

At a later meeting the secretary reported that he had received a letter from Mr. Arthur Fricker's agent intimating that Mr. Burrows had seen him respecting the renting of the cellars. As agent, he did not object as long as the Committee were willing to enter into an agreement with Mr. Fricker, stating that when they came to hand over the premises they should do so in their entirety, with all damage made good. In November 1885 the Association resolved that the secretary write to Mr. Fricker expressing the Committees' readiness to comply with the terms of his letter and to enter into the agreement.[455]

As Mrs. Turner was very ill and no longer able to act as housekeeper, the Association engaged a Mr. Bull and an official agreement was signed. As was customary he would receive an allowance for special meetings held in the Kingston rooms.[456] Due to Mr Clements' illness, the Committee also had some difficulty in getting a quorum. In the end Mr. Clements resigned just before Christmas but died soon afterwards.[457]

Christmas Day Celebrations

Mr. Stringer took four days' holiday at Christmas starting on December 24, 1885. On Christmas Day the Association invited seventy people who were living in the lodging houses and who were visited by the young men of the Association every

Sunday evening, to an annual dinner. This would take place at the Association rooms in Union Street. The Association provided a meal of beef and plum pudding. Miss Edmonton addressed a few words to the company, and Mr. Frank Newson read to them. They served tea at five-thirty p.m., and Miss Harty, Miss Lea and Mr. Bonson sang a selections of songs.

A few days later Mr. Britton gave a free tea to a large number of the lodgers from Bridge Street and the back lanes, and spoke of the pleasure he gained from meeting his friends who were gathered together. 'He was thankful for the attention that was given him when he visited the lodging houses on a Sunday, for the behaviour was always as good as it would be in any church or chapel.'[458]

January 1886 – August 1887

It is unclear when the Committee decided that Mr. Stringer was not suited for the role of general secretary of the Kingston and Surbiton Y.M.C.A. Mr. Stringer had come back from Christmas leave to deal with the annual report. During the following months requests to use the rooms continued as before. On June 21, 1886, the results of the election of the new Committee were not minuted, and the only indication that an election had taken place was a note stating 'the result of the election of the new Committee was announced and Mr. Frank Gaydon, and Mr. H. J. Bristow were appointed scrutineers to see that the returns were correct. The meeting was then closed with prayer.' [459] In July the Committee agreed that the secretary should attend the Bristol Conference.[460] Rather than giving a full report, however, he presented only a brief account of the proceedings of the conference, stating that a full report would be published in the October number of the *Monthly Review*. He considered that the spirit characterised at the meetings was one of determination and that more than ever the work of the Associations should be 'Christ for young men and young men for Christ.'[461]

In September 1886 Mr. Bull said he was willing to take charge of the Surbiton rooms three nights a week and suggested that the Committee should grant him some payment. The Committee agreed that the Surbiton rooms should be open every evening from October 1, and that Mr. Bull should be employed to take charge of them three nights a week and when the secretary was absent. Mr. Bull was to receive 2/- a week, with a one month trial, and that the arrangement should continue during the winter if it worked.[462] By November 1886 the secretary had obviously found coping with the visitations to young men impossible given all the other duties he had to perform. He therefore proposed that there should be a visiting Committee. Each full member should look after four to six young men. Each should have a book in which to record each month the results of each call made to members. The whole Committee should meet monthly to compare notes. He also proposed in January 1887 that the Association procure a number of boards to be exhibited gratis by friends of the Association, and that they should be affixed if possible, to the railings of churches, announcing the time and place of meetings. A small slip giving the name of the speaker and the subject should be pasted on the board every week. He thought these actions would increase attendance on a Sunday, and generally advertise the Association. He suggested that Mr. Bull the caretaker might do the posting. The minutes, which Mr. Stringer wrote, state 'It was agreed that the idea was a good one and the secretary was requested to see how many boards could be exhibited in the manner suggested.'[463]

Sir Charles Douglas Fox and Mr. E.W. Stringer

The *Surrey Comet* announced the death of George Cavell on January 1, 1887. Mr. Cavell of Grantham Lodge, Surbiton Hill, was one of the original founder members of Christ Church. He was also the president of the Surbiton Y.M.C.A. The Association unanimously agreed that they should send a letter of condolence to Mrs. Cavell and the family, and ask Captain Cundy to act as president of the amalgamated Associations. In reply Captain Cundy suggested Sir Douglas Fox would be a good new president. The Association asked the secretary to write to Captain Cundy expressing a hope that he would still continue as president.[464]

At the February meeting the secretary announced that George Williams had promised to preside at the annual meeting on Wednesday, March 30 and suggested that the Clapham Gospel male choir should assist. Mr. Morten, seconded by Mr. Salisbury, said that the Clapham male choir were not to be invited but that the secretary communicate with Mr. P. Salisbury to arrange for local help as needed.[465] The secretary then reported that he had received a letter from Captain Cundy in which the latter stated that he would continue president only until another gentleman accepted the post. Acting on this statement, the secretary had written to Sir Douglas Fox, who replied as follows:

> Coombe Springs —
> To the Secretary Kingston and Surbiton Y.M.C.A. near Kingston on Thames
>
> Dear Sir — Kindly convey to the committee my appreciation of their having offered me the important position of president of this Joint Association, and to say that if it is the unanimous wish of the members I shall be happy to serve.
>
> Yours sincerely, Douglas Fox.

The secretary explained that Captain Cundy had suggested the name of Sir Douglas Fox for the Post.[466] The Committee endorsed the decision, and it seems as if all the members were pleased that Sir Douglas would replace Captain Cundy as new president, but the impression is given that the Committee had not been consulted before the invitation.

Sir Charles Douglas Fox, who preferred to be known as Sir Douglas Fox, was born in 1840 in Smethwick in Staffordshire. His father was a civil engineer whose company Fox and Henderson had won the contract to build the Crystal Palace designed by Joseph Paxton. Fox studied at Kings College London and Trinity College Cambridge, but his education ended abruptly when his father went bankrupt. He became articled to his father, who had set up an engineering consultancy. Thereafter Sir Charles Fox and Sons designed railway viaducts and bridges. Later, after his father died in 1874, Douglas was involved in the construction of the Snowdon Mountain Railway and the extension of the Great Central and several of the London's early tube lines. He was knighted at Windsor Castle by Queen Victoria in March 1886 and, during the 1880s, lived in Coombe Springs, Kingston. Later his company, Sir Douglas Fox and Partners, served as the London based consultants involved in the design of the Victoria Falls Bridge, the main arch being linked in 1905.[467]

Sir Douglas was a member of the Church of England and involved in the Church Mission Society and therefore more than worthy of taking over the presidency. Although it is impossible to confirm, it appears that the secretary had acted on the advice of Captain Cundy before the Committee, who should have authorised him to write the letter, had discussed the situation. At the general Committee Meeting on 14, March 1887, Mr. Morten reported that Mr Stringer had been requested:

> To tender his resignation of the office of Secretary, to take effect not later than 2 August also that a letter had been received by the committee from Mr. E.W. Stringer tendering his resignation in accordance with the terms of the aforesaid resolution.[468]

At the same general meeting on March 14, 1887, Mr. Newson tendered his resignation because he was moving from the neighbourhood. Although the minutes are somewhat muddled, Mr. Stringer continued to attend the Committee meetings and wrote the minutes for the meetings up to and including July 11, 1887. These meetings included an annual members business meeting held on June 29, 1887, when Sir Douglas Fox took the chair. In these minutes Mr. Stringer not only listed all the names of the new Committee but he also gave their addresses.[469] A *Surrey Comet* report in July gives more detail about Mr. Stringer's departure and shows that the members were not happy about this situation. Mr. Stringer was very popular with many of the members. The *Surrey Comet* reporter writes that:

> Mr. Bristow interrogated the committee as to the reasons why the secretary Mr. Stringer was asked to resign, and moved a resolution expressing regret at the action of the committee. This was seconded by Mr. J.W. Colverson, and from the way in which the remarks of these gentlemen were received it was evident that the action of the committee is disapproved of by many of the members.[470]

These were difficult times, and Mr. Newson obviously felt that the time had come for him to leave the Kingston Association. Nevertheless, although he gave in his notice in March 1887, he did not leave Kingston and Surbiton Y.M.C.A. until July 22, 1888. Mr. Stringer worked out his notice period quietly and without rancour, leaving on August 3, 1887, for Brighton. A week later on August 8, Mr. Robert Cowdery joined the Y.M.C.A. as general secretary. The minutes do not report how he was chosen. The 1891 census reports his age as twenty-nine, that his wife was called Kate and his two children Lettie and Harold, aged one and five months respectively, were all living in Warwick Lodge, Eden Street.

WILBERFORCE BRYANT – VICE-PRESIDENT
KINGSTON AND SURBITON Y.M.C.A.
1886 – 1888

The Bryant Family and Francis May

The Gables in Surbiton was built for Wilberforce Bryant in 1877. It was designed by Sir Rowland Plumbe, erected by T.J. Meesom of Twickenham and built in red brick replacing the property previously erected on the site.[471]

The story of the Bryant family, who lived in Surbiton during the second half of the nineteenth century, starts with William Bryant, the son of a starch and polish maker, who was born in 1804 in Tiverton in Devon. It also includes initially Francis May, who became his partner and who began his career as a tea dealer. Both men were Quakers and sometime during 1839 they set up as general merchants in London. Among their products they sold matches, which they imported from Carl and Johan Lundstrom's match factory in Sweden. By 1853 they were selling large quantities of matches and in August 1855, Francis May acquired the British rights on a design produced by Lundstrom. The match was very successful and in 1861, William Bryant took a lease on a factory named Fairfield Works in Fairfield Road, Bow.[472] An inspection by a Royal Commission reported that it was 'remarkable for the excellence of most of its arrangements both for the health and comfort of the workpeople.' Francis May was a kind employer, during the early 1860s the factory workers were invited on a day-trip to his home in Reigate. Part of the fun was a visit to the Reigate Caves. The landlord of the Bats and Bulls public house organized a visit to the old sand mines and for a fee of 2d lit them with candles for the excited factory workers.

After Wilberforce and his brothers became involved in the business it soon became obvious that the Bryant family were anxious to buy out May. A dispute took place that lasted from 1864 to 1875 and although two Quaker Friends acted as arbitrators there was no agreement. May's wife Jane died in 1872 and a year after William Bryant's death in 1874, not wanting to go to law, May left the business. Further information about Francis May is limited other than he continued to live in Reigate amongst his large family of five daughters and two sons.[473] He died in December 1885 at the age of 82, remembered as a 'mild-mannered and kindly' man, the Quaker who provided Reigate with a school.[474]

In 1871 William Bryant was living in Oakenshaw, Oak Hill, Surbiton with his wife Anne. He described himself on the census as a 'Manufacturer of Chemical Lights', employing one-thousand-five-hundred people. William's sons Wilberforce aged thirty-three, Frederick and Theodore aged twenty-eight also appear on the 1871 census. Arthur, another son, was twenty-nine in 1871, a widower and is described as a merchant who lived in the Ewell Road. By 1876, following William's death in 1874 and May's departure in 1875, the firm Bryant and May, were significant East End employers. The 1881 census shows all four sons retaining properties in Surbiton, although Arthur died during his early forties, leaving behind his second wife and six children.

30. The entrance to the Hillcroft College, formerly The Gables, owned by Wilberforce Bryant   (**AG 2013**)

Quarterly Meetings

The Kingston and Surbiton Y.M.C.A. asked Wilberforce Bryant to be a vice-president in January 1886, and by March of that year he had accepted the position.[475] The Association then began to use his gardens and accommodation for their quarterly meetings. It was a normal circumstance for the Committee to send out invitations to notable people at appropriate periods during the year to ask them to be vice-presidents. They invited Lord Tankerville to fill this role at the same time as Bryant, but there is no further mention of his name. Some vice-presidents were not proactive; others were and together with presidents such as Captain Cundy gave continuous assistance and financial help over long periods of time. A resident of Wimbledon during his latter years, by December 1887 Sir Joseph Bazalgette had become president of the SW (Suburban) District Union of the Y.M.C.A.[476] Sir Joseph was the chief engineer of London's Metropolitan Board of Works, having created the sewer network for central London. Known for his hard work, Sir Joseph would have taken his role as president very seriously.[477]

Although remaining on the register of the Society of Friends, Wilberforce Bryant had by this time become a member of Christ Church Surbiton and was a patron of the Church of England Temperance Society.[478] However there may have been another reason for his being invited to be a vice-president. This was because in 1884 he had set aside a portion of his estate to be used as a meeting room and a theatre and had said 'any useful or religious body' could use these facilities freely.[479] The house and the grounds would have offered a delightful change from Zoar Chapel for the Association's increasing social activities.

The front entrance of The Gables, now Hillcroft College, is shown in Figure 30. The *Surrey Comet* records the first use of the venue by the Association on March 27, 1886:

> By kind permission of Mr. Wilberforce Bryant, the quarterly social meeting in connection with the Kingston and Surbiton District Branch of the Young Men's Christian Association was held at the Gables. Each member was accorded the privilege of taking a friend of either sex, and there was consequently a large gathering. Refreshments were served in the lower hall, under the direction of the energetic secretary Mr. E. Stringer, and an adjournment was subsequently made to the large upper hall which was well filled. The chair was occupied by Mr. G. Cavell, one of the presidents of the association, and those present included Capt. Cundy, the other president, Mr. Wilberforce Bryant, Revd. W. Baster, Mr. J.S. Morten, and Mr. Furse, who attended as a deputation from the central association. The National Anthem was first sung, and was followed by one of Sankey's hymns, after which prayer was offered by Capt. Cundy. The Chairman then gave a cordial welcome to the visitors, and expressed the pleasure he felt in seeing so many ladies present. He spoke with earnestness upon the importance of immediate decision for Christ, pointing out that the language of the gospel was "Now." Procrastination was invariably dangerous, but it was especially so in reference to religion, for life at best was short and uncertain, and he had noticed throughout his long life that men who appeared the strongest had frequently been smitten down the soonest. Miss Maud Lea sang very

tastefully 'O rest in the Lord,' Mr. E.W. Stringer evinced the possession of an excellent memory in reciting 'The chronicles of angels'; Miss Harty evoked much applause by her successful rendition of 'The Better Land'; and Mr. W. Hayward sang with considerable taste Grounod's 'Nazareth.' A capital exhibition of tasteful part singing was given by Miss Harty, Mrs. J.T. Hayward, Mr. J.S. Morten, and Mr. W.E. Gardener who sang a quartet,"A Song of Salvation," being No. 258 in Sankey's collection. Another hymn was sung, after which Mr. Furse addressed the meeting at length upon the subject of entire sanctification ... a hearty vote of thanks was accorded to Mr. Bryant for the use of the rooms. Mr. Bryant gracefully acknowledged the compliment, and said he should be happy at any time to place the rooms at the disposal of the association. A very interesting and successful gathering terminated with the benediction. Miss Harty kindly and efficiently acted as accompanist. [480]

Repairs to the Kingston Premises

During the summer of 1886 the (Union Street) Brick Lane rooms needed further maintenance. In July the Association asked the landlord to undertake repairs, which again he appeared to ignore. In August, as he had not replied, the secretary again wrote to Mr. Willmott. Mr. Fricker inspected the premises and said that, while he advocated letting them tumble down, he would send a man to do something. They thereafter repaired the building. They then gave Mr. Bull the task of renovating the hall and, in February 1887, the landlord sent Mr. Parslow a cheque of £2. 4. 4d to cover expenses. [481]

Despite the repairs, the rooms must have been unsuitable for social meetings particularly when ladies were present. Using The Gables for these occasions would have been very enjoyable. In October 1886 the Association held the quarterly social meeting on the Bryant estate again. In January 1887 an interesting lecture illustrated with coloured views was also held at The Gables, whilst in October 1887, September 1888 and again in 1889 the Association met socially in what they undoubtedly thought were beautiful surroundings. [482] As we shall see later, Mr. Wilberforce Bryant was no longer living on the estate in 1889.

The Factory, 'Lucifers' and the Strike

The year 1888 was of particular significance for Bryant and a period when he, his brothers and the Bryant and May factory in Bow were at the centre of a controversy that continues to retain a prominent place in the history books. In July 1888 one-thousand-four-hundred matchmakers, mostly young women and girls, walked out of the Fairfield factory in Bow as a protest against their appalling employment conditions. [483] Although reports during the early 1860s found the factory to be spacious and airy with the workers getting proper lunch breaks; it has been suggested that major changes had occurred after William died.[484] Yet even before 1874 the company had expanded rapidly, taking over smaller businesses, and by 1876 Bryant and May were the largest employers of match workers in Britain, with official endorsement from the Factory Commission as a model employer in 1876. The company had made inroads into the American market by 1883, and, during the next year, the brothers set the business up as a limited company. By 1885 it had become so dominant that the company was selling matches to Australia, India and the Far East. The prosperous middle classes, who found the return from their dividends a very lucrative twenty-three per cent, continued to support the company, whilst the shares by 1887 had risen from their original price of £5 to £18. 7s 6d.[485] Having achieved a monopoly, Bryant and May reduced the wages of their workers. Whereas in 1876 the company claimed to pay between ten and twelve shillings a week, by 1888 the earnings of female employees apparently ranged from four to nine shillings a week reduced by a series of fines imposed by male foremen for faulty work. The public were not aware that a proportion of the workers, in particular those who did the 'dipping', were exposed to phosphorous poisoning. The company had hidden this fact by dismissing workers showing signs of this condition. The inhalation of phosphorous caused yellowing of the skin, loss of hair and 'phossy jaw' bone cancer of the face and jaw.[486]

Recently Louise Raw, in her book *Striking A Light*, has overturned the traditional interpretation of events, by arguing that Annie Bessant (the nineteenth century political activist) did not encourage the girls or lead the strike. It was the women themselves who decided to walk out of the factory in protest and used Bessant through her newspaper *The Link* to achieve public recognition of their appalling work conditions.[487] However the *Surrey Comet* hardly mentioned the incident although many other newspapers reported the strike. The only mention of the incident in the *Surrey Comet* is in an article on July 21 concerning a meeting that the Merton branch of the Socialist League organised and held in the Broadway. A Mr. Mercer, who was a London City missionary, severely criticised the company, and a collection was made totalling £2. 12s 4d.[488] The fact that there was little criticism from the local area is not surprising given that Wilberforce Bryant had lived in Surbiton for more than seventeen years, worshipped at Christ Church and would have known and been known by most of the social elite.[489]

The Bryant and May strikers returned to work after their managers agreed to most of their demands including the abolition of fines and right to eat their meals away from the workplace. After the 1888 strike Bryant and May protested that they would have preferred to manufacture 'safety matches', but the public preferred the 'Lucifer.'[490] The government continued to support the company because it thought that banning the 'Lucifer' would result in an increase in the import of foreign matches. In 1891 the Salvation Army opened its own match factory in Old Ford, East London. They only used red phosphorus and paid double the wages the Bryant and May employees received. In only a short period of time the Old Ford factory was producing six million boxes of matches a year.[491]

Although on marching out of the Bow factory the match workers found a place in the history books, most of the Kingston and Surbiton residents would have been unaware of these events. As we shall see in the next chapter, the Y.M.C.A. had problems of its own, in particular the building scheme it had to abandon also in mid-1888. It continued to request the use of The Gables as a venue for its activities, although the Association had moved into Warwick Lodge by September 24, 1890. Mr. Alfred Cooper, a tea merchant, was then living in the house with his wife, three children, mother in law, two visitors and eight servants (not including another eight servants who lived in accommodation within the grounds). Bryant had left Surbiton in 1887, having purchased the five-hundred-and-seventeen acres of the Stoke Park estate as his private residence. By 1892 he was a justice of the peace, High Sheriff of Buckingham and president of the local agricultural shows which were held on the Stoke Poges estate.[492] The Bryants spent many thousands of pounds improving the estate, which was later featured by Edward Rose in the *Illustrated London News* in 1896.

> To reach it, one crosses the green loveliness of an English park, barred halfway to the house by a narrow lake overhung with trees: a lake invented by the famous Capability Brown, and much visited by gleaming swans and ducks in modest blacks and greys. The ancient manor house is a little to the right, by the waterside; great trees stand here and there, shadowy in the hot sun; splendid deer come up, tame and inquisitive, to stare at the visitor.[493]

Bryant and most of his family did not frequent Surbiton after 1888, and the minutes never again mention that he was a vice-president.

A BUILDING SCHEME
JULY 1884 — SEPTEMBER 1884
AUGUST 1885 — JULY 1888

Looking for New Premises; July — September 1884

Finding new premises away from their dilapidated rooms in Brick Lane proved a hard task, causing the Association considerable difficulties, time and expense before its quest was finally accomplished. On July 14, 1884, a long discussion took place about the future of the Y.M.C.A. in Kingston, with the Association debating whether to build new premises or to rent an empty house.[494]

Members mentioned various options. Mr. Knapp said that the late Inland Revenue office had been taken and recommended Dr Biddell's late house in St. James Road. Mr. Parslow and Mr. Salisbury suggested that the Association should build a place of its own. The meeting suggested that a deputation should wait upon Mr. George Williams, Mr. Samuel Morley and other rich philanthropic men to endeavour to enlist their aid in the undertaking.[495] Mr. Samuel Morley was a mill owner, a Liberal and a Congregationalist. He was one of those who had given £5,000 to buy Exeter Hall, and in 1882 he had guaranteed the National Council of the Y.M.C.A.[496]

After much discussion, the Committee appointed two members to visit the various houses to let in the neighbourhood, to find the lowest rent and report back. On July 21, 1884, a report was received and discussed:

that there was no place available in the Market place.

that Mr. Clement's house known as Warwick Lodge, Eden Street was to let but he (the reporter) did not deem it suitable.

that the premises formerly occupied by the London County Bank and later by Prescotts situated in High Street were to let, but that the rent asked was £100 per annum.

that the premises lately occupied by Salvin Taylor & Co. & the adjoining shop were to let and that the rent was £45 per annum. Mr. Gaydon deemed that the house in St. James Road was the most suitable for the Association's purposes. However Mr. Philip Salisbury reported that he had been over Dr. Biddell's late house in St. James Road but the great obstacle was that the basement was flooded occasionally.

The Association agreed that they should inspect Prescott's late premises in the High Street and Salvin Taylor and Hewitt's late premises in St. James Road at the earliest possible opportunity and that members meet at half past six at the Association's rooms, the keys having been procured to enable an inspection.[497] Following this inspection, no one considered the various buildings suitable. Although the house lately occupied by Dr. Biddle in St James Road was fit for purpose the flooded basement represented a serious deterrent. Captain Cundy was also not happy about the Association moving there. Later they found that the house was no longer available. They then considered Clattern House and agreed that the secretary should write to the corporation to find out whether they would let a portion of the building and at what cost.[498]

The minute book ends abruptly on September 8, 1884, and, when the minutes were restarted in a new book on May 9, 1885, the Committee had united with Surbiton and the Association was involved in choosing and welcoming their new secretary.

Selecting a Site; August 1885 – July 1888

On August 21, 1885, the subcommittee of the building fund met to discuss the proposed building of a new Y.M.C.A. in the Kingston area. Messrs Northcroft, Newson, Parslow and Stringer, who was at this time the new general secretary, attended the meeting. Mr. Newson said that very little had been done to promote the scheme up to the present time, but that Captain Cundy had signified his approval. The difficulty had been procuring a suitable site. The general opinion was that the most convenient site would be in St. James Road, and Mr. Northcroft, who was a building surveyor, undertook the task of seeing Mr. Roles, who owned land in this location. As they did not know Mr. Roles address, Mr. Parslow offered to procure it and forward it to Mr. Northcroft. They also discussed finance. A sum of £225 had already been promised (£50 of this conditionally), and Mr. Clements (who was a solicitor and a member of the Committee) had agreed to advance the required money at five per cent for the purchase of a site and the erection of a building, guaranteeing that he would not call in the finance for twenty years. He also offered to do the legal work for free.[499]

On August 9, 1886, Mr. Newson announced that Mr. Rutland Saunders had advised the Association that the plot of land next to the Drill Hall was on the market. A former member, Rutland Saunders had left the Association in September 1880. The subcommittee had met privately after having received this information and decided to make a bid for the plot not exceeding £300. At a Special Committee meeting to consider the matter, Rutland Saunders produced rough plans both of the ground and the suggested building. A further meeting took place on August 16, with Rutland Saunders being present.[500] There were objections to the site as it was feared that some of the young men connected with the Association might be drawn away by the attractions associated with the Drill Hall.

The secretary read a letter from Mr. George Cavell, who also disapproved of the scheme. Mr. Northcroft also wrote, regretting that he could not attend the meeting owing to a swollen foot, but saying he would fall in with whatever the Committee might eventually decide. Mr. Newson explained the scheme at length in a letter read by the secretary, and several members spoke concerning the quietness of the neighbourhood. The chairman, having decided that the Drill Hall wasn't a problem, authorised Mr. Saunders to make an offer of £250 for the site in Orchard Road to increase it to £270 at his discretion if necessary.[501] A month later at a General Meeting held on October 13, 1886, Mr. Newson reported that the owner of the Orchard Road site was unwilling to accept the offer of £270, and the meeting instructed Mr. Saunders to offer £320. This meeting also mentioned sites in Ashdown Road and Clarence St and requested Mr. Gardener to make enquiries about them and report back.[502]

On November 8, 1886, the Association found that the owner of the Orchard Road site was erecting buildings to let. The Committee had recently viewed a site in Brook Street, currently the subject of negotiation. Mr. Gardener reported that the Clarence Street property that he had viewed had a frontage of forty feet and a depth of forty feet. The price was £1,100. The frontage of the site in Ashdown Road measured one-hundred-and-eighteen feet, and the greatest depth was ninety-five feet declining somewhat. The price was £800. The Association resolved that Mr. Rutland Saunders should attend to the Ashdown Road site as well as that of Brook Street.[503] They discussed other properties, and Mr. W. C. Gardener stated that he had enquired as to the Ashdown Road property and found that Mr. Street would be willing to sell three lots to the Association for £400. The Association produced and examined a plan of the property. They decided to communicate with Mr. Rutland Saunders in the matter forwarding him also the plan of the estate.[504]

On January 10, 1887, the Association unanimously resolved that 'an offer of £350 be made for the plots in Ashdown Road subject to being certain that the amount had been fully guaranteed.' Mr. Saunders asked if they could give some idea of the accommodation that would be required. He thought that there should be two classrooms, a reading room and library (in one), a secretary's room and two rooms for the caretaker. A member made an offer to guarantee the interest of £100 for ten years if the complete scheme were undertaken and the building had a hall in the accommodation. Finally the members unanimously agreed to place the matter of the building in the hands of a committee of three, Messrs Northcroft, Newson and Henderson.[505]

A Decision

On January 24, 1887, a Special Meeting reported that Mr. Street had declined to take less than £400 for the site in the Ashdown Road but at the same time it was mentioned that a site in Denmark Road was available, and that this might be obtained cheaply. The meeting discussed this possible option at length. Mr. Northcroft had written to the Committee saying he would be 'willing to fall in with whatever decision the committee might arrive at.' Mr. Parslow and Mr. Gardener wanted Mr. Newson to see Mr. Hind Smith to ask if the Association could borrow £100 and, if it could, make an offer of £400 for the three plots in Ashdown Road. Mr. Salisbury moved an amendment negating the motion, and the Association eventually agreed (five to two) to ask Mr. Henderson to see the Butlers, the family who had offered the site in Denmark Road and to report back at a future date to the Committee. The Denmark Road location then became the preferred site for the future Kingston and Surbiton Y.M.C.A.[506]

On February 21, 1887, Mr. Newson had called on Mr. Street, the owner of the Ashdown Road property, to ask if he would be willing to keep the property open until December 31, 1887, promising to pay £25 if the purchase did not go through but they had not been able to obtain a reply. The meeting listened to a letter from Mr. Henderson, stating that he had called on the Butlers regarding the Denmark Road site and a telegram from Mr. Gerald Butler in which he said:

> you shall have the ground required at one quarter of the price at which it may be valued on condition of the Buildings being erected subject to our approval.'[507]

The General Meeting on March 14, 1887, had a busy schedule of business. The Association had asked the secretary, Mr. Stringer, to tender his resignation, and he had complied by the time the meeting took place, although he continued to take the minutes. Mr. Newson also tendered his resignation stating that he had moved, but later minutes show that he continued to be involved with the building scheme. Mr. W.E. Gardener said he had a letter from Mr. Street in which he asked for a definite reply respecting the property in the Ashdown Road. A letter from Mr. Rutland Saunders commented on the offer by Mr. and the Misses Butler to sell the Denmark Road site to the Association, a site with a fifty feet frontage at £5 to £6 per foot according to depth.[508] Mr. Rutland Saunders had lived at Brooklyns, in Denmark Road at the time of his marriage and so would have known the area.[509] Unfortunately the minutes do not indicate the details of his comment on the site owned by the Butlers. Mr. Parslow wasn't happy about these proposals. He suggested that it would be worthwhile to entertain a proposition for the purchase of the Wesleyan Chapel in St. James Road. He said he understood that, whereas the original sum required was £1,500, they might now buy the chapel for £1,000. However the Denmark Road site appeared to be a very good offer. Mr. Newson estimated that the actual cost of the site would be about £75, being one-fourth of its estimated value. The meeting defeated Mr. Parslow's objection by nine votes to two, and agreed that:

> this committee accept with thanks the kind offer of Mr. and the Misses Butler of Adelaide Road, Surbiton, which offer is a plot of land 50 feet frontage and about 50 feet depth at one fourth of its value such value having been stated at £5 to £6 per foot frontage according to depth and would feel grateful if such plot can be the one nearest the proposed diverted footpath – Grove Road End.[510]

The Butlers

The Butlers were a young family who in 1871 lived in Bleinham Lodge in Adelaide Road with their aunt Isabella Butler who was in her fifties. The family originally came from Wickham Market in Suffolk where their father Weeden Butler was the Vicar of the Anglican Church of All Saints. Their mother Frances appears to have had ten children seven girls, including twins, and three boys. As Henry and Percy born in 1849 and 1857 do not appear on the 1861 census, it is possible that they did not survive and by 1871, both Weeden and Frances Butler were also probably dead. The older girls had left home as they would have been in their late twenties. The Butler children in Adelaide Road in 1871 consisted of four girls and a boy called Gerard, by this time nine years of age. The eldest girl Julia was twenty-three and three other daughters—Florence, Gertrude and Annie —were fourteen, nine and seven respectively. In the family there was also Frances Christee (the sister of Isabella Butler) aged fifty-nine. The two aunts had been born in Chelsea, as had Weeden Butler. There were three servants, one of whom was Eleanor Newson aged fifty-six who had been born in Suffolk and lived in the family home both in 1851 and 1861. During 1881 Blenheim Lodge was empty apart from two servants. Gerard Butler was studying at Trinity College, Cambridge, whilst his sisters Florence, Gertrude and Annie were staying in Hastings with their aunt Isabella, now aged sixty. Eleanor Newson was also found in the family. On the 1891 census Florence, thirty-four, had returned to Bleinham Lodge in Adelaide Road, now living apart from her sisters but still retaining Eleanor Newson as her servant, now seventy-five. The finance detailed during October 1887 suggests that only three of the Butler siblings were involved in this generous gift. However why this land was offered to the Association at such an advantageous price remains a mystery.[511]

31. Bleinham Lodge in Adelaide Road, home of the Butler family, now a nursing home.   **(AG 2012)**

The Denmark Road Site

Mr. Frank Newson reported to the Committee on April 18, 1887. He had written to Mr. Butler making an offer and had viewed the land in his company. Mr. Butler explained that, on the advice of the surveyor, the plot they were willing to let the Association have must be confined to a spot about two-hundred feet from the Springfield Road. The minutes state that the Committee agreed to:

> ask Mr. Newson to see Mr. Butler again and endeavour to obtain an additional frontage of 5 or 10 feet at the reduced price but to obtain no more than 5 feet if Mr. Butler required the full price. They also agreed that the Deed of Conveyance should be made over to Sir Douglas Fox, Captain Cundy, Messrs H.T. Northcroft and J. F. Henderson. They then heard a letter from Mr. Rutland Saunders giving a rough ground plan of the proposed building and resolved that such plan be submitted to Mr. Butler as expressing the views of the committee and that the building would comprise of a ground floor and first and second floor. The question of raising the funds was then considered when it was resolved that Mr. Newson be assisted by Mr. W. Macfarlane and those who can help.[512]

32. Looking towards the Bridge in Springfield Road—the proposed Y.M.C.A. building would have been in Denmark Road, to the left.   **(AG 2013)**

On May 9, 1887, Mr. Newson reported that he had called on Mr. Butler, who had promised to see his surveyor. Mr. Butler was willing to allow the Association an extra five or ten feet of land at one-fourth the estimated value, such value now stated at 5 guineas per foot. Mr. Newson said he had written, offering to pay full price for the additional land required, but Mr. Butler had expressed his willingness to let the Association have it at the same price per foot as proposed for the original quarter. He also stated that Mr. Butler was willing to recognise the full amount in the conveyance and to return three-fourths to the Association. Mr. Newson said that he had called on Mr. Wilberforce Bryant regarding funds but Mr. Bryant had not replied. He had therefore, asked Mr. Hind Smith to use his influence with Mr. Bryant in the matter.[513]

33. Looking along Denmark Road. The flats are roughly where the building would have been situated.   **(AG 2012)**

Finance and Organisation

The Association suggested that drawing room meetings should be held to encourage residents of the neighbourhood to raise the necessary funds. Mr. Newson produced a copy of the Trust Deed used by the National Council. He also reported that Sir Douglas Fox, Captain Cundy and Mr. Northcroft had all signified their willingness to be trustees, but that Mr. Henderson's answer had yet to be received. The meeting resolved to place a six by four foot board on the site and to obtain tenders for its erection. The subject matter should read as follows:

> Site for the Kingston and Surbiton District Young Men's Christian Association Building. Subscriptions which are earnestly solicited may be paid to: The London and County and Messrs Shrubsoles' Bank or to W. Macfarlane, Esq., Hon Treasurer, Richmond Road, Kingston on Thames.

The meeting also unanimously agreed to elect Mr. W. Macfarlane as treasurer of the building fund along with Mr. Newson and to add Mr. Macfarlane to the building subcommittee. They agreed to ask Sir Douglas Fox, the mayor (Ald. Sherrard) and Captain Cundy to initiate the proposed drawing room meetings but to leave details to the subcommittee. Mr. Newson also reported that Mr. Hind Smith had suggested the name of a gentleman willing to undertake the solicitor's work with the conveyance etc, free of charge. The meeting unanimously agreed to add Mr. F. Pitts to the Board of Trustees, the board to consist of five members, with the Association to have the authority to add more.[514]

On May 23, 1887, Mr. Newson read a letter from Captain Cundy. It was understood that the ground could be returned to Mr. and the Misses Butler should the Association be unable to raise the funds. Mr. Butler was eager to see the plans as soon as possible. Mr. Newson read a letter from Mr. Butler that stated that the total amount promised was £470, this amount to include the reduction in the price of the land by the Butlers. Mr. Northcroft said that they now required the elevation. He thought it would be well to pay down one quarter of the price and that the legal preliminaries should be settled first; in short, the Association needed to 'acquire the land.' Mr. Northcroft then proposed that the trustees be 'empowered to acquire the site in Denmark Road which will be two-hundred feet from the Springfield Road, sixty feet frontage beyond that, by its depth.' Mr. Macfarlane seconded the proposal and the meeting agreed it.

A copy of the Trust Deed was produced, and the meeting agreed that the trustees should pass it round one to another, but then to take the opinion of the General Committee before making any decision. During a discussion as to the contents of the building Mr. Northcroft produced a list of what he thought would be required. Mr. Newson reported that a Mr. Hayward had expressed his willingness to undertake the legal work free of charge, excepting out of pocket expenses. He had also written to Mr. Butler.

The following subscriptions to the building fund were reported: R.T. Bond, Esq., £25, Miss Walter £5, G. Foot Esq, £5, J.S. Morten Esq., £20. Mr Saunders produced plans of the proposed elevation and plans of the various floors. The meeting fully considered these plans and asked Mr. Saunders to prepare reduced plans to come within £1,200, for the first section exclusive of cost of land. Mr. Parslow moved as an amendment, 'that £1,350 be the figure upon which Mr. Saunders work out his elevations and that he submit the same with cost thereof as nearly as possible to the Committee.' Mr. Macfarlane seconded, but only two voted for the amendment and the original motion was carried by four to two.[515] In August Mr Saunders produced fresh plans. These were inspected and approved and Messrs. Northcroft & Co., were requested to take out the quantities for the first section of the building.

Complications

Complications started to arise at this time. On September 5, 1887, Mr. Newson read a letter Mr. Hayward had sent that ran as follows:

> Dear Sir - Abstract of Title has been sent therein from which it appears that the land which the Society are buying having belonged to different owners the Title is somewhat complicated. ... You know the vendors perfectly well, please therefore write me whether under the circumstances you require me fully to investigate the Title or whether you will take the conveyance without this,
> Yours truly

The meeting passed a resolution to the effect that the Title as submitted by the abstract to Mr. Hayward be accepted, together with the necessity of a fence being put upon both sides of the land, but agreed that it should be a post and rail fence at present. Mr. Newson reported that Mr. Butler's solicitor agreed to accept £10.10/- to cover his own and Mr. Dawson's expenses. The meeting also agreed to secure the right of light over ten feet of land on the western side and seven feet on the eastern side, for the amount of £10 or £11, only Mr. Parslow dissenting.[516]

On November 7, 1887, the Association resolved to deposit the Deeds, Abstract of Title and copy of the letter given by the trustees to the vendors (to the effect that upon a sale of the property such portion of the land as might then be unbuilt on shall be re-conveyed to the vendors) in a small tin box at the London and County Bank, for so long as they should act as the Association's Bankers.[517] On October 26, 1887, Mr. Newson reported that the estimate for expenditure connected with the erection of the first section of the building (including the cost of the land) amounted to about £1,500 and that about £600 had been paid or promised by the following:

Captain Cundy	£100	Sir Douglas Fox	£50
Messrs F. Newson	£50	F. Pitts	£50
W.G. Grattan	£50	Bedford Marsh	£25
R.S. Bond	£25	J. S. Morten	£20
Miss Walter	£3	Mr. and Misses Butlers (3)	£78.15 – each
Total	£611. 5s 0d.		

In January 1888 the Association submitted the following list of tenders:

Henley & Sons	Kingston	£1698
Gladwell	Hornsey	£1678.14s 5d
Wall Chas	London	£1627
Oldridge & Sons	Kingston	£1493
Havell J.F.	Kingston	£1475
Snelling H.	Kingston	£1445
Higgs J.	London	£1387
Constable G.	Kingston	£1378
Judd D.	Kingston	£1122

After considerable discussion Mr. Judd's tender was accepted. Mr. Parslow preferred Mr. Constable but this preference was not seconded.[518]

During February 1888 both the chairman and the secretary were also involved with various difficulties relating to the building scheme, in particular trying to raise a loan. However, Mr. Parslow confounded the situation by enquiring:

> if the Committee knew whether the piece of land purchased would afford a foundation suitable for the building as he had been informed that the river once ran through it and that the land was water logged. Mr. Newson stated that the land (though at one time partly covered with water) had never formed part of the river bed and he did not apprehend any difficulty in connection with it. He had already asked Mr. Saunders to test it, but this had been omitted. Mr. Parslow proposed Mr. Gardener seconded and it was resolved that two trial holes be dug immediately.

A letter from the borough surveyor following an inspection of the plans by the Improvement Committee stated that the building line must be ten feet from the boundary and that no part of the building must project beyond such line.[519] Consequently the contract was left unsigned.[520]

In April 1888 the secretary reported the trial holes had contained water about one and a half feet deep. Although a firm bottom had been found Mr. Rutland Saunders, not having seen the ground without water, could not state positively that the foundation was good. At this point in the meeting the chairman, Mr. Northcroft said that it might be possible to secure a piece of ground nearer the town. Mr. Newson stated that the Corporation Improvement Committee would meet on the following day and decide how far the buildings must be put back. Mr. Gardener said he thought it would be far better to secure a site nearer the town, whilst the secretary reported a strong feeling on the part of the members was against the present proposed site. Mr. Newson thought the Committee was under no legal obligation to build on the present site but could allow it to stand in abeyance for three years before re-conveying it to the Butlers or re-conveyancing the land.[521]

In June the Butlers said that they were prepared to allow the building to be erected forty feet nearer Springfield Road, provided the Association paid the expenses and the legal points could be satisfactorily arranged. The meeting also learned that the site in St. James' Road 'could not be had.' Mr. Newson stated that his brother believed that they were empowered under the Special Corporation Act. (The brother would have been Harry Newson who was a barrister at law and was Frank Newson's senior by two years.) Mr. Newson stated:

> The Builder who had made the trial holes reported a solid foundation at a depth of 6 ft. 54 ft. back and he thought that the building had better be moved higher up, as it was the best procurable site and would be in a good position for the Norbiton men when the bridge was built.

Mr. Northcroft recommended that they leave the matter until they definitely settled whether the bridge would be built. The road bridging the Hogsmill was erected in 1893, five years later. The notice attached to the bridge showing the actual date of its erection is shown in Figure 34. Mr. Parslow said he thought the proposed site very unsuitable. Mr. Morten thought that they should generally consider the opinions of the members. Mr. Parslow moved, and the meeting resolved that 'the matter be adjourned with a view to bringing it before the members at the General Meeting on the 27th inst.'[522]

The Annual General Meeting — June 27, 1888 — Differences of Opinion

The fourth annual meeting of the Kingston and Surbiton Y.M.C.A.took place on June 27, 1888, after which the General Committee met and announced the new committee. After a preliminary notice the chairman Sir Douglas Fox said:

> he thought a word of explanation was necessary in reference to the hope he had expressed at the last Meeting in relation to the New Building. At that

time there was a reasonable expectation that it would speedily be erected but unforeseen difficulties had arisen in connection with it which had caused much delay. He would now ask Mr. Newson to kindly report the present position.

Mr. Newson made a statement to the following effect, that a piece of land in the Denmark Road had been offered by Mr. and the Misses Butler to the Committee at one fourth of its value, which offer had (after consideration) been accepted by them on the understanding that the Building should be erected right up to the road boundary line, but upon the plans being submitted, the borough surveyor gave notice that the building must be set back 10 feet. As it was found impossible to get any concession from the Improvement Committee as to the distance, Mr. and the Misses Butler had kindly consented to allow the Building to be shifted 40 feet nearer to the Springfield Road where there was greater depth, and where the building would be consequently farther from the water, charging only the cost of the transfer ... the question was now brought forward for discussion owing to difference of opinion as to the suitability of the site ... (the) arrangement had been made for the retransfer of the land to the vendors after the lapse of three years if the building was not erected during that period. The Chairman then asked Mr. Rutland Sanders to report as to the respective capabilities of the two sites. Mr. Rutland Sanders who submitted plans said that he did not apprehend any difficulty in erecting the building upon the present site although some extra expense for foundation would of course be entailed, that he should certainly recommend moving 40 feet nearer to the Springfield Road, as the extra depth would doubtless prove to be very advantageous, affording an additional 5 or 6 feet. The Chairman then invited discussion on the question, observing that he thought it would be best, before considering details in connection with the building, to decide as to the suitability or otherwise of the position of the present site.

The meeting became extremely heated at this point, and various members blamed the Committee for what had occurred. They argued that a members' meeting should have been called, and individual members said that the site in Denmark Road was unsuitable. In reply Mr. Newson said he 'still believed that it would be best to build upon the present site.' After a long discussion the meeting proposed and passed the following resolution:

That the Committee be requested to make arrangements for disposing of the land acquired in Denmark Road, and seek a more central and suitable site.

The meeting continued to be very tense and heated, with Mr H.T. Northcroft expressing his 'disapprobation of what had been said,' and saying that he intended to step down from the Committee and resign. Mr. Morten then praised Mr. Northcroft for his valuable assistance to the Association during the building scheme, as had other members of the Committee.

In closing the chairman said that he thought a wise decision had been made respecting the new building; he believed a more central site would add greatly to the usefulness of the work. He also urged the members to remember that when they met together, whether at a devotional or business meeting, they met as Christian men, and should ever strive to manifest a Christ-like spirit.[523]

34. The Bridge was built in 1893 and opened in 1894. Notice attached to the north side of the Bridge.   (**AG 2012**)

A picture on the front page of a leaflet shown in Figure 35 indicates how the building would have looked. The description and details of the finance involved, page 2, appears as Figure 36. Two plans of the interior design of the building, shown at the top of the front page are of interest. These show both the ground and first floor.

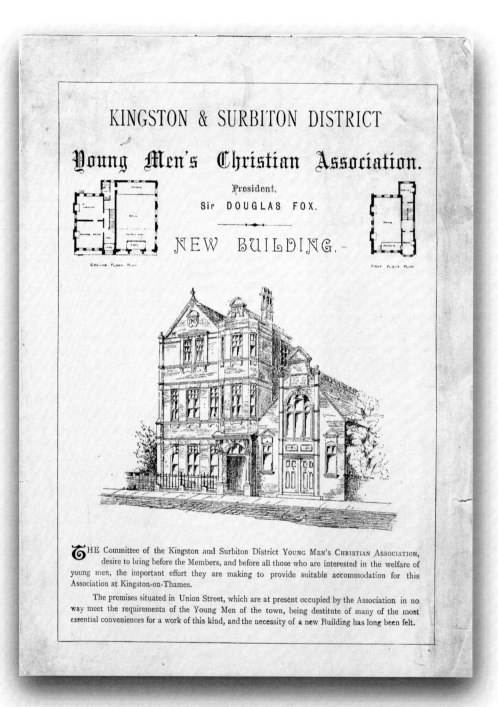

35. The building that was never built, p.1.   **(YMCA)**

At length, by the kindness of MR. and the MISSES BUTLER, a suitable plot of Land has been secured in the Denmark Road, and the Committee now earnestly appeal for Funds, so that the Building Scheme may be brought to a successful issue.

At the head of this Circular, a sketch is given of the front elevation of the proposed new Building, and also plans showing the accommodation on the ground and first floors of the main Building, which will contain the Reading Room, Library, and Class Rooms, with accommodation for the Secretary and Caretaker. It is proposed to fit up the Hall adjoining, so that it can be used both as a Lecture Hall and as a Gymnasium, thus meeting a want long felt in the town.

So far as can at present be computed, the total cost of the Buildings (including the value of the land and also the furnishing) will be about £2,500, towards which upwards of £600 have been already subscribed or promised. Taking into consideration the present size of Kingston and its Suburbs, and its rapid extension, as also the number of young men who are employed or resident therein, the Committee think that it will be generally conceded that £2,500 is a very moderate sum to be expended on this object, and therefore ask for the generous support of all interested in this work amongst young men.

On the opposite page will be found some testimonies of public men to the value of the Young Men's Christian Association, which the Committee recommend to the consideration of such as may not be intimately acquainted with its objects.

The following are amongst the amounts already given or promised :

Captain Cundy	£100
Mr. Gerard W. Butler	78
Miss Butler	78
Miss F. Butler	78
Sir Douglas Fox	50
Mr. F. Pitts	50
Mr. F. Newson	50
A Member	50

Subscriptions to the Building Fund will be received by the London & County Banking Co., Ld., Market Place, Kingston, or by the General Secretary,

MR. R. W. COWDERY,

Y. M. C. A. ROOMS,

UNION STREET, KINGSTON ;

Or by the Hon. Treasurer,

MR. FRANK NEWSON,

13, OVAL ROAD,

GLOUCESTER GATE, LONDON, N.W.

36. The building that was never built, p.2.   (YMCA)

On the left of the ground floor to the front of the building would have been the reading room, behind that at the back, the library. There would have been a hall to the right with a gallery at the front and a platform at the back. The toilets would have been at the back of the hall. Upstairs on the first floor there would have been a large room to the left with a platform at the front, a small room to the right and an office at the back. Page 2 mentions accommodation that could be used for the secretary and caretaker, probably these would have been on the second floor and are not shown in the form of a plan. This then is how the building would have looked had the Committee not voted against the continuation of the build on June 27, 1888. Certainly this building would have been a prominent feature on Denmark Road, and, there would have been easy access from the centre of Kingston once the bridge over the Hogsmill was built in 1894 and later also from Surbiton.

On July 2, 1888, the secretary reported that he had written to Mr. Northcroft, who now might reconsider his decision to withdraw from the Committee, which he later did. Mr. Newson handed to the chairman a letter of resignation but consented to remain treasurer (presumably of the building fund) until the Committee appointed someone else. Mr. W.G. Carn did resign. This last resignation was to result in a decision on July 30, 1888, that had long-term repercussions for many Kingstonians. Mr Carn wrote to the Committee stating that the Saxons football club would in future be carried on apart from the Y.M.C.A. The meeting resolved that the letter be 'acknowledged and the Club thanked for the gift of lavatory fittings.'[524]

BUSINESS AS USUAL

PAPER WORK AND OBLIGATIONS

JULY 1888 – MARCH 1890

Business As Usual

Whilst dealing with the Denmark Road building scheme the Association continued with more mundane work. Mr. Stringer left in August 1887 and was replaced by Mr. Cowdery who, it appears, managed to fit seamlessly into the running of the Kingston and Surbiton Y.M.C.A. despite, as we shall see later, having religious views differing from some of the members. The Association continued much as they had always done, dealing with the day-to-day events including occasional difficulties with individual members.

One of these difficulties occurred at the beginning of 1888 due to frequent loud talking in the reading room. This was not allowed, particularly when a meeting was taking place in the room adjoining. The Committee decided to put up a notice stating that they would regrettably be compelled to close the reading room during meetings if the loud talking continued. The notice was defaced soon after it appeared. In spite of enquiries and the questioning of the two members known to have been in the reading room on the Saturday evening in question, the Association never identified the culprit. They agreed to place a notice on the board expressing the deep regret of the Committee at such an occurrence and saying that were they to discover who had defaced the notice they would ask him to resign. Two months later they still had not found the responsible person although the Committee had its suspicions.

The Caretaker reported one of the associate members who lived in Eden Street had made false and disrespectful statements concerning the Committee. After taking steps to find out more particulars about this young man, the Committee decided to ask him to attend the next Committee Meeting. This did not happen as before the meeting the secretary received a letter which read as follows:

Dear Mr. Cowdery

In answer to your letter in asking me to attend at your Committee Meeting on Monday, I have had the decision of the Members not to attend and also that we shall be glad for the Committee to call a Meeting and then we shall perhaps have an understanding between the Members and Committee about the insulting notices that have been posted upon the Notice Board. We ask as a body of Members that Mr. Parslow shall be asked to resign from the Committee as he is the means of having such notices placed and also causing unpleasantness between Members and Committee.

We shall be glad for the Committee to call a General Meeting of Members in a time if convenient.

Yours very truly,

The Committee at their next meeting called in Mr. Bull the Caretaker to ask him what he had heard about the associate member who had written the letter. Mr. Bull reported hearing him use very offensive and insulting language on several occasions. The Committee therefore resolved that, 'In accordance with Rule 12 the young man must be excluded from the Association and that the secretary give him intimation to that effect.' Rule 12 can be found in Appendix XVII, page 230. This action appears to have occurred, and the minutes make no further mention of the young man.[525]

A more worthwhile incident occurred after this event. Mrs. A.C. Bryant asked for help from the members to assist her in giving teas to the lodging house poor. Mrs. Bryant may have been Mrs. Arthur C. Bryant, widow of Arthur Bryant and sister in law of Wilberforce Bryant. The teas were to take place at the Wood Street schools over a period of two days at the beginning of March. The secretary agreed to ask the members to give their utmost assistance.[526] Thereafter at regular intervals the minutes note the attendance of members at lodging house teas. (Although no further mention is made of Mrs. A.C. Bryant in the minutes a Mrs. A.C. Bryant continued to give a yearly donation to the Y.M.C.A. during the 1890s.) During March the Committee had to repair the harmonium at an estimated cost of thirty shillings. In April Mr. Lea sent a postcard stating that the next quarterly conference of the South Western District Union would be held in Wimbledon on April 24, 1888. In April the treasurer also announced that the General Fund accounts were £3.13s.6d in deficit and that they needed contributions by members to close this gap. Fortunately by May the Association had closed the gap and was able to balance the books for the previous year. The minutes note that the National Council conference was to be held in Stockholm and the annual secretaries' conference in Croydon. The Committee agreed that the secretary should go to the latter but not to the former. They requested the secretary to attend the Metropolitan Council meeting at Exeter Hall and in October bought a new doormat for the Kingston premises.[527]

Negotiations

In the last chapter we saw how the members responded to the difficulties relating to the Denmark Road site. At the meeting on July 2, 1888, they decided that the negotiations that needed to be opened up with Mr. Butler with the view to transferring the land back to the family should be left for the present. However the Butlers were obviously very approachable and amenable people, and, on July 30, 1888, the meeting resolved that Mr. Newson should meet with Mr. Butler. The secretary also reported that, following an interview with Mr Rutland Saunders, it was thought that the amount owing to him for his fee as architect would be £60. The Committee had clearly expected a much lower figure, and Mr. Northcroft said that he would advise getting a detailed account. Mr. Parslow said that he remembered hearing Mr. Newson say that Mr. Saunders would do all preliminaries free of charge and that charges would only commence when plans were started and the site definitely settled.[528] It was agreed to write to Mr. Saunders asking for particulars of his charges to the present time, 'as the business was now in abeyance.' Mr. Parslow was asked to fill the role of treasurer, taking over from Mr. Newson. This he accepted but only if the office were *pro tem.*

The Committee did not meet again until October 1, 1888, when they heard that a letter had been received from Mr. Saunders stating that he had not yet made out his account. The Butlers, on the other hand, consented to the re-conveyance of the land in Denmark Road, with the Association paying £5 in full settlement of all costs coupled with an agreement by the Association to burn the deeds. The fencing around the site had been removed, and the Committee asked Sir Douglas Fox and Mr. Northcroft to sign a letter authorising the bank manager to deliver up the deed box and then to send the deeds to Mr. Newson who was given the responsibility of destroying them.[529] Mr. Parslow told the meeting that he had written to Mr. Hayward (the solicitor who acted in the conveyance to the Association), pointing out the circumstances under which the Association was labouring and asked if he would kindly accept a nominal sum. In December they received a letter from Mr. Hayward who had given Mr. Hicks his costs amounting to £5. 5s. 0d and, although Mr. Hayward appears to have originally charged more, his final charge was £3. 3s. 0d. The Committee resolved that they should instruct Mr. Parslow to send Mr. Hayward a formal receipt.[530] The Association up to this moment had managed to extricate themselves from the Denmark Road situation without incurring too much expense.

Paying the Accounts

In February 1889 Mr. Rutland Saunders submitted his account to the chairman, the total sum being £99.18s 9d. At the meeting on February 18, 1889, the Committee discussed the bill or rather the amount of the bill at length. Members said that they had understood that Mr. Saunders had transacted the preliminary business as a friend of the Association and not officially. The minutes show, however, that this young architect and surveyor had spent much time and effort in preparing and negotiating on behalf of the Association. For nearly two years between August 1886 and June 1888 he had been available for consultation, had made visits to numerous sites, written copious notes and eventually prepared a Specification of Works. Mr. Saunders, who worked with his father in their London office, was used to dealing with high profile clients. He had clearly used a clerk who would have expected to be paid. [531] Moreover from his comments at the General Meeting in June 1888 he obviously thought that erecting a building on the Denmark Road site near Springfield Road presented no major problem.

Inadequate finance and the time it took, not only to find an affordable site in a good position but one fit for purpose, lay at the heart of the problem. The last two or three years of the 1880s was an extremely difficult period in which to buy land in Kingston, particularly on a limited budget. It has already been noted that Kingston was becoming overcrowded due to the arrival of the London and South Western Railway in 1863. The arrival of a more direct line to London from Kingston station in 1869 prompted the British Land company to buy up an area to the north of Kingston station, divide the land into building plots and sell on these plots. In this way railway-linked speculation was producing rapid profits. Between 1871 and 1891 the population living to the north of Kingston Station had grown from 694 to just under 4,000. Many changes were about to take place, some of which would alter the structure of the town. In 1888 the council gained powers to purchase land for street improvements and, when the Housing of the Working Classes Act came into force in 1890, local authorities were ordered to demolish unfit housing and provide alternative accommodation. In this way some, but not all, of Kingston's slum areas were improved by the turn of the century.[532] As we shall see later, these changes may have forced the Association out of Zoar Chapel in the following year. Although not in the centre of the town, the site in Denmark Road could have been suitable as there may have been the possibility for expansion later once the bridge had been built. It was unfortunate but understandable that the members considered that the path of the Hogsmill was too close to risk building on the site.

37. The Bedford Institute in Quaker Street, Shoreditch, London, designed by Rutland Saunders and built in 1894.   (**AG 2012**)

38. The ornate door frame   39. The ornate windows

Bedford House — A Grade II English Heritage Building   **(AG 2012)**

Mr. Saunders' bill was not the only one outstanding at this time. Mr. Northcroft also thought that the Association should initially consider the £33.13s 0d owing to Mr. Judd. Mr. Judd was the builder chosen to undertake the build in Denmark Road, there having been a three per cent liability upon Mr. Judd's tender.[533] Mr. Saunders was in no hurry to discuss his bill but eventually the matter was resolved after Mr. Frederick Pitts, a merchant living in Liverpool Road and one of the Committee, offered to see him to talk the matter over. Mr. Saunders agreed to accept £77 and to supply the Committee with a complete set of plans and specification (either original or copies) and forms of tender. The Committee asked Sir Douglas Fox to draw cheques for this amount and £28 3s 6d in favour of Messrs H.T. Northcroft & Co., for preparing quantities. Mr. Northcroft kindly offered to hand Mr. Saunders the cheque and to receive the plans.[534]

The 1891 census shows Rutland Saunders twenty-eight years old living in Hackney. In 1894 a 'handsome red brick gabled building constructed to a florid English Renaissance design', replaced the Quaker Meeting House that had been built in 1656 in Quaker Street, London. Current pictures of the building designed by Mr. Saunders can be found in Figures 37, 38 and 39. The building was erected to house the Bedford Institute and named in honour of Peter Bedford, a Quaker silk weaver and philanthropist who had formed a society for Lessening the Causes of Juvenile Delinquency. Designed by Rutland Saunders this magnificent, imposing building was used between 1894 and 1947 for all kinds of charitable activities. These included educational classes to alleviate poverty among those living in Shoreditch. Bedford House is now a listed, Grade II English Heritage building.[535] Recently a number of homeless young people occupied it, but currently it appears to stand empty.[536]

There are no plans in the Y.M.C.A. archive. It is therefore uncertain if any were passed to the Committee, although there is the 'Specification of Works', a forty-two page file thirteen by eight inches in copperplate writing with alterations, some in pencil, others in ink, made in another neat hand. There is also a large two-page notice entitled Kingston & Surbiton District Young Men's Christian Association New Building. The front cover carries a picture of the proposed structure that might have been the Y.M.C.A. in Kingston, see Figure 35, page 168.[537] Although the Y.M.C.A. building would have been much smaller than Bedford House, it is possible to find similarities of style and ornamentation between the two designs.

A further person had concerns about events in Denmark Road. Captain Cundy wrote, declining to preside at the Social Meeting on September 25, as he was displeased with the action of the Committee concerning the £100 subscribed by him to the Building Fund. Mr. Morten offered to see Captain Cundy about his letter, and the Committee instructed the secretary to write to him expressing members' regret over his not attending and saying that Mr. Morten would shortly call upon him. Mr. Morten reported seeing Captain Cundy, and satisfactorily explained how matters were and promised that the Committee would let him know when they had taken any fresh step about the new building.[538]

ROUTINE, CREATIVITY
AND PROCRASTINATION
NOVEMBER 1888 – MARCH 1890

Routine

The more mundane, yet necessary, work of the Association continued during the negotiations. This included the payment of debts outstanding due to the change of plans relating to the Denmark Road project. At a November 1888 meeting a letter from the town clerk was read expressing concern about the provision of adequate exits from public halls. The secretary reported that Mr. Parslow had taken the matter in hand.[539] The National Council wrote, announcing a week of prayer from November 11 to 18, and asked for financial assistance. The Committee sent a subscription of a guinea. The secretary reported that a cabman called concerning the cabmen's shelter at Kingston station and requested the corners of the tables might be rounded off. Mr. Brown kindly promised to have them rounded off and received thanks for his kindness on completion. The Association announced that the Sacred Choral Society intended giving a public performance of 'The Daughter of Moab' in the Albany Hall and decided to assist the Choral Society in any way they could. In December 1888 they asked members who had not paid their subscriptions to do so by the end of the month. The secretary was allowed a week's holiday as he was getting married.[540]

The secretary asked whether another daily paper might be substituted for the *Daily Telegraph* as it had of late written largely against all that was good and true in matters of religion. The *Daily Chronicle* was taken in its place.[541] In May the secretary reported that about ninety books were missing from the Association library and asked whether the bookshelves might be fitted with wire doors. The Committee thought it undesirable to lock up the books and decided to put up a notice over the library to stop members taking books without the librarian having registered them. They asked those with books to return them.[542]

The annual business meeting on June 26, 1889, reported that the Committee had received no new nominations for the ensuing year, so Mr. George M. Walker and Mr. George Jolly took the places of those who had resigned. The Committee also asked the members to support the Association by voluntary subscriptions 'in addition to the members subscriptions the lowest of which shall be 5/- per annum.' This request was agreed.[543]

A New Idea — Visiting Committee and Provident Fund

On July 1, Mr. Morten proposed the formation of a visiting subcommittee, which was to be comprised of three Kingston and three Surbiton members empowered to assist the general secretary in visitation and to formulate a scheme for the raising of a provident fund for the help of members who might be in need.[544] At a members' meeting on October 22, 1889, Mr. Northcroft said that the object of the meeting was to invite new members and to afford relief to 'any of its members in times of real need arising either from sickness or inability to obtain employment.' The Association made a house-to-house canvas in both the Kingston and Surbiton districts, with the view of finding young men living in the area and giving to each a personal and hearty invitation to the meetings.[545] By March 1890, £3.12s.2d, had been subscribed, £2 of which had been deposited in the Post Office savings bank.[546]

Literary and Debating Society

In November 1889 the Association proposed a literary and debating society with 'a diversity in the programmes,' including an occasional evening considering the life of Longfellow or other poets, plus recitations or readings from their works, with a small subscription to be made.[547]

National Council Protest Against Gambling

Following a resolution passed by the National Council against gambling, it was resolved that 'at Meetings of this Association where unconverted young men are prominently present we should do all in our power by prayer and protest against the grievous sin of gambling and betting.'[548]

Lodging House Work and the Cabmen's Shelter

In December 1889, the Association held a lodging house dinner in the Kingston rooms, spending £3 on the meal.[549] The secretary reported that Mr. Creed had arranged more regular attendance at the lodging houses, and the result had been very satisfactory.[550] Following the death of Miss Ranyard a letter from her executor confirmed the Association's title to the cabmen's shelter.[551]

Procrastination

The Committee refused to consider moving. At the annual business meeting on June 26, 1889, the chairman said that the new building question was still in abeyance and asked whether any instructions to give to the Committee were proposed. They resolved that the Committee be 'requested to continue looking out for a new site and that the thanks of the Meeting be tendered to them for their past services.'[552]

The Kingston rooms in Union Street were becoming increasingly unhealthy. In November 1889 the caretaker had complained that the water was unfit to drink and Mr. Parslow asked to see or write to the landlord respecting it.[553] This situation may have prompted Mr. Bull to seek other employment, and Mr. Parslow gave notice informally that Mr. Bull was applying for the post of caretaker at the Tiffins' School. Mr. Bull vacated the rooms having secured the position, and the Association secured the services of Mr. and Mrs. H. Brown, whom they employed on the basis that they were thoroughly suitable persons.[554]

In December 1889 Mr. Burrows sent in a letter suggesting that the rooms lately held by the Conservative Club were vacant and suitable for the Y.M.C.A. and offering a donation of £10 towards expenses of removal if the Committee carried out his suggestion. It will be remembered that Charles Burrows lived next door to the Association rooms and was leasing the cellar for £5 per annum. Mr. Parslow wrote back that the Committee 'do not see their way clear to move at present' but thanking him for his kind offer. At the same time a member asked if any members of the Committee were taking steps to secure a site for the proposed new building. The secretary replied that nothing had as yet been done in that matter since the Committee thought the Association was not currently in the position to take such a step.[555] This situation was to change in March 1890 when an incident forced both the Committee and the members into action.

MOVING TO WARWICK LODGE
PROGRESS OF THE EARLY CLOSING
MOVEMENT
MARCH 1890 – SEPTEMBER 1890

Notice to Quit

In March 1890 Mr. Sherrard, the Solicitor, sent the Association a letter giving them 'Notice to Quit' their premises by June 1890. This notice may have been connected with the Housing of the Working Classes Act 1890. Mr. Parslow immediately wrote back informing Mr. Sherrard the Y.M.C.A. had a yearly tenancy. Mr. Sherrard had replied acknowledging that Mr. Parslow was correct and the Association had the right to retain the use of the premises until June 1891, but the letter continued: 'he trusted they would find it convenient to vacate them by Christmas 1890.' The Association thereafter resolved to make no further communication until after the next Committee Meeting on May 5, 1890.[556]

Options and Discussion

The Association had various options. They knew that the Conservative club premises had been vacated but the rent would be £65 per annum, and Mr. Parslow pointed out that with the addition of rates and taxes this would amount to a considerable sum. Mr. Northcroft asked Mr. Bristow if he could inform the Committee whether it would be possible to secure the Leopold Coffee Tavern. Mr. Bristow said that he was not sure but would enquire. Mr. Parslow asked if the Committee would again consider the matter of securing another site to erect premises. This was bearing in mind Sir Douglas Fox's remark at the last annual meeting 'a home of our own would be very beneficial to the Association's work.' The land on Ashdown Road was therefore also considered. It was resolved that Mr. Bristow and the secretary see the owner of the Leopold and that Mr. Parslow check about the Ashdown Road Site.[557]

The Leopold Coffee Tavern was situated at Bridge Foot in Kingston and advertised as 'good accommodation for Parties, Bicyclists, Bean-feasts &c &c.' in the *Coffee Public-House News and Temperance Hotel Journal*.[558]   Mr. Northcroft reported having communicated with Mr. Taylor, the freeholder of the Tavern, regarding his willingness to sell the freehold and Mr. Taylor in reply had referred him to Messrs Wilberforce and Theodore Bryant, the latter referring him to a Mr. Bristow the present lessee. Most of the members of the Committee, having viewed the Leopold, gave their opinions as to the suitability of the accommodation after which:

> Mr. Northcroft was asked to write to Mr. Taylor for the price of the freehold and if unwilling to sell, to state whether he would let the premises at the present rental for 50 years or longer on lease, with option to alter the premises to suit the Associations requirements.

Mr. Parslow reported an interview with Mr. Street regarding the site in the Ashdown Road. Mr. Street was not eager to sell, yet expressed his willingness to consider the matter again and his inclination 'to sell the same piece of land as before at the same price.'[559]

Between May 19, and June 25, 1890, the members discussed the prospect of new premises. They inspected the Leopold Coffee Tavern and considered it to be suitable for the purposes of the Association. The owner, however, said he would not sell the property or let it to a Committee. He would only negotiate with a gentleman or such gentlemen as would be deemed by his solicitor a satisfactory security for the rent. The Committee thought it best to set aside the question of procuring the Leopold. It also learnt that another person was in treaty for the premises lately occupied by the Conservative club.

The owner of a plot of land opposite the Kingston Railway Station had expressed his willingness either to sell sufficient of the land for the erection of a new building for the sum of £500 or to let a similar portion of land at a peppercorn rent if the Association would erect a building and grant him the use of the ground floor. One member strongly recommended consideration of these options. The secretary reported that a piece of land with a frontage of eighty feet opposite to the land previously mentioned might be bought for £375, but the shape was very awkward. The general opinion was that the Association was not in a position to build. Mr. Walker said that premises now occupied in St James Road by Mr. Edgell would soon be available. Some of the members were against this idea as the noise of the printing machines next door would be objectionable.[560] Nevertheless they asked Mr. Northcroft to see Mr. Edgell about the possibility of securing his offices for the temporary use of the Association.[561]

A Choice Between The Leopold Coffee Tavern and Warwick Lodge

After the annual general meeting the chairman read the correspondence that had passed between him and the solicitor of the owner of the Leopold Coffee Tavern about securing the lease for the Y.M.C.A. The owner was willing to let to one or more responsible gentlemen on a lease of twenty-one years at a rental of £110 per annum. The chairman then invited the members freely to express their opinions on the subject. Mr. Morten felt that the Leopold would be the right place for the carrying on the Association's work and he could strongly recommend that the negotiations for securing it be continued. Others disagreed because of its proximity to the back lanes and the class of men that usually stood at the corner of the street.[562]

The Association proposed to take a poll of the whole of the members to learn whether the majority of them were in favour of the Leopold or otherwise. After a discussion it was suggested that they inspect Warwick House, Eden Street. Between the date of this meeting on June 25, and the meeting on July 7, they contacted Mr. Betts, the owner of Warwick Lodge, and asked him about the long-term prospects of the site and the removal of certain fixtures. On July 4, Mr. Betts replied, although the secretary appears only to have received the letter on the date of the meeting, July 7, when the result of the poll was announced as follows:

For Warwick Lodge	26
For the Leopold	7
Against the Leopold	2

After discussion the meeting resolved to instruct the Committee to negotiate with the present Lessees of Warwick Lodge. The chairman suggested that Mr. T.L. Hodgson should see the owner Mr. Betts to ascertain at what price he would sell the freehold. Mr. Parslow produced a plan of the Ashdown Road site and suggested that the purchase of that for the erection of the suggested new building would be preferable to buying the freehold of Warwick Lodge. Mr. Harvey proposed that an effort should be made to raise a third of the sum if the freehold of Warwick Lodge could be secured at a fair price and the remainder borrowed from a building society.[563]

The Early Closing Movement and the Meeting in the Assize Courts
While the Y.M.C.A. considered its move, another important activity affecting many of the young people in the Kingston area had begun. As on previous occasions, the *Surrey Comet* had received correspondence relating to the Early Closing Movement, which led to a public meeting in the Assize Courts, reported in the paper on May 10, 1890. The mayor, councillor James East presided,

supported by the Rev. A. S. W. Young (the vicar of All Saints Church) and other notable individuals. One of these was Mr. Cowdery, the Y.M.C.A. secretary who acted as the representative of the young men who worked as assistants in the retail trade in Kingston.

The meeting started with the mayor saying that, as a former assistant, he sympathised with those who were seeking to shorten the hours of labour. He then called upon Mr. Young to address the meeting. The Vicar, whom the meeting cordially received, said:

> he was very happy to respond to the invitation to attend the meeting, and to express his views on the question. He imagined they had come together for a friendly conference, which was the best way to carry out any movement of the kind; not to have mass meetings to the Fairfield, or wild harangues at the Coronation Stone, but to meet together and talk it over in a quiet way... It could not possibly be good, morally, that anyone should be so completely tied to business as to have no time for anything else. The objection was sometimes raised by people who knew nothing about the conditions of the question, that to turn young people loose in the town in the evening hours was opening up to them all sorts of opportunities of doing mischief and getting into harm; but he said most emphatically that no one ought to listen to such an objection for a moment. (Cheers.) It opened up opportunities for good. Of course those opportunities might be abused, but they could not help that. They would never make people better by shutting them up in prisons, or by tying them to any business, and restricting their natural desire for liberty and recreation, light and air. He was always inclined to trust the better side of human nature, and he felt sure that if the opportunities were given they would be used for good and not for harm (Cheers.) For these reasons he heartily supported the movement.

A letter from Councillor A. Nuthall, J.P. stated that his firm closed punctually at five p.m. on Wednesdays, ten on Saturdays, and eight every other evening. Mr. Duncalfe, a Clarence Street Draper, thought that it would require:

> strenuous and combined effort to carry the point. In addition to the demon of competition ... they had to deal with the demon of selfishness, and his experience was that the public were very selfishly inclined in this matter.

Alderman Hide the market dealer upholsterer said:

> he took great interest in the movement for a long time, but at last he got so disheartened at the contracts being so continually broken down, that he fixed his own hours and kept to them (Applause) ... He thought that the local authorities ought to have the power to enforce the closing of shops at a certain hour, upon the requisition of three-fourths or seven-eights of the traders. ... He believed that seven-eighths of the tradesmen in every town in England would be glad to close their shops at a reasonable hour, and he

could not see why the remaining one-eighth should be allowed to tyrannise over them.

Mr A.M.Levy, a Thames Street jeweller added:

> a great number of the resident population were gentlemen whose business took them to London during the day. They returned to Kingston from 6 to 7 o'clock and after a meal took a stroll in the town ... A great many of the accidental population came down to Kingston to reside during the summer months, going on the river during the day, and returning in the evening, when they looked at the shops and made their purchases ... a great deal too much money went out of Kingston now, and some of the most ardent advocates of the early closing movement took their money to the co-operative stores. ... There were many poor people who could only do their shopping late.

Mr. Crossfield an outfitter and boot maker on Kings Road said he was:

> one of those unfortunate individuals who did next to nothing during the day and his trade usually began at 6.30 and did not end very often until 9.

Councillor Carn moved an amendment in favour of closing at 2 p.m. on Wednesdays, when scarcely any business occurred in Kingston. He argued:

> even if they could close punctually at 8 there would only be a few weeks in the summer when it would be light, and what could they do in the dark? (Great laughter.) He was afraid many of them would go to places which they would be better out of. If the shops closed at 2 on Wednesdays, it would give masters and assistants the chance to get some genuine recreation.

Mr. Cowdery, the Y.M.C.A. secretary speaking on behalf of the assistants, supported the original motion: 'it was the last half hour or hour which made all the difference to the health of the assistants. He argued that whenever early closing had been introduced, it had had the effect of elevating the young people both morally and physically.' Only the tradesmen voted on the amendment, which the meeting rejected by fifteen to ten. The original motion, which was put three times stated that:

> in the opinion of this meeting it is desirable that an effort be made to induce the tradesmen of Kingston to close their shops at a fixed hour, 8 o'clock in the evening, except on Wednesday and Saturdays, when the hours should remain as at present, and that a committee be appointed for the purpose of carrying out the details necessary to the attainment of the object in view.

The tradesmen adopted this motion twenty-five votes to five, the assistants and the general public proving unanimous in their support.[564] Following the meeting,

Mr. William Carn wrote a letter which also appeared in the *Surrey Comet*, stating that he thought closing at two p.m. on Wednesdays would be a much better proposition than eight p.m. in the evening. Closing at eight p.m. would deprive many tradesmen of their best business hours.[565] On May 31, 1890, the *Surrey Comet* printed a list of those shops whose owners had signed to support shortened hours in Kingston. The numbers in each road are as follows:

Thames Street	24	Market Place	17
Clarence Street	25	Church Street	09
Richmond Road	21	Acre Road	01
Park Road	11	London Road	37
Kingston Hill	11	King's Road	01
Canbury Park Road	01	Surbiton Road	18
Eden Street	20	Brook Street	06
High Street	07	St. James' Road	01
Hampton Wick	09		

More than two-hundred shops had agreed to close at eight p.m. on Monday, Tuesday, Thursday and Friday.[566] On June 7, 1890, the paper included a letter to the Editor entitled 'Earlier Closing of Shops in Kingston and Neighbourhood.'

> To the Editor—Sir,
>
> Will you kindly allow us to report to the public the progress that has been made in this matter … As a matter of fact, the number of dissentients is not more than six or seven. We do not want to do anything disagreeable so we will not ask you to publish the names of these: we are confident that their number is too insignificant to imperil the success of the movement…
>
> James East, Mayor of Kingston, A.S.W. Young, Vicar

There followed a list of subscribers who had collectively raised £17. 5 9d. All the donations were under £1 except one from a Mrs. E. Powell, who gave £5, and some people who had given to the fund only allowed their initials to go forward. The article also included the following:

> Something approaching a demonstration amongst the assistants of the town took place last evening. The fact is the employees recognised that unless the early closing movement was unanimously adopted last evening, when an increase of business is usually anticipated, the efforts of the committee would in all probability, be nullified. Hence the exceptional interest aroused. Assistants were busily engaged distributing hand bills early in the evening, and about 8.30 a number of them congregated around Mr. Hart's (boot maker) establishment in Thames street, which remained open after 8.

Hooting was indulged in; a barrel organ brought upon the scene; and at times some pasty substance was thrown at the assistants connected with the establishment. When at length the shop was closed a little before 9.0, the crowd, now considerably augmented, moved into Clarence street, where Mr. Carn, another dissentient also came in for unfriendly notice, and thence to Richmond-road, where a demonstration was made in front of Mr. Mason's. The crowd, which had assumed very large proportions, afterwards returned to Clarence street and dispensed.[567]

The paper of July 26 reported that 218 shops had signed to say that they would close at 8 p.m. throughout the week except on a Saturday and a Wednesday. Shops did not open on Sundays.

In 1904 the Shop Hours Act gave local authorities the power to fix trading hours on condition that two-thirds of the traders involved agreed, whilst in 1911 the Shops Act specified that all employees must finish early one day each week.[568]

The Y.M.C.A. Secures Warwick Lodge

Although Mr Parslow appears to have preferred the Ashdown Road site, during the three weeks following the Meeting on July 7, he worked hard to facilitate the move to Warwick Lodge. On July 28, he reported his achievements to the Committee at a general meeting.[569] The Committee resolved that Mr Parslow should complete negotiations on the best terms he could obtain. Mr Parslow acknowledged the Committee's vote of thanks and moved a resolution which was carried, 'That the proposed draft Deed of Assignment as submitted be adopted.'[570]

The Committee informed Mr. Brown the caretaker that he was no longer required but that they would pay his expenses for removal to another house and lodging for a fortnight.[571] Mr. W.B. Browne did the painting, papering and repairs, and the Committee asked Mr. Northcroft to secure plans for an iron building capable of holding about two-hundred people. They also asked Mr. Morten to select and buy carpet for the premises and detailed the secretary to find somebody to rent the kitchen garden.[572] On August 18, the secretary produced plans of iron buildings with an estimated cost of a building to hold two-hundred being £200 or one to hold one-hundred and forty-four people at the lower price of £165. The Committee decided that the Room built should be capable of holding at least two hundred people.

Furniture, Carpets, Linoleums, Bedsteads, Bedding.

SMITHERS & SONS,

104 to 114, London Rd., KINGSTON.

Removals and ↗

ESTABLISHED 1845.

Warehousing.

SMITHERS & SONS,

104 to 114, London Rd., KINGSTON.

40. Smithers & Sons Advertisement—Abstract of the Thirtieth
Annual Report 1902-3, p.28.   (**YMCA**)

Our Cosy Rooms.

——— A SECOND HOME.

Open 10 a.m. till 10.30 p.m.

YOUNG MEN are cordially invited to call at Warwick Lodge to visit the Rooms and make the acquaintance of Y.M.C.A. men.

A FREE TICKET ———

Will be given to any young man, suitably introduced, entitling to the use of the . .

COSY AND HOME-LIKE ROOMS,

and other advantages of the Association for one month.

Young men may call on the Secretary any time and he would be glad to hear of and welcome any Young Men coming into the town, or to give introductions to kindred Associations to those leaving.

Hollanders worden vriendelijk uitgenoodigt tot de vergaderingen der Christelijke jongelings vereeniging. De President is bereidt raad en uitkomst te geven in geval van moeilijkheid.

Junge Deutsche Männer sind herzlich eingeladen, anden Versammlungen des Vereins, teilzunehmen und dem Verein sich anzuschliessen. Der Verein bietet Christlichen Anschluss und Gemeinschaft und sucht dabei auch die körperliche. Entwieklung des jungen mannes nach kräften zu fördern.

ARTHUR HILL, Sekretär,
Warwick Lodge, Eden Street,
Kingston-on-Thames.

41. Our Cosy Rooms — Abstract of the Thirtieth Annual Report 1902-3, p.29.   **(YMCA)**

Mr. Hayward's offer of £10 per annum for the kitchen garden was accepted but he was asked to contribute extra 'for the ripe fruit.' The letting of the stables and the coach house was left until later. Mr. Brown was asked to make a new set of bookshelves for the reading room. It was agreed to amount the noticeboard from Union Street on legs, paint it and buy fenders and table covers for the reading room and parlour.[573]

Mr. Parslow reported that Mr. Smithers had consented to remove the Association's property free of charge except for the men's time. Mr. Smither's advertisement found in the Thirtieth Annual Report 1902-3 is shown in Figure 40.[574] Warwick Lodge opened on Wednesday, August 13, 1890, and immediately began to provide a second home for all young men of whatever nationality residing in the area. [575]

WARWICK LODGE–A SECOND HOME
1890–1908

42. Warwick Lodge circa 1897 – Twenty-fifth Annual Report 1897-8 p.1.   **(YMCA)**

At the opening of Warwick Lodge the *Surrey Comet* described the building as:

> standing in large grounds, which will be very useful, especially in the summer months. During the past fortnight alterations have been made to the interior of the building. The billiard room has been turned into a reading room and the dining room into a library, while the drawing room will serve as a secretary's office.[576]

43. Warwick Lodge games room, circa 1898,   **(YMCA)**

Later in 1903 it was described in an annual report as:

> in a good position in the town (Eden Street is a thoroughfare to Surbiton) and upon ground with a frontage of 96 feet, but much wider at the rear – 130 feet – and a depth of about 200 feet, abutting property on Fairfield West. The property consists of house, small hall (capable of holding 200 persons) and by 1903 a handsome building erected and equipped as a Gymnasium two years ago through the munificence of Captain Cundy, the president. The building when used for concerts or meetings will seat about 500 persons. The property as it stands is a very valuable asset of the Association and is capable of considerable development for building purposes when means are forthcoming.[577]

The First Committee Meeting was held on September 15, 1890. Mr. Parslow reported that he had been unable to extract further concession from Mr. Sherrard and therefore had settled the assignment accordingly, the papers then going into a deed box. Mr. Walker reported that he had taken steps to secure a second hand iron building but, having failed to obtain one suitable, he had begun negotiating for the purchase of a new one from a firm in Bermondsey. Mr. Morten reported that the furnishing had been done in as reasonable way as possible.

Mr Morten offered to present the Association with twenty-four Bibles and it was resolved that one-hundred of the larger Sankey's Hymn Books be purchased. Mr. Morten also lent an excellent organ for use, another member presented a set of quoits and a lamp for the outside of the Association was promised. It was also resolved that a twenty light gas meter be hired from the gas company. [578]

Incompatibility with Church Membership and Resignations

Shops may have stayed open very late of Saturdays, but they shut on Wednesdays at five p.m. and at eight p.m. on other weekdays, the Early Closing Movement apparently moving in the right direction.

Unfortunately, the difficulties previously experienced by the Association did not disappear when they moved into Warwick Lodge. The annual report for the year 1892 to 1893 states that not only had Mr. Northcroft moved from the district and Mr. R.W. Cowdery (the secretary) resigned, but the Committee also regretted that they had been deprived through resignation on account of differences of opinion of the valuable support of Mr. J.S. Morten and others who have long been connected with the Association. 'Such differences are always to be regretted, but your Committee are glad to be allowed to report that those who withdrew did so as THEY considered it in the interest of the Association and in a perfect spirit of brotherly love.'[579]

The only information about the exodus comes from Walter Hill's account included later in this chapter, which shows that the problems relating to doctrinal differences clearly remained and continued after the move in 1890, and by 1900 the following was added to the annual report:

> Inasmuch as the increasing publicity resulting from the growth of Young Men's Christian Associations and the extension of their work renders it desirable that the relation in which these Associations stand to the Churches should be clearly defined and understood:
>
> It is hereby resolved and affirmed – "The Young Men's Christian Association recognize the Churches of God which ... are in Christ Jesus, as existing by divine appointment of the maintenance of the institutions of public worship and for the ministry of the Word of God, and earnestly disavow any

intention or desire to enter upon functions proper to the Churches. The Associations seek to be and desire to be regarded as helpers to the Churches in effort and service directed towards a class of persons not easily reached by ordinary Church agencies, and consider it to be alike their privilege and their duty to lead young men into fellowship of the Churches and under the influence of the Christian ministry." [580]

The Association therefore reaffirmed its 1900 its intention to attract into membership those not easily reached by the churches and thereafter lead them into the fellowship of a church.

The Closure of the Surbiton Rooms

The annual report for the year 1892 to 1893 also mentioned that:

In consequence of the withdrawal from the Association of several Members who took active part in the work at Surbiton, and being for some time without a Secretary, they considered it best to suspend the meetings there from October last. It is their intention, however, to hold a meeting of Members and others belonging to Surbiton shortly, and if sufficient support is forthcoming to continue the work there.

The minutes of this meeting remain undiscovered. Mr. Morten had given the general fund a sum of £40 in 1892, but, even with this extra amount, the Association had a deficit of £33. 2s. 2d. An annual report for the years 1893 and 1894 have not been found in the archive, and subcommittee minutes do not mention the Surbiton rooms. By July 1895 buying the freehold of Warwick Lodge served as a main topic for discussion at Committee meetings. [581]

Mr. Arthur Hill

In 1893 the Association selected Mr. Arthur Hill as secretary, a role that he accomplished with great skill and dedication until his retirement in 1927. Born in Upper Mitcham and formerly secretary of the 'Christian Progress' Scripture Reading Union, Mr. Hill had more recently served as hon. secretary to the Sidcup branch of the Y.M.C.A. and a lay missioner in the parish of Mitcham. Mr. Hill's son Walter was three years old when the family came to Kingston. Some years later he wrote:

In 1890, to meet the needs of adequate accommodation, Warwick Lodge, a house in Eden Street standing in its own grounds, was taken on a lease of five years and was formally opened in August of that year. This provided very suitable accommodation, with a large garden for summer activities. It also provided living accommodation for the Secretary. The following year a hall, known as the "Iron Room" was built on vacant land adjoining the house, to be used for gymnastics and other activities.

In 1891 Sir Douglas Fox resigned as president and was succeeded by Captain James Cundy. In the following year Mr. R.W. Cowdery resigned as Secretary and was succeeded by my father, Mr. Arthur Hill, in January 1893.

It was at this time the writer of these notes came into the picture at the early age of three years. My first contact with Warwick Lodge was on a very wet day in February, my mother's birthday, when we took up residence and my father started his life's work of over thirty years.[582] The family took up residence in a flat prepared for the purpose within Warwick Lodge. On account of several doctrinal differences several of the members had resigned with Mr. Cowdery and in consequence the situation my father had to deal with was not an easy one. However with the support of the President and members of the Association, steady progress was made.

A General Council and Subcommittees were eventually formed, covering religious work, a literary and debating society, choral society, gymnastics, and the football club in 1885 which must rank among the oldest sports clubs in the district. A former Mayor of Kingston, W.G. Carn, was the first captain of the football club. (This is incorrect as it was W.G. Carn's son who was Mayor.) They were subsequently known as "The Saxons" Football Club (Y.M.C.A.)[583] Considerable support was given by shopkeepers in the town, some of whom joined as members and took an active part in the work of the Association. Prior to the arrival of large multiple stores, the custom was for the staff to live over the shop premises and many of the young men so employed very much appreciated the welcome given to them by my mother in our large kitchen for supper on many evenings during the week.

Among this number were two young men who subsequently became President of the Association and occupied positions of importance in the town, W.G. Eggleton, who became Mayor of Kingston, and Leonard Bentall, who developed Kingston's biggest store. A very successful evangelistic meeting was started in the Iron Room after church services on Sunday evenings and continued for some years until similar gatherings were started in the churches. A large open-air meeting was held at the Clarence Street end of Eden Street until the coming of the trams in 1906. A Cabmen's Shelter at Kingston railway station was a liability rather than an asset. Visits to the common lodging houses were made and for some years a regatta was organised including rowing, swimming and life saving, with considerable success. It was eventually amalgamated with the borough regatta. Cycling was very popular and many excursions were made, often including an open-air meeting in the town visited.

The Jubilee of the formation of the Young Men's Christian Association by George Williams (later Sir George) was celebrated in 1894 and, by gracious invitation of Queen Victoria, a large international gathering was held in Windsor Castle. The President (Sir Douglas Fox), Mr. G.A. Barrett, my father and mother were present from Kingston. Hospitality for visiting delegates was also made available.[584]

Walter Hill

44. Mr. Arthur Hill, Secretary of Kingston and Surbiton Y.M.C.A, 1893—1927 (**YMCA**)

45. The garden Warwick Lodge, circa 1898, picture in various annual reports

(YMCA)

Mr. W.G. Eggleton's Reminiscence

William Eggleton joined the Y.M.C.A. in 1890 at the age of twenty-five. He later became president of the Association, a deacon and superintendent of the Sunday School at Bunyan Baptist Church and mayor of Kingston in 1949 and 1951. He wrote:

> It was always the YM when I joined in 1890 and the name survives, Warwick Lodge, a great old world garden at the rear, replete with tempting fruit trees and bushes. There was a quoits patch alongside a high wall. Memories: One can appreciate the tact and blind eye of Arthur Hill. Those Sunday evenings informal gatherings when he led the singing on his violin

and those homely chats in the kitchen. Somehow it was always the kitchen we made for, be it button, darn, cocoa or cake, it seemed more like home, particularly to us young fellows who had left home. Mrs. Hill was a real mother to us and old members will lovingly remember her. For the privilege of having known Arthur Hill, for his help, sympathy, counsel and comradeship, one gives thanks and carries on.[585]

Spiritual, Mental, Social and Physical

The 1892 annual report stated that the object of the Association had been changed:

> Many members have felt that the social side of the Association has not in the past been sufficiently used as a means of drawing young men to the rooms, and so getting them under the spiritual influence of the Secretary and Members. Believing that this was the fact, your Committee have lately developed the social side, and with very encouraging results, several young men being attracted by these agencies have joined as Members and Associates, and regularly attended the Religious Meetings.

In October 1894 a Special Committee met to revise the Kingston rules, shown in the 1898-99 annual report:

> 1. That this Association be called the Kingston and Surbiton District Young Men's Christian Association.

> 2. That the object of the Kingston and Surbiton Association, was now considered to be the **spiritual, mental, social and physical wellbeing** of young men. [586]

A break down of the work in 1895 to 1896, is as follows:

The Spiritual
Prayer, Bible Study and Conference
The Annual Week of Prayer for Young Men
Foreign Missions
The Sunday Afternoon Conversational Bible Class
Mission Work at Home
The Sunday Evening Meeting
The Thursday Evening Meeting

The Mental   Chess Draughts
The Literary and Debating Society

The Social   Social Gatherings during the year

The Physical   The Gymnasium
Quoits   The Athletic Club
Boating,   Swimming

The Athletic club provided boating, cricket, cycling, rowing, football and gym work, ambulance classes, life saving and swimming. There was also a lodgings register, which had been used by twenty young men. [587]

Captain Cundy Pays for the Gymnasium; 1899

About this time the gymnasium became an important part of the Y.M.C.A. activities. The thirty-seventh report, 1882, states that Exeter Hall did have a gymnasium, but it had been kept in the background. It had had only one display, and visitors would not necessarily be aware of its existence, although it had done good work.[588] In 1888 the Exeter Hall gymnasium transferred to Long Acre and was opened by the Prince of Wales accompanied by several notables. At the Dublin Conference of 1889, it was claimed that athletics was necessary for the purity and strengthening of the body and that a healthy body contained a healthy mind.'[589] Athletics had become an important ingredient in the well-being of young men. Originally the Kingston and Surbiton Association had used the Iron Room for gymnastic work, but it was too small. Therefore, after the annual meeting held in the Assembly Rooms in 1899, Captain Cundy announced that he would pay for a gymnasium. The Kingston and Surbiton gymnasium opened in 1900. The 1899–1900 annual report shows that the number of members had reached three-hundred and ten, of these one-hundred and sixty were full members and one-hundred and fifty associates.

46. Reading room Warwick Lodge taken before 1898   **(YMCA)**

The Association in 1902–1903 — Annual Report   (YMCA)

Sunday Afternoon.   2.30 P.M.

A . . .

Conversational Bible Class

Is held at WARWICK LODGE.

Lessons on the Life of our Lord

Jesus Christ.

1903.

Aug. 2	"Nicodemus"	John iii.	1–21
„ 9	"Men of Samaria" ...	John iv.	1–42
„ 16	"The Nobleman of Capernaum"	John iv.	43–54
„ 23	"The Prophet in his own Town"	Luke iv.	16–30
„ 30	"The Call of the Fishermen"	Matt. iv.	12–22
Sept. 6	"The Leper"	Matt. viii.	1–4
„ 13	"The Roman Officer's Great Faith"	Luke vii.	1–10
„ 20	"The Widow's Son of Nain"	Luke vii.	11–16
„ 27	"The Paralytic" ...	Mark ii.	1–12
Oct. 4	"The Call of the Publican	Matt. ix.	9–17
„ 11	"The Cripple at Bethesda"	John v.	1–16
„ 18	"At Jerusalem—Persecution"' ...	John v.	
„ 25	"The message from John the Baptist"	Matt. xi.	

NOTA BENE.—The Class lasts one hour every Sunday afternoon, and when the weather is favourable, is held on the Lawn.

Young Men are cordially invited.

ARTHUR HILL, *Leader.*

Sunday Evening. ———— **8 O'CLOCK.**

A UNITED . . .

Evangelistic

Meeting ~

IS HELD IN THE . . .

Y.M.C.A. HALL,

Or, when the weather is favourable, in the

Open-Air ^{AT THE}_{END OF} Eden Street,

Kingston=on=Thames.

Short Addresses.

Singing ^{LED BY} Mr. G. H. NORRIS,

Christians are cordially invited to support this Meeting by their presence and to constrain others to attend.

ARTHUR HILL, *Conductor.*

Thursday. ─────── 8.45 P.M.

A . . .

Men's Meeting.

Bible Readings and Prayer,
Missionary Addresses,

Helps and Encouragement to Young Men in the Christian Life and Work at home and abroad.

Difficulties and Questions Doubts
Prayerfully Considered. Dismissed.

ALL MEN WELCOME.

Saturday. ─────── 8.30 P.M.

A MEN'S

Praise & Prayer Meeting

Specially for Young Christians.

Young Men are most earnestly invited.

─────

We would earnestly remind our Members of the suggestions, printed on the Members' Cards, for regular daily supplication to God on behalf of the work of the Association.

ARTHUR HILL, *General Secretary.*

Miscellaneous Announcements.

THE Y.M.C.A. CHORAL SOCIETY

The Members have arranged to spend the Afternoon at

ST. GEORGE'S HILL, WEYBRIDGE,

On Wednesday, August 19th.

Trains from Surbiton at 2.10 & 2.50.   Cyclists start at 2.30 p.m.
All Y.M.C.A. men and friends are invited.

A meeting of the members and friends will be held on Tuesday, September 29th, 1903, to consider arrangements and appointments for the ensuing season.

Ladies and gentlemen wishing to join the Society are invited to attend.

GEO. H. NORRIS, *Conductor*.

Y.M.C.A. Bible Reading Union.

The Union provides the **New Testament Calendar (1d.)** This is an Annual Course of short portions for *any* year, and comprises *the whole* New Testament.

Old Testament Calendar, 1d.   In same style, but forming *Two* Annual Courses, embracing *the whole* Old Testament.

Young men find this special arrangement most helpful, and we strongly urge its immediate adoption and permanent daily use by all not previously pledged.

AN EARNEST WORD TO YOUNG CHRISTIANS.

"Take heed to thyself."
"Give attendance to Reading."
"Take heed to the Doctrine."
"Neglect not the Gift that is in thee."
"Be diligent in these things."

Y.M.C.A. Missionary Union.

Work by and for Young Men in Heathen Lands.
The duties of the Members are—

1 **Regular Prayer.** 2 **Regular Reading.** 3 **Regular Giving·**

Meetings for united prayer are regularly held.   A News Letter is prepared periodically.   Boxes and Cards provided to receive the Weekly Contributions.

WILL MORE OF OUR MEN CONTRIBUTE?

Boxes and Calendars for above can be had on application,

ARTHUR HILL, *Gen. Secretary*.

Y.M.C.A. Athletic Club.

AMBULANCE.

Instruction in **"First Aid to the Injured"** has been given by Dr. A. M. DALDY.

Seventeen men attended the early Lectures but only ten presented themselves for the Examination. Of these there were two candidates for Medallions, one for a second Certificate, six for first Certificate and one Junior.

All the men, except one for a first Certificate, passed, and will receive the St. John Ambulance Awards at a Meeting to be held on Aug. 26th.

BOATING.

Members and Associates can have Boats at reduced rates at Mr. BURGOINE'S Boat House, High Street, Kingston, on showing cards.

CYCLING.

Wednesday Run.	Saturday Run.
Start 3 p.m.	Start 3 p.m.
Aug. 5—Oxshott, Bookham.	Aug. 1—Oxshott, Cobham.
,, 12—Box Hill.	,, 8—Chertsey, Virginia Water.
,, 19—St. George's Hill.	,, 15—Dorking, Silent Pool.
,, 26—Oxshott	,, 22—Slough, Windsor.
Sept.2—Ripley, Guildford.	,, 29—Reigate, Betchworth.
,, 9—Reigate Hill.	Sept.5—Cobham, Fetcham.
,, 16—Slough, Windsor.	,, 12—Ewell, Ashstead.
,, 23—Ashstead, Headley.	,, 19—Weybridge, Woking.
,, 30—Addlestone, Woking.	,, 26—Box Hill, Dorking.
THOS. DYKE, *Hon. Sec.*	G. H. NORRIS, *Hon. Sec.*

Cycling Party. A Week's Holiday on Wheels.

Day Out-and-Home Circular Runs.

Start at 8 a.m. each day.

Sept. 21—Burnham Beeches.	Sept. 24—Reigate, Horley.
,, 22—Aldershot.	,, 25—Caterham Valley
,, 23—Hindhead.	,, 26—Leith Hills.

ARTHUR HILL, *Conductor.*

Y.M.C.A. Athletic Club *(continued)*.

PHYSICAL CULTURE. ⸺

Mondays. 8.45 P.M.

Sandow's Exercises & Physical Drill

In our large and well-equipped

G Y M N A S I U M.

Mr. J. J. CUTMORE, ⎱ *Hon.*
Mr. W. E. HILL, ⎰ *Instructors*

Fridays. 8.45 P.M.

PRACTICE, under the direction of Mr. A. J. MERCER.

SWIMMING. ⸺

The "**Nisbet Challenge Cup**" Competition, and other **Races**, will take place at the **Corpora= tion Baths**, on **Wednesday, Oct. 21st, 1903.**

Tickets for the Baths at half price can be obtained by Members and Associates at Warwick Lodge.

LIFE SAVING. ⸺

A Class for the Instruction in the methods of **Rescue and Resuscitation** of the apparently drowned commenced July 29th in the Y.M.C.A. Hall, for Land Drills, and will continue every **Wednesday**, at 8 o'clock—August and September.

Men who can swim are invited to join at once.

Athletic Club Garden Party

❧

At WARWICK LODGE,

On Wednesday, August 26th, 1903.

All further information *re* **Athletic Club** can be obtained from ARTHUR HILL, *General Secretary.*

Men Wanted!

𝔜𝔬𝔲𝔫𝔤 𝔐𝔢𝔫 are heartily invited to join the Association either as Members or Associates, and to avail themselves of all the advantages set forth in this Programme.

𝔐𝔢𝔪𝔟𝔢𝔯𝔰.—All Christian Men (see "Basis," page 15) should join as members and take part in the work and the management of the Association.

𝔄𝔰𝔰𝔬𝔠𝔦𝔞𝔱𝔢𝔰.—Any respectable young man over 15 years of age may join as an Associate and be entitled to all the privileges except that of the management of the Association.

Subscriptions.

MEMBERS   ...   .   6/– per ann.
ASSOCIATES from 15 to 18 years of age, 2/6   ,,
  ,,   ,,   18 years of age   ...   4/–   ,,

The Subscription may be paid half-yearly, and dates from joining.

A larger subscription would be very acceptable from any who can afford it.

THE SECRETARY'S OFFICE IS UPSTAIRS.

- -

FORM FOR JOINING
THE
Y. M. C. A.

Name in Full—Mr. ....

Private Address ....

....

....

Business Address ....

....

Reference to Mr. ....

(Insert age, if under 18, and whether Member or Associate.)

Captain Cundy Clears the Mortgage - 1908

The 1895 to 1896 report noted that the lease on Warwick Lodge expired at Michaelmas. To deal with this far-reaching question, the Association appointed a house committee, which immediately opened negotiations with the owner of the property, Mr. Thomas Betts, as to terms for a new lease or for acquiring the freehold. The Y.M.C.A. had decided to purchase the freehold of the property for £1,750 on the following terms: '£300 to be paid down on account, and £1,450 to remain on mortgage for seven years with Mr. Betts, at 4 per cent. per annum.' Through the liberality of Capt. Cundy, the Misses Du Pre, Mr. R.S. Bond and Mr. Clayton and the contributions of twenty or more other friends, the Association raised the £450 and left £1,000 on mortgage. In 1908 Capt.Cundy, aged eighty-four said that he had concluded that the Association should have a new president: 'I desire to make the payment of the mortgage (£1000) a parting gift to the Y.M.C.A. and so end my responsibility, with the exception of a moderate annual subscription while I live.' He died in March 1909.[590]

WHAT THE . . . . . .

Kingston and Surbiton District

Young Men's Christian Association

Provides for the

Leisure Hours of Young Men.

A Second Home.   **A Cheerful Place of Resort.**
Desirable Friendships.
Counsel in times of Difficulty and Doubt.
Openings for Christian Work.

Sea-side Holiday Homes.
Social Gatherings.
Introduction to Kindred Associations.

Addresses.   Debates.   Lectures.   Music.
Singing.   Games.
Reading Room.   Writing Room.   Library, &c.

Summer and Winter Recreations.
Boating, Cricket, Cycling, Swimming, Quoits,
Football and Gymnasia.

A Free Ticket, entitling to the use of the Rooms
   and other advantages, for One Month.

Apply Personally to—

ARTHUR HILL,

Warwick Lodge,   General Secretary,
Eden Street,
Kingston-on-Thames.

KNAPP, TYP., KINGSTON, SURBITON AND WIMBLEDON.

CONCLUSION

This book has been written for two main reasons. The first is to create a comprehensive synopsis of an important body of primary sources and to place it firmly in the Kingston location. The second reason is that this is a story that should be told. When combined with information found in the *Surrey Comet*, these records contain a considerable amount of information relating to nineteenth century society in Kingston and Surbiton. It includes not only details of the work of the Y.M.C.A. but also that of the Early Closing Movement. Other information such as the difficulties relating to poor accommodation, property prices and numerous other mundane pieces of detail are included, some of which will be of interest to those involved in the history of the area.

Apart from writing a history of the Y.M.C.A. in Kingston and Surbiton, I have sought to provide an opportunity to meet the members. These members may have differed culturally and socially from us but they seem very similar in many of their hopes, ideals and aspirations. Some, such as the founder of the first Y.M.C.A. in Kingston in 1858, the Congregational minister the Rev. Lawrence Byrnes, who might have gone to Lincoln but chose Kingston instead, stand out. Mr. Byrnes, for example, not only ministered to his church members but also encouraged the building of a Congregational Church in Maple Road, reformed the church in Cobham and in 1855 replaced the 'little, obscure, building' (the old Congregational Chapel in Kingston) with the church that stands in the centre of Kingston today. In 1858 he also initiated the beginning of the Y.M.C.A, only fourteen years after George Williams started the London Association in 1844.

In February 1859 at the fourteenth annual meeting of the Association in Exeter Hall it was reported that the London Association consisted of one thousand, five hundred young men and was divided into nine districts.[591] Although Kingston did not register with the parent body until the early 1860s, this early Association must have predated many others in the country. After he left the area, Byrnes became 'the 449th climber to ascend Mont Blanc from Chamoney,' achieving this on August 26, 1871.[592] He kept in touch with members of the Congregational (now the United Reformed) Church in Kingston and would have known about the Association's move to Warwick Lodge in 1890 and the progress made by the Early Closing Movement in the same year. He died aged eighty on July 4, 1902.[593]

The young men who initiated the Y.M.C.A. in 1874 obviously thought that separating from the group attached to the Baptist Church in Brick Lane was important. The latter Association had started in 1872, after the Rev. Lawrence Byrnes had left Kingston, and had focused solely on religious activity. The new 1874 Association encountered many difficulties during the 1870s and 1880s. These included the problems associated with leasing Zoar Chapel, a very old building in constant need of repair, and later the problems associated with trying to build new premises. Without the perseverance and dedication of Mr. Frank Newson, a shipbroker's clerk, and Mr. William Parslow, a solicitor's general clerk, the 1874 Kingston Association would not have continued.

I also introduce their counterparts who started the Surbiton Association in 1868, the accountant Mr. George H. Lea; his friend a Surbiton gardener, Mr. John King, who later ran a greengrocer's shop in 3 Paragon Terrace, Berrylands Road and the Rev. Edward Garbett, (later Canon Garbett) the first vicar of Christ Church. Darwin's book *The Origin of the Species* published in 1859 confused and frightened many people. An outstanding theologian Edward Garbett told members of the Surbiton Y.M.C.A. 'if any one felt any difficulty with reference to God's Word, if they came to him he would do his best to assist them, and should always feel honoured and happy to do so.'[594] The generous Mr. Morten is also mentioned. On several occasions he paid for the redecoration of the Surbiton rooms, whilst Captain Cundy, paid for a gymnasium and, in 1908, gave the Association one thousand pounds to clear the mortgage on Warwick Lodge. Although disagreements arose and individuals left the Association, the contributions of many former members show that their appreciation endured beyond their time in Kingston. Mr. Newson gave £4. 4s. 0d annually, Mr. Carn 5s. The year after Captain Cundy's death Mrs. Cundy, donated a further one hundred pounds and continued to give yearly thereafter. In 1927 Leonard Bentall, who joined as an associate member in 1893, gave the Association seven hundred and fifty pounds from himself, his wife and his staff. He gave this at a time when the Association was unable to raise sufficient money towards the building programme that followed after the demolition of Warwick Lodge.[595]

The book reveals that the Kingston Association was slow to appreciate the need to move towards a programme that encompassed 'the whole man.' However, this omission does not appear to have been peculiar to Kingston and Surbiton. Whereas as early as 1866 the New York Association revised their constitution with the aim to improve the 'spiritual, mental, social and physical condition of young men,' we know from Binfield that the move towards a similar programme in England happened much more slowly and was only achieved much later.[596] However what is obvious from reading the history of the Kingston and Surbiton movement is that by the turn of the century the Association was revising its programme, and throughout the twentieth century continued to adjust to the needs of the community, a situation that has continued up to and including the present day.

A report from 1917-18 documents the change that had taken place by the end of World War I in 1918. The report is not signed but it is possible that Arthur Hill's son wrote the report, which reads as follows:

> This centre of the Y.M.C.A., upon which "The Red Triangle is fixed, still stands as it has stood for many years past for the true well-being of Men — Body, Soul and Spirit.
>
> The symbol does not present any new principles but indicates that the centre is actively engaged carrying out in a very practical way, the meaning and message of "The Red Triangle" especially to the men of H.M.Forces. Hundreds of men fresh from good homes, some for the first time "joining up", men from the front "home on leave", men who have given a good account at the front, and now in our Local Hospitals; all find Our Centre to be "The Soldiers' link – with – home."
>
> Here a sailor or soldier may drop in, leave his cumbersome kit for a while, get a wash and begin to feel comfortable before he visits his friends. Or if it is food, rest or lodgings that are required, he can be supplied or advised where to go. The lounge with all sorts of games and music, writing accommodation, and where concerts are given, is very much appreciated.
>
> The military officers and the men confirm this.
>
> An officer writing to the Secretary, under recent date, says "On behalf of all men in my command since some time in 1916, I wish to convey to you and your Committee thanks for pleasure and entertainment your Y.M.C.A. centre has afforded at Kingston."
>
> A Matron writes also recently "I should like to thank you for your kindness to our Wounded Soldiers. They say that they are made so welcome and comfortable when they visit the Kingston Y.M.C.A. The men much appreciated your kindness and are very grateful."
>
> The usefulness and popularity of the centre here is growing every week and we have received much help and encouragement in having a constant supply of voluntary helpers, who work very hard in the Canteen, and others who entertain the men. 65 ladies have assisted in Canteen and others, regularly at the Sunday Song-Service after tea in the Lounge, and various friends have provided Concerts and entertainments.
>
> All these helpers have spontaneously come to our assistance and this feature is particularly pleasing and calls forth the best thanks of the Committee and the appreciation of the Sailors and Soldiers who use the Rooms.

It is estimated something like 2,000 VISITS ARE MADE TO THE ROOMS WEEKLY.
The place is open all the day and the men freely come in and out as they would in their homes. The returns of the Canteen are now enormous in comparison with last year, and increasing monthly.

A Comparison (A Week End)

Last Year	This Year
7 doz. 1d Cakes including Buns	2,200 1d Cakes including Buns
9 Loaves of Bread	62 Loaves of Bread
3 lbs of Tea per Month	3 lbs of Tea per Day

This year (1918) we have given away 47,000 sheets of writing paper

3,000 Letter Cards	3,000 Post Cards
1,000 Gospels	Sold £110 Postage Stamps

This continuing adjustment to the needs of the community was also evident towards the end of the World War II in 1946 when Mrs. Alice Kendall, our neighbour, took me—aged ten—on a Saturday, to the Y.M.C.A. in Eden Street to help in the kitchen.[597] Warwick Lodge had been demolished, and the Association had built premises with two shops at the front of the building providing the Association with rent. During the week and on Saturdays the place was filled by hungry young men in uniform eating or waiting to be fed by a resolute number of ladies recruited from all walks of life. The Y.M.C.A., in particular the members of the Women's Auxiliary, did incredible voluntary work during this period. As there was no hostel accommodation, several of the ladies would offer young men a bed for the night in their own homes and breakfast in the morning to counteract the lack of overnight stay. In the Y.M.C.A. archives a pamphlet shows Mrs. Alice Kendall as well as Mrs. Hilda Woods, the chief cook with others were given 'The Order of the Red Triangle,' at a ceremony that took place on April 10, 1946 in the Guildhall in Kingston with the mayor and corporation in attendance.

Some years later when I was in my late teens, I joined the Women's Auxiliary, working behind the counter on a Saturday. By this time it was mostly Kingston people who came through the swing doors between the two shops in Eden Street. Various dignitaries would come and mingle. Gladys who worked in the shoe shop at the front of the building, would spend her ten minute mid-afternoon break having a cup of tea in the kitchen. The duty policeman, who was making certain all the buildings behind the premises were locked and secure for the weekend, would frequently bang on the window and 'a cuppa' would be poured from the large brown metal teapot, allowing him to have a quick drink at the back door. By this time various billiards and snooker tournaments took place at the London Central Y.M.C.A. there were footballers, numerous clubs, activities, evening entertainment and at the front counter, a continuous assembly of young men, their friends, girl friends, wives and children. Occasionally one of the well-known Kingston tramps would also arrive, throwing a few pennies on the counter and receive in return a bacon sandwich with extra thick bread and a full thermos of tea. The Y.M.C.A. seemed at the hub of Kingston's social activity.

In retrospect these appeared to be halcyon days. The war was over, and expectations were high. However for some expectations were realised, for others they were not, as I discovered when I attended in 1961 a Y.M.C.A. conference for young people with my future husband. The then secretary, Frederick Daldry, encouraged and organised our trip which we paid for ourselves. The conference took place on idealic Mainau, an Island on Lake Constance. After the first day a feeling of unease started to spread throughout the delegation. Early one morning towards the end of the week, a coach and a number of cars pulled up at the main door of the Island Palace. After being quickly boarded by about thirty delegates, one of whom was a young girl in tears, the convoy sped away having waved good-bye to the remaining delegation. Although it was not initially clear what was happening, we later learned that the Berlin Wall was about to be erected, and those who had left the Conference had managed to get home, to their families, just in time. Although the wall was removed after 1989, little has changed and the world continues to be a place of conflict, fear, destruction and extreme deprivation for many.

The Y.M.C.A. is the largest and oldest charity working with young people in the world with women now included as members. It currently operates in one-hundred and nineteen countries, reaching fifty-eight million people. In England there are one hundred and fourteen associations with programmes supporting the perceived needs of local communities.[598] The Kingston and Surbiton District Young Men's Christian Association is currently part of one of the largest Y.M.C.A.s in Europe and called 'Y.M.C.A. London South West.' This Association includes the Y.M.C.A.s in Wimbledon, Surbiton, the Hawker Centre and the Hampton Pool with Youth Centres at the 'Basement' in the John Bunyan Baptist Church, Kingston, and the John Innes Youth centre in Wimbledon. It is the largest provider of supported housing for the homeless in South West London.[599] It works in partnership with the National Health Service, Kingston Churches Against Homelessness and Age UK. Supported by government grants, every year it helps hundreds of people. The hostels provide a safe place for the young and for the more mature who require respite, thereby giving people the means to rebuild relationships or to receive more individualised help in times of stress. Its other services include life skills classes, foundation learning, apprenticeships, volunteer schemes and social activities, all of which it funds from the surpluses (profits) of the gyms, childcare service and cafes. In a world where 'loving your neighbour as yourself' is scarce, the Association aims to treat each person as an individual, holistically mindful of body, mind and spirit.[600]

APPENDIX I

At a meeting held at the Gospel Hall, Applemarket, Kingston, on Saturday evening 10th January 1874, it was arranged to open a Reading Room for the use of Young Men employed in Kingston and the neighbourhood.
The minutes continue:
In order to carry this properly into effect the following resolutions were:

1. That a committee be appointed consisting of:

L. Stringer	J. Newson	J.Morten
F. Lardelli	H. Rimer	H. Maxwell
H. J. Hapgood	J. Dale	H. Carter

    With power to add.
2. That a treasurer and secretary be also appointed-

Treasurer	L. Stringer
Secretary	J. Newson
3. That a reading room be opened for the purpose of gathering together the young men of Kingston and neighbourhood, and affording them an opportunity of spending their leisure evening hours with profit and pleasure.
4. That all be invited to attend the Sunday afternoon Bible Class with which this Reading Room is connected.
5. That the said room be called the Young Men's Reading Room.
6. That the room be opened on Thursday next 15th inst. to commence with a tea at 8.15 p.m. (to which special invitations be taken round.)
7. That the following Gentlemen be invited to give us their presence and some to speak on the occasion.

Rev. A. Williams	Rev. H. Bayley
Rev. J. F. Osborne	Capt. Cundy
Rev. Akroyd	Mr. Norton
8. That L. Stringer and J. Newson provide all necessary eatables and drinkables for the tea.
9. That the following notices be placed somewhere in the room.

    Notices:
    This room will be open free to all young men employed in business from 7 o'clock p.m. to 10 o'clock p.m. every evening (Sunday excepted.) Books, papers, periodicals &c. will be provided which are not to be taken away from the room.

    Special:
    There will be a class for the study of the Scriptures, held every Sunday afternoon between 3.30 p.m. and 4.30. p.m. at which all are earnestly invited to attend.

L. Stringer.

Y.M.C.A. Minute Book 10 January 1874 — 25 September 1879, pp.1 - 4

APPENDIX II

The Rules of the Young Men's Christian Association as agreed on the 3 October 1878:

1. That the Association be called "THE YOUNG MEN'S CHRISTIAN ASSOCIATION,' Kingston-on-Thames Branch.
2. That the object of the Association be the improvement of the spiritual and mental condition of young men.
3. That the means to be employed for the attainment of this object be the individual effort of each Member of the Association in his daily calling, and the holding of meetings in the Rooms of the Association for Prayer, Biblical Instruction, Preaching the Gospel, mutual edification and encouragement.
4. That the affairs of the Association be in the hands of a Committee of Management, a Treasurer, and Secretary, to be elected from amongst the Members of the Association.
5. That the Committee consist of nine Members (including the Treasurer and Secretary), of whom four shall form a quorum.
6. That the Committee be elected annually by a majority of Members assembled at a General Meeting of the Members of the Association, to be called for that purpose the last week in September, or as soon after as can conveniently be arranged.
7. That in the event of the removal or resignation of any of the Committee, it be in the power of the Committee to fill up vacancies, subject to confirmation at the next General Meeting of Members in September.
8. That an annual meeting be held, at which a report be given of the proceedings of the Association.
9. That any one be eligible for Membership upon giving decided evidence of his conversion to God.
10. That any one desirous of becoming a Member be proposed by a Member of the Association, and that the proposal (in writing) be sent to the Secretary of the Association, and that the proposal (in writing) be sent to the Secretary for presentation at the next meeting of the Committee.
11. That the Committee be empowered to elect a Member after due consideration and enquiry as to his suitability.
12. That the Committee be empowered, by a unanimous vote, to suspend or exclude any Member whose conduct is found, in their judgment, to be inconsistent with his Christian profession.
13. That the Rooms of the Association be also used for a Reading Room and Library, and that the same be under the control of the Committee of the Association, who shall appoint a Librarian.
14. That the Librarian be authorised to receive subscriptions towards the expenses of the Reading Room and Library.

N.B. There is no fixed subscription for Membership, the means of the Members varying, but it is expected that all will contribute.

Y.M.C.A. Minute Book 10 January 1874 – 25 September 1879, p. 69 - 71

APPENDIX III

The Rules of the Reading Room and Library as agreed on the 27 December 1878

1. That an Attendance Card be furnished, in due course, by the Librarian to each Subscriber of One Shilling per quarter, (paid in advance), towards the expenses of the Reading Room and Library.
2. That the Reading Room be open to any young man, engaged in business, in Kingston and neighbourhood, upon production of his Attendance Card, showing that the quarterly subscription had been paid.
3. That any Subscriber who pays an additional sum of 3d. per quarter, be entitled to borrow one Book per week from the Library.
4. That the time for changing Books be from 7.30 to 8.30 p.m. every Thursday Evening.
5. That all Books be returned to the Librarian at the expiration of 7 or 14 days, and if kept for a longer period a fine of One Penny per week be paid by the Subscriber.
6. That any Subscriber who loses or damages a Book be required to pay for a new copy of the same.
7. That the Librarian submit a list of the names of all intending Subscribers, to the Committee of the Young Men's Christian Association for approval, before issuing Attendance Cards, (addition) and that the Committee be empowered to object to Candidates for enrolment as Subscribers, to expel anyone behaving in a disorderly manner, and generally to enforce the Rules.

Y.M.C.A. Minute Book 10 January 1874 – 25 September 1879, pp.87 - 8

APPENDIX IV

The Rules for the Discussion Meetings

1. That a Chairman be appointed by the Committee: having the control of the Reading Room and Library, whose decision, upon all questions of order, raised at any meeting shall be final, subject however to an Appeal to the said Committee on important questions.
2. That the subjects for debate be first submitted to the said Committee for their approval
3. That the Chairman of each meeting be allowed to exercise his discretion in allowing others to speak after the Members have concluded.
4. That no Speaker be allowed more than 8 minutes except the opener of the debate who shall be allowed 15 minutes.
5. That a Secretary be appointed who shall take the management of the Class.

N.B. The Elocution and Discussion Class fee of 1/- per quarter is to be paid to the Librarian.

Y.M.C.A. Minute Book 2 October 1879 – 13 January 1882, pp.25 - 7

APPENDIX V

The Rules for the Elocution Class

1. That a Secretary be appointed who shall take the management of the class, and be responsible to the Committee having control of the Reading Room and Library for the way in which the class is carried on.
2. That the pieces &c: to be read or recited be first submitted to the said Committee for their approval.
3. That no one be permitted on any one evening to occupy the time of the Class for more than 10 minutes unless with the sanction of the Secretary.
4. That any complaint as to the conduct of the Class be addressed to the Committee above mentioned.

Y.M.C.A. Minute Book 2 October 1879 – 13 January 1882, pp.28 - 9.

APPENDIX VI

The Rules as agreed 27 November 1880 - Young Men's Reading Room & Library
Brick Lane Kingston. In connection with the Young Men's Christian Association (Kingston on Thames Branch)
Open every evening from 7 till 10 o'clock (Sundays excepted)
Rules

1 That the Subscription to the Reading Room be one shilling per quarter (payable in advance) and that Attendance Cards be furnished by the Librarian to young men paying that sum.
2. That the Reading Room be open every evening as above to Subscribers who must if required produce their Attendance Cards.
3. That Newspapers be provided, and that the Books of the Library, Chess &c be for the use of Subscribers only.
4. That no smoking shall be allowed in the Room nor anything done therein which may be an annoyance to those present.
5. That any Subscriber who pays an additional sum of 3d per quarter (in advance) shall be entitled to borrow one book at a time from the Library subject to Rule 7.
6. That the time for changing Books be from 7.30 till 8.30 every Thursday Evening.
7. That if any Book be not returned to the Librarian within the period stated thereon a fine of one penny per week or part of a week shall be paid by the Borrower.
8. That any Subscriber who loses or damages a Book shall pay for a new Copy of the same.
9. That the Librarian shall have the General Management of the Reading Room and Library under the control of the Committee of the Young Man's Christian Association and that he be empowered to expel anyone behaving in an objectionable manner and generally to enforce the Rules.

Y.M.C.A. Minutes 10.1.1874 – 25.9.1879, pp.135 - 7.

APPENDIX VII

Revision of Rules - 3 February 1882

Rule 2   The words "social" to be added after "spiritual."
Rule 4   The words "a President and other officers" to be substituted for a "Treasurer and Secretary."
Rule 5   The words "and a Chairman" to be inserted after "Secretary" and " o f whom four" to read "four of whom."
Rule 6   The word "June" to be substituted for "September"
Rule 7   The words "subject to confirmation ... September" to be omitted.
Rule 8   The words "early in each year" to be inserted after the words "meeting be held"
Rule 9   The words "young man over 15 years of age" be substituted for "one" and the word "satisfactory" for "decided."
Rule 13   The words "of the Association" after Committee be omitted.
Rule 14   to be called Rule 15
Rule 14   That young men over 15 years of age of good moral character be admitted as Associates on payment of a fixed subscription entitling them to all the privileges of membership except the right of voting at meetings.
Rule 15   The former Rule 14 to be now Rule 15.

(see Appendix II for previous rules)

Y.M.C.A. Minutes 2.10.79 – 3.2.1882, pp.142 – 3.

APPENDIX VIII

Kingston Y.M.C.A. Cricket Club Rules 7 July 1882

1.   That the Club be called the Kingston Y.M.C.A. Cricket Club.
2.   That the management of the Club be in the hands of a Sub Committee and officers to be appointed by the General Committee.
3.   That the Club be open to non members of the Association whose names shall be subject to the approval of the Subcommittee.
4.   That the Subscription of the season be 2/6d
5.   That the Club colours be amber and black.
6.   That Monday, Wednesday and Friday at 7 o'clock and Saturday afternoon at 3 o'clock shall be recognised for practice. No practice shall be held unless a number of the Sub Committee be present.
7.   That the Captain shall select the team to play in matches subject to the approval of the Sub Committee.
8.   That any Subscriber failing to play in a match after having promised to do so shall be fined 1/- unless the Committee be satisfied with the reason given for his absence.
9.   That the Sub Committee be empowered to expel any subscriber conducting himself in an improper manner.

Y.M.C.A. Minutes 3.3.1882 – 8.9.1884, pp.29 – 31.

APPENDIX IX

Rules of the 'Open Air' Branch

Motto "Do all in the name of the Lord Jesus" Col.III, 17.)

1. That the Committee appoint a leader of this Branch, with whose directions all the workers must comply. Should any member have a grievance he must comply with the leader's directions during the remainder of the Service, but can lodge his complaint with the Sub Committee for the Open Air Branch, who will give the matter due consideration.
2. That speakers be careful always to preach the great truths of the Gospel, and that their addresses be short and definite.
3. That the workers obey the directions of the leader both as to the opening and closing of meetings.
4. That to avoid late hours the recognised time for assembling for the prayer meeting at the Association Rooms be seven o'clock and that the meetings in the open air commence at 7.30 precisely and at the Lodging Houses at 7.15.
5. That to avoid confusion any worker wishing to speak shall first communicate with the leader.
6. That the suggestions (fancied by the Open Air Mission) be strictly followed: viz

1. Do not attempt fine language or artificial manners, but speak in a natural tone and explain and persuade.
2. Study the character of your audience, which will sometimes be a very mixed one, and adapt your address accordingly.
3. Always speak courteously both in preaching to a group and in speaking to individuals.
4. Never resist the police.
5. Avoid noisy singing, unseemly tunes, shouting and ridiculous gestures.
6. If a person wishes to debate, walk and talk with him or get one of your group to do so, or arrange for a private conversation, or if necessary request the postponement of a discussion until after your address is done.
7. Always speak reverently of God and avoid anything trifling in manner. There is much in the open air to disturb serious thought.
8. Do not attempt to make open air preaching so much a source of worship as an evangelistic effort to bring thoughtless and careless persons to give heed to the things of God.
9. Never thrust tracts at persons; but offer them politely to all who may be willing to accept them.
10. When the Open Air Service is finished do not remain gossiping, but if you have occasion to speak to individuals observe suggestion 6.

Qualifications

1. A good Voice
2 Naturalness of manner
3 Self possession
4 A good knowledge of Scripture and of common things.
5 Ability to adapt himself to any congregation.
6 Good illustrative powers.
7 Zeal, prudence and common sense.
8 A large loving heart
9 Sincere belief in all he says.
10 Entire dependence on the Holy Spirit for success.
11 A close walk with God by Prayer
12 A consistent walk before men by a holy life.

Y.M.C.A. Minutes 3.3.1882 – 8.9.1884, pp.40 - 43.

APPENDIX X

Cricket Club Rules 7 April 1884

1. That the Club be called the Young Men's Christian Association Cricket Club.
2. That the management of the Club be in the hands of a Committee of 8 who shall be elected annually at a General Meeting of the members, such Committee to have power to add to their number.
3. That the club be open to non-members of the Association, who shall be elected by ballot of the C.C. Committee 2 black balls to constitute rejection.
4. That the subscription for the season be 5/- (could be 8/-)
5. That the Club colours be plain white with gold monogram on a black ground.
6. That the ground be open for practice every evening at 6 p.m. and on Saturday 2 p.m. but that no practice take place unless a member of the Committee be present.
7. That the Secretary shall select the teams to play in matches subject to the approval of the Captain.
8. That any member failing to play in a match after having promised to do so, be fined 1/- unless the Committee be satisfied with the reason assigned for his absence.
9. That the committee be empowered to expel any member conducting himself in an improper manner.
10. That no Committee Meeting be held unless four of the members be present.
11. That a Committee Meeting be held on the first Wednesday in every month.
12. That the Association Committee shall have full control over all the affairs of the Cricket Club and can at anytime take such steps as they may deem necessary in the interests of the Club.

Y.M.C.A. Minutes 3.3.1882 – 8.9.1884, pp.160 - 1.

APPENDIX XI

Mr. G.H. Lee's Visit to Amsterdam Y.M.C.A. Conference in August 1872.

Mr. Lee … drew a graphic account of his journey to Amsterdam. Embarking at Harwich he arrived at Rotterdam on Tuesday, August 20, and proceeded without delay to Amsterdam, the place of conference. Having reported himself to the Secretary of the Conference in a building called "Diligentle" plans of the city, 13 hymns in polyglot fashion in four languages (Dutch, German, French, and English), and programmes of the proceedings were presented to him. The conference opened almost immediately, and continued for six successive days. The delegates were from many countries – England, Ireland, Scotland, Germany, France, Switzerland, and America, had sent their representatives, and nearly 300 delegates from these various countries had met together in the hope of advancing the eternal happiness of Christian young men throughout the civilised world. The president of the Dutch association was chosen president of the conference. Proceedings were opened each day by singing some hymns, each nationality singing their own words to the same hymn, and then would follow extempore prayer in English, Dutch, French, and German. It was during these impressive scenes, said Mr. Lee, that he experienced the grand realisation of the confusion of tongues, as the good old book says. The time of conference was fully occupied by speeches and reading essays in reference to the mode of treating young men, with the object of making them happy in this world, and eternally happy in the next. For the benefit of English speaking delegates, speeches in foreign tongues were translated off into good English, and here Mr. Lee contrasted the linguistic feats of foreigners as compared with ourselves. He says it was no uncommon thing to meet delegates, French, German, and Dutch, capable of translating and speaking off hand two, three, and even four languages. Much information and many valuable hints were gathered from these essays and speeches. Each speaker or essayist detailed the mode of treating young men in the country or province whence he came. From the Germans it could be gathered that they differed from other associations, inasmuch as they combined healthy recreations of mind and body with food for the soul, nor did they neglect the temporal wants of Christian young men. The German associations were also societies of reference, for if a member went from one town to another, or from one country to another, he would receive letters of introduction. The Dutch were not unlike the German associations, save one exception – they only embraced as members unmarried men; when once married they ceased membership. The aim of the associations in England was unfolded very clearly by an English delegate, Mr. Williams, who said, in an essay of rare ability, that the scope and object of the Young Men's Christian Associations in England, were the salvation of young men, the mixing them in one bond of brotherhood, so as to become missionaries and workers in all departments of Christian labour. The Associations of America differed from those among them other than Christian young men, and had a network of agencies employed, and their direct aim did not appear to be that nature which was the pith and essence of the English Associations. They appeared not only to undertake general evangelical work of all kinds among all classes, but to provide for mental improvement, healthy recreation, and amusement generally. Paid agents were legion amongst them. Mr. Lee gave also some interesting details of the modes of conducting the Dutch Associations – the agencies and difficulties. Many of the means and agencies employed are similar to our own, but the associations are composed of 'younglings," i.e. unmarried men. The Dutch have about 150 societies, with 2,600 members. Prayer meeting are almost wholly unknown; bible classes fortnightly, and members read papers on biblical and other subjects. The associations for the most part are poor. Mr. Lee concluded a most interesting and able address by stating that previous to the departure of the delegates to their various homes and countries, they were invited to dinner by a young man – a Bremen merchant; and whilst assembled for the last time, they, one and all, reaffirmed the Paris basis of action. Thus ended a most remarkable conference in the interest of pure religion and the moral and social good of society.

Surrey Comet Saturday 12 October 1872 p.3.

APPENDIX XII

Surbiton Estimated Population and the Death Percentages At Five Year Intervals

Year	Population (Estimated)	Year	Deaths	Percentage Deaths/ Population
1855	4198	1855	58	1.38
1860	5202	1860	73	1.40
1865	6180	1865	161	2.61
1870	6996	1870	136	1.94
1875	7602	1875	115	1.51
1880	9300	1880	139	1.49
1885	10700	1885	106	0.99

R.W.C Richardson *Thirty-Two years of Local Self-Government 1855 – 1887*, pp.143, 144.

APPENDIX XIII

Extract From Annual Reports of Owen Coleman M.D., Medical Officer of Health 1880

During the latter part of the year we had to deplore two outbreaks of diphtheria, resulting in ten deaths. These outbreaks have been the subject of special reports, and have been fully discussed by your Board, so that it is not necessary for me to do more than briefly allude here to the facts.

The disease commenced during the month of October, and it was found that with-out exception every single house that was invaded had milk from the same dairy. Investigation brought to light the fact that two cases had occurred in the dairyman's house, and that one had ended fatally. The milk supply was stopped, an impure well on the premises closed, and no more cases appeared at that time. Then, with the exception of a single case, probably caused by insanitary conditions, there was an interval of three weeks, when the disease reappeared. This time another dairy was implicated, an overwhelming proportion of the invaded houses being supplied from the same source. Every endeavor was made by the sanitary authorities to ascertain how the milk became infected, and every assistance to that end was afforded by the dairyman and the cow-owner, but without effect.

A communication appeared in the local journal on January 1, advising that all milk should be boiled, and the last case that I am acquainted with was on January 3. Since then I am glad to be able to say no fresh cases have come to my knowledge. In the first outbreak there were 12 cases and two deaths, and in the second 44 cases and nine deaths, but one case having commenced in the new year is not included in the returns for the past year.

Richardson pp.123 - 4

APPENDIX XIV

Statistics of Deaths in Surbiton Compared with London, England and Wales

	1877	1878	1879	1880	1881	1882	1883	1884	1885	1886
Small-pox	0	0	0	0	0	0	0	0	0	0
Measles	8	1	0	0	2	7	0	0	0	1
Scarlet Fever	2	1	0	0	1	0	1	4	0	0
Whopping-cough	2	2	1	5	0	7	0	6	2	1
Diphtheria	0	1	0	10	1	1	0	4	2	0
Fever, typhus	0	0	0	0	0	0	0	0	0	0
Fever, enteric	2	0	0	2	2	2	1	0	0	1
Diarrhoea	4	3	4	3	1	1	2	1	0	5
Sub Total	18	8	5	20	7	18	4	15	4	8
Mortality from phthisis	11	15	14	18	8	5	12	10	12	7
" from other lung disease	14	26	22	31	16	9	15	27	16	27
" from heart disease	12	11	11	6	11	14	14	14	12	8
" cancer	1	5	10	5	6	5	2	1	2	3
" violence	2	6	6	·5	4	1	1	1	1	4
	58	71	68	85	52	52	48	68	47	57
Total deaths	114	112	114	141	100	118	111	125	104	123
Total percentage death-rate	1.26	1.24	1.26	1.43	1.06	1.18	1.08	1.19	0.97	1.14
London	2.15	2.31	2.26	2.17	2.12	2.13	2.04	2.03		
England & Wales	2.03	2.16	2.07	2.06	1.89	1.96	1.95	1.96	1.9	1.93

Richardson p.127

APPENDIX XV

Rules of the Surbiton Young Men's Christian Association

Agreed on 14 July 1882 at Mooresfort, Berrylands.

1. That this Society be called "The Surbiton Young Men's Christian Association."
2. That the object of the Association be the mutual edification of its members and the promotion of the cause of Christ among young men.
3. That the means employed for the attainments of these objects be meetings, for prayer, for the study of the Bible and for other similar purposes.
4. That the arrangement of the Association be vested in a Committee (including Treasurer and 2 Secretaries) who shall be elected annually by a majority of members and that 5 members shall form a quorum for the purpose of such elections.
5. That a Chairman by chosen by the committee for each meeting and that all meetings shall begin and end with prayer.
6. That at all ordinary meetings any young man shall be welcomed but that it shall be in the power of the committee to hold meetings from time to time for members only.
7. That the committee shall have power to suspend or exclude any member whose conduct is considered by them to be inconsistent with the Christian character.
8. That any young man over 15 years of age desirous of becoming a member be proposed by a member of the Association and that the proposal (in writing) be sent to one of the Secretaries for presentation at the next meeting of committee.
9. That the committee be empowered to elect a member after due consideration and enquiry as to his suitability.
10. That the Association be supported by an annual subscription of 1/- from each member payable in advance, and by voluntary contributions.

Accepted at the General Meeting Friday Evening, Surbiton Y.M.C.A. Minutes 14 July 1882

Mooresfort Berrylands.

APPENDIX XVI

2 July 1884

Question "Would any Alteration in the Meeting be conducive to greater success?

1.   that the times of the Sunday afternoon Meetings should be altered to 3 p.m.
2   that the members should be invited to pray
3   that reading round of the passage be dispensed with
4   that difficult subjects contained in the Bible should be considered and that endeavours should be made to secure really first rate speakers
5   that essays should be occasionally read followed by discussion thereon
6   that occasional amalgamations of the various Bible classes should take place if possible
7   that the time of the Sunday morning Prayer Meeting be altered to a more suitable one.
8   that distribution of invitations be made on Saturday evenings &c
9   that steps be taken to enlist sympathy of the Local People.

Minute Book 3 March 1882—8 September 1884, pp.180 - 1

APPENDIX XVII

Rules of the Kingston and Surbiton District Young Men's Christian Association 1 July 1885

Basis:

The Young Men's Christian Association seeks to Unite those Young Men, who, regarding the Lord Jesus Christ as their God and Saviour according to the Holy Scriptures, desire to be his disciples in their doctrine and thief life, and to associate their efforts for the extension of his kingdom amongst Young Men.

RULES OF THE ASSOCIATION

1. That this Association be called the "Kingston and Surbiton District Young men's Christian Association.'

2. That the object of the Association be the improvement of the spiritual, social, and mental condition of young men.

3. That the Agencies employed for the attainment of this object be the personal efforts of the Members of the Association in the sphere of their daily calling, Devotional Meetings, Classes for Biblical Instruction, and for Literary Improvement, the delivery of Lectures, the diffusion of Christian Literature, Libraries for reference and circulation, and any other means in accordance with the Holy Scriptures.

4. That all Meetings of the Association be commenced and closed with prayer.

5. That the management of the Association be vested in a Committee to consist of 15 Members of the Association, who shall be elected annually by a majority of the Members in such manner as may be deemed advisable, and that the result of such elections be declared at a General Meeting of Members to be held during the month of June or as soon after as can be conveniently arranged. Of the members so elected not less than 6 shall be resident in the Kingston and not less than six in the Surbiton District.

6. That the President, Treasurer, and General Secretary be ex-officio Members of the Committee. That the number to constitute a quorum shall be eight, three of whom must be members resident in the Kingston and three in the Surbiton District.

7. That in the event of the removal or resignation of any of the Committee, it be in the power of the Committee to fill up vacancies.

8. That an annual Meeting be held early in each year, at which a report be given of the proceedings of the Association.

9. That at all ordinary Meetings any young man shall be welcomed, but that it shall be in the power of the Committee to hold Meetings from time to time for Members only.

10. That any young man over 15 years of age be eligible for Membership upon giving satisfactory evidence of his conversion to God.

11. That any one desirous of becoming a Member be proposed by a Member of the Association, and that the proposal (in writing) be sent to the General Secretary for presentation at the next Meeting of the Committee, who shall be empowered to elect Members after due consideration and enquiry as to their suitability.

12   That the Committee be empowered, to suspend or exclude any Member whose conduct is found, in their judgment, to be inconsistent with his Christian profession, but that such member shall have the right of appeal to the general body of members.

13   That young men over 15 years of age, and of good moral character, be admitted as Associates on payment of a fixed subscription, entitling them to all the privileges of Membership, except the right of voting at Meetings, that the Associates subscription be fixed at 2/6 per annum.

14   That the Association be supported by an annual Minimum Subscription of four shillings from each Member, payable in advance or quarterly, and by voluntary contributions.

N.B. The Committee are empowered to exercise their discretion in remitting part or whole of the subscription due from any Member who may be sick or otherwise unable to contribute.

Minute Book Kingston and Surbiton 9 May 1885 – 5 December 1887, pp.18 - 9

Founder Members of the Y.M.C.A. in 1874

Age	Meeting Date					
	10.1.1874	21.1.1874	11.2.1874	20.5.1874	17.6.1874	14.7.1874
19	l. Stringer	L. Stringer	E.L. Stringer	E.L. Stringer	E.L. Stringer	
22	J. Newson	J. Newson	J. Newson	J. Newson	J. Newson	J. Newson
22	J. Morten					
23	F. Lardelli	F. Lardelli	F. Lardelli		F. Lardelli	
36	H. Rimer	H. Rimer	H. Rimer	H. Rimer		
29	H. Maxwell	W. Maxwell				Maxwell
23	H.J. Hapgood	H.J. Hapgood				
	J. Dale				W.A. Fitzpatrick	W. Wallis
	H. Carter	H. Carter	H. Carter			G. Siggers
						R. Wright

Table 1.

Kingston Committee — October 1879 — September 1880

Age	Forename	Surname	Occupation	Address
44	William	Bowskill	London City Missionary	Gibbon Road
31	Frank	Hertslet	Officer Metropolitan Board of Works	Eden Street
19	Walter Th.	Lea	Tutors Assistant	The Laurels, London Street.
22	Frank	Newson	Shipbroker's Clerk	Knights Park
20	William H.	Parlow	Solicitor's General Clerk (Law)	Oak Lea Passage
16	Rutland	Saunders	Clerk	Alexandra Road
64	Charles	Sparkes	House Proprietor	Cambridge Cot. Tudor Road
25	William	Walter	Solicitor	No.11, St. James Road, Surbiton
67	Edward Pope	Williams	Retired Publisher	Surbiton Road

Table 2.

Kingston Committee — September 1880 — September 1881

45	William	Bowskill	London City Missionary	Gibbon Road
18	Robert	Buchanan	Bank Clerk	Ardoch House,Langley Road
19	S. Herbert	Fry	Manager to Photographic Artist	Grove Crescent
25	Alfred	Gaydon	Watchmaker	Thames Street
32	Frank	Hertslet	Officer Metropolitan Board of Works	Eden Street
20	Walter Th.	Lea	Tutors Assistant	The Laurels, London Street
23	Frank	Newson	Shipbroker's Clerk	Knights Park
21	William H.	Parslow	Solicitor's General Clerk (Law)	Oak Lea Passage
26	William	Walter	Solicitor	No. 11 St. James Rd. Surbiton

Table 3.

Kingston Committee September 1881 — June 1882

46 William	Bowskill	London City Missionary	Gibbon Road
19 Robert	Buchanan	Bank Clerk	Ardoch House,Langley Road
26 Alfred	Gaydon	Watchmaker	Thames Street
18 Bedford	Marsh	Articled Clerk to Solicitor	Cadogan House Cadogan Road
24 Frank	Newson	Shipbroker's Clerk	Knights Park
22 William H.	Parslow	Solicitor's General Clerk (Law)	Oak Lea Passage
23 William	Sessions	Mercantile Clerk Tuto (Teacher)	1 Agincourt Villas, London Road
27 William	Walter	Solicitor's Heneral Clerk (Law)	No. 11 St. James Road, Surbiton
27 George Vincent	Wright	Solicitor	Shrublands, Park Lane, West Croydon

Table 4.

Kingston Committee July 1882—June 1883

47	William	Bowskill	London City Missionary	Gibbon Road
20	Robert	Buchanan	Bank Clerk	Ardoch House,Langley Road
27	Alfred	Gaydon	Watchmaker	Thames Street
19	Bedford	Marsh	Articled Clerk to Solicitor	Cadogan House Cadogan Road
25	Frank	Newson	Shipbroker's Clerk	Knights Park
23	William H.	Parslow	Solicitor's General Clerk (Law)	Hope Cottage, Richmond Park
24	William	Sessions	Mercantile Clerk Tuto (Teacher)	1 Agincourt Villas, London Road
28	William	Walter	Solicitor's Heneral Clerk (Law)	No. 11 St. James Road, Surbiton
28	George Vincent	Wright	Solicitor	7, Southbridge Place, Croydon

Table 5.

Kingston Committee July 1883 — June 1884

23	Jas. Henry	Coulthwaite	Printer Compositor	Smithers Cott. Church Road, N.
28	Alfred	Gaydon	Watchmaker	Thames Street
31	Walter G.	Gratton	Booksellers Assistant	Kings Road
26	Frank	Newson	Shipbroker's Clerk	Suffolk Cottage, Knights Park
24	William H.	Parslow	Solicitor' General Clerk (Law)	Oaklea Passage
18	Frank	Pittam		Devon House, Eden Street
25	William H.	Sessions	Mercantile Clerk Tutor (Teacher)	1 Agincourt Villas, London Road
28	William	Walter	Member of the Stock Exchange	No. 11 St. James Rd. Surbiton
20	Wise	Alfred	Telegraphist Cl.	1 Elm Terrace, Elm Road.

Table 6.

Kingston Committee July 1884 – June 1885

	Oliver	Britton		4, Church Street
18	J.W,	Colverson	Railway Clerk	Norbiton
29	Alfred	Gaydon	Watchmaker	Thames Street
16	Charles	Knapp	Student	Clarence Street
25	William H.	Parslow	Solicitor' General Clerk (Law)	Oaklea Passage
27	Edward	Salisbury	Clerk	1, Springfield Road
23	Philip	Salisbury	Clerk	1, Springfield Road
26	William H.	Sessions	Mercantile Clerk Tutor (Teacher)	1 Agincourt Villas, London Road
21	Wise	Alfred	Telegraphist Cl.	1 Elm Terrace, Elm Road.

Table 7.

Surbiton Committee 1871—1872

35	George H.	Lee	Accountant Official Trustee Dept.	Worple Road, Wimbledon
37	Benjamin	Eve	Grocer (Master)	Alpha Road
55	George	Foot	Linen Draper	Berrylands Road
41	Joseph	Friend	Linen Draper	Ewell Road
32	Finlay	Gibson	Tutor in Classic/ Mathematics	The Laurels, London Road South
26	William	Maxwell	Law Publisher	Berrylands Road
40	George A.	Mills	Banker's Clerk	Adelaide Road
48	Charles E.	Norton	Clerk to Colonial Merchants	Cadogan Road
30	George	Parfitt	Mason	Victoria Road
48	Samuel Benjamin	Poole	Florist and Seedsman	Alpha Road
42	Peter	Lake	Annuitant	4,Cisiter Cottages, Ewell Road
33	John	King	Gardener (Servant)	4 Paragon Place

Table 8.

Surbiton Committee — May 1882

60	George	Cavell	Stockbroker	Grantham, Ewell Road
64	James A.	Strachan	Stockbroker	Penrhyn, Victoria Road
20	Thomas D.	MacDonald	Carpenter	6, Alpha Road
27	A.W.	Maxwell	Clerk Insurance	Highfield, The Avenue
22	George	Walker	Bank Clerk	Mooresfort, Berrylands.
20/59	Robert	Buchanan	Bank Clerk/ Manager	Ardoch House, Langley Road.
54	William	Charles	Carpenter	5 Cisiter Cottages, Ewell Road.
32	Joseph	French	Clerk Insurance	67, Alpha Road
	James A.	Godfrey		
26	Joseph	Kitt	Colporteur	21, Browns Road
30	John S.	Morten	Mealman	Frascati, St. James Road
32	William	Webb	Schoolmaster	No.2 Hill Vill Berrylands Road

Table 9. It is uncertain whether the Robert Buchanan who sat on this committee was the 20 year old Bank Clerk or his 59 year old father the Bank Manager.

Kingston and Surbiton Committee 1885–1886

18/57	William	Charles	Stationer/ Carpenter	5 Cisiter Cottages, Ewell Road
29	George	Clements	Solicitor	Lawn Lodge, Clarence Street
30	Alfred	Gaydon	Watchmaker	Thames Street, Kingston
33	John S.	Morten	Mealman	Frascati, St. James Road.
28	Frank	Newson	Shipbuilder's Clerk	Knights Park
70	Henry T.	Northcroft	Building Surveyor	Glenroy, The Avenue
26	William H.	Parslow	Solicitor's Clerk	Hope Cott., Richmond Park Rd.
22	Arthur	Passey	Bronze Metal Worker	Woodside Cottage, Tolworth.
32	George	Poole	Mercantile Clerk	9, Paragon Terrace.
40	Harry	Rushworth	Builder	1 Matilda Villa, Ewell Rd.
28	Edward	Salisbury	Clerk	Alexandra Road
24	Philip	Salisbury	Clerk	Alexandra Road
25	George M.	Walker	Bank Clerk	Moorefort, Berrylands
36	William Hy	Webb	Schoolmaster	Alpha Road
22	Alfred	Wise	Telegraphist CL	1, Elm Terrace, Elm Road, Kingston.

Table 10. It is uncertain whether the William Charles who sat on this committee was the 18 year old Stationer or his 57 year old father the Carpenter

Kingston and Surbiton Committee June 1889 – May 1890

18	Arthur	Babbs	Builder's Clerk	22, Warwick Grove, Surbiton
38	William B.	Browne	Carpenter	10 Albert Road, Norbiton
21	Charles	Creed	Upholsterer	Victoria Road, North
24	Frederick	Fry	Plummer and Gasfitter	Oilnill Lane Kingston
48	Joseph	Grindley	Patent Firefighter Manu.	124, Acre Road, Kingston
36	James F.	Hayward	Carver Gilder/ Frameworker	29 Victoria Road
33	Walter	Hoare	Hatter	6 Thames Street, Kingston
	George	Jolly		Walpole Villa, Worthington Road
24	John W	Langford	Corn Merchants Assistant	c/o Messrs. Marsh, Market Pl. ,Kingston
37	William	Lewis	Dealer Toys and Games	58 High Street, Kingston
36	John W	Morten	Salesman	Frascati, Surbiton
74	Henry T.	Northcroft	Building Surveyor	Glenroy, The Avenue, Surbiton
42	Frederick	Pitts	Merchant	Salvadore, Liverpool Road, Kingston Hill
30	George M.	Walker	Stockbroker	Carfax, King Charles Road.

Table 11. Officers—Sir Douglas Fox; W. Charles; W.H. Parslow.

Kingston and Surbiton Committee June 1890 – May 1891

19	Arthur	Babbs	Builder's Clerk	22, Warwick Grove, Surbiton
28	Albert J.	Ballen	Florist	Hill Cottage, Berrylands Road, Surbiton
22	George C.	Bristow	Assistant in Coal	London Street, Kingston
39	William B.	Browne	Carpenter	10, Albert Road, Norbiton
23	Charles E.	Creed	Upholsterer	4 Masons Cottages, Victoria Road, Norbiton
32	Charles E.	Crook	Grocer's Assistant	c/o Mr. Grace, 3 Victoria Road, Surbiton
22	Henry	Grantham	Wheelwright	79 Richmond Park Road, Kingston
17	David	Hallett	Articled Pupil Architect	1 Laurel Villa, Ashdown, Kingston
22	Henry W.	Kedge	Carpenter	3 Crooks Cottage, Victoria Road, Norbiton
38	John	Morten	Salesman	Frascati, Surbiton
74	Henry T.	Northcroft	Building Surveyor	Glenroy, The Avenue, Surbiton
33	Henry	Pharo	Gas Engineer and Lamp Manu.	Overdale, Manorgate Road, Norbiton
43	Frederick	Pitts	Merchant	Salvadore, Liverpool Road, Kingston Hill
	A.W.	Smart		71, Canbury Park Road, Kingston
31	George M.	Walker	Stockbroker	Carfax, King Charles Road, Surbiton.

Table 12. Officers – Sir Douglas Fox; W. Charles; W.H. Parslow.

Committee Members included in the Tables without age and occupation were found in the Minutes but not on the Census.

NOTES

1. *The Fifth Report of the Surbiton Young Men's Christian Association for the Spiritual Improvement of Young Men 1871-72,* (Kingston: Knapp, Steam Printer, 1872), p.10.

2. C. Binfield, *George Williams and the Y.M.C.A: A Study in Victorian Social Attitudes,* (London: Heinemann, 1973), pp.11-23.

3. E.T. MacDermot, *Great Western Railway, (1927). Volume 1 1833-1863,* "Appendix 1" (London: Reprinted Ian Allan: 1982), pp.130-1, <// en.wikipedia.org/wiki/ Great_Western_Railway#cite_note-12> (Retrieved 18.8.2012).

4. Binfield p.261.

5. *Y.M.C.A. Minute Book January 1874 to September 1879,* p.1, p.9.

6. *Surrey Comet* (SC) 1.6.1861, p.4; 12.10.1867,p.4.

7. *Kingston and Surbiton District Young Men's Christian Association 27th Annual Report, 1899-1900,* (Knapp Typ. Kingston, Surbiton and Wimbledon), p.15.

8. K. Tiller, *English Local History,* (Gloucestershire Alan Sutton Publishing, 1992), p.1.

9. Tiller, p.171.

10. J. Tosh, *The Pursuit of History,* 3rd. ed. (Harrow: Longman, 2000), pp.6-8..

11. History in Focus: The Open University, - What is History? Arthur Marwick, The Fundamentals of History, <www.history.ac.uk/ihr/Focus/ Whatishistory/marwick1.html> (Retrieved 6.2.2012)

12. C. Surman, The Surman Index On-Line, <www.english.qmul.ac.uk/drwilliams/surman/ intro.html> (Retrieved 8.3.2015).

13. A.C. Sturney, *The Story of Kingston Congregational Church,* (Stourbridge: Mark & Moody, 1955), p.34.

14. Sturney, p. 34.

15. SC. 27.9.1862, p.4.

16. E.E. Cleal, *The Story of Congregationalism in Surrey,* (London: James Clarke & Co., 1908), pp. 188-9; Isaac Watts 1674-1748 wrote 600 hymns including "Our God, Our Help in Ages Past". The hymn with the words 'Nor fear the wrath of Rome and Hell,' is entitled 'God the glory and defence of Sion' <//www.wholesomewords.org/ biography/biorpwatts.html> (Retrieved 4.9.2012).

17. Cheshunt College catered for students of any non-conformist denomination, was strongly evangelical and over time became associated particularly with the Congregationalist ministry. <www.british-history.ac.uk/report.aspx? compid=66624> (Retrieved 27.4.2011).

18. SC 11.2.1860, p. 4; 8.5.1869, p. 5.

19. William Paley, (1743-1805), was a philosopher-natural-theologian, who argued that the nature of God could be understood through his creation, the natural world. Born in Peterborough, Northamptonshire, he graduated from Christ's College, University of Cambridge, in 1763, returning as a tutor three years later. He later became Archdeacon of Carlisle and Canon of St. Paul's.' At Christ's College, the portraits of Paley, Milton and Darwin hang together as they all graduated from the same College. William Paley's *Evidences* was required reading for Theology students at Cambridge University. It is not known whether it was at Cheshunt College but because of Byrne's enthusiasm for Paley's work this seems probable. <www.wmcarey.edu/carey/paley/ paley.htm> (Retrieved 12.6.2011); Hart, T.E., The Victorian Web, Natural Theology of Paley, <http://www.ucmp.berkeley.edu/history/ paley.html> (Retrieved 27.4.2015)

20. Butters S., *That Famous Place: A History Of Kingston Upon Thames*, (Kingston: Kingston University Press, 2013), pp.208-19.
The current Surbiton Station was opened in 1838 and was at first called 'New Kingston Station,' until the line reached Kingston in 1863. The terminology 'Pastoral Office' is used in the Minutes of the Church written on January 23, 1851.
21 S. Butters, *The Book of Kingston*, (Oxon: Barron Birch for Quotes, Finmere 1995), pp.89-110.
22. A.C. Giles, *The Failure of a Speculative Builder: The Downfall of Thomas Pooley of Surbiton, 1838-1844*, (Issue 1. 2000, Occasional Paper, Number 1/03, Centre for Local History Studies, Kingston upon Thames).
A.C. Giles, Audrey C., Surbiton: The Development of a Middle Class Suburb, (M.A. dissertation, Kingston University 2002).
23 P. Reading , Reluctant Reformers: Politics and Society in Kingston upon Thames, 1830-1900, (PhD thesis, Kingston University, 2008), pp.73-4.
24 J.R. Davis, *The Great Exhibition*, (Gloucestershire: Sutton Publishing Ltd., 1999), book cover, pp.134-8, 170-7. Davis writes that before passports it was difficult to know how many people came into Britain. It has been estimated that in the three years before the Great Exhibition there had been an annual average of around 21,500 foreigners entering the country..
25 Binfield, pp.172-3; P. Bayless, *The Y.M.C.A. at 150: A History of the YMCA of Greater New York, 1852-2002*, (YMCA of Greater New York: 2002), pp.1-3.
26 Sturney, p. 34.
27 It is unknown where the church in Cobham stood as the current Cobham United Reformed Church was only formed in 1962. Cobham United Reformed Church, About us

<http://www.cobhamurc.org.uk/about-us/> (Retrieved 27.4.2015)
The 'Tea Meeting'is recorded in Kingston United Reformed Church Minutes October 5, 1855, (Kingston U.R.C. Eden Street, Kingston).
28 Cleal, pp.189.
29 M. Freeman, *Railways and the Victorian Imagination*, (London: Yale University Press, 1999), p. 58.
30 R. Chambers, *Vestiges of the Natural History of Creation: The Bodies of Space, Their Arrangements and Formation*, <www.gutenberg.org/dirs/etext04/vstc10h.htm> (Retrieved 8.12.2011); *Vestiges of the Natural History of Creation*, //en.wikipedia.org/wiki/Vestiges_of_the_Natural_History_of_Creation#cite_note-Darwin (Retrieved 2.3.2013).
31 Walter E. Houghton, *The Victorian Frame of Mind 1830-1870*, (New Haven and London: Yale University Press, 1957), pp.58-9.
32 SC. 1.6.1861, p.4; SC. 12.10.1867, p.4.
33 I am grateful to John Fisher, Kingston United Reformed Church archivist, for this information.
34 SC. 1.6.1861, p.4.
35 SC. 24.5.1862, p.4.
36 SC. 21.6.1862, p.4.
37 SC. 5.7.1862, p.4.
38 W.Y. Fullerton, The Spurgeon Archive, *Charles Haddon Spurgeon: A Biography*, Spurgeon's College, <http://www.spurgeon.org/misc/bio11.htm> (Retrieved 11.9.2012).
39 Spurgeon's College is currently situated at 189, South Norwood Hill, SE25 6DJ.
40 The Spurgeon Archive.
41 SC. 15.1.1859, p.4.
42 SC. 28.5.1859, p.4.
43 SC. 28.5.1859, p.4.
44 SC. 6.6.1863, p.4; 25.7.1863, p.4.
45 SC. 17.9.1859, p.4.

46 Binfield, p.65.

47 Binfield, p.71.

48 Binfield, p.65.

49 Found on the 1861 census.

50 Binficld, pp.155-6.

51 SC. 17.9.1859, p.4.

52 SC. 10.9.1859, p.4.

53 SC. 17.9.1859, p.4.

54 SC. 24.9.1859, p.4.

55 SC.22.9.1860, p.4.

56 SC. 3.11.1860, p.4.

57 SC 1.6.1861, p.4.

58 R. F. Holmes, *Pubs, Inns and Taverns of Kingston,* (Wildhern Press: 2009), p.146.

59 Binfield, p.267; Bournemouth YMCA Christian Faith in Action <http://www.bournemouthymca.org.uk/about-us/history-of-the-ymca/> (Retrieved 23.2.3014).

60 World YMCA Empowering Young People <http://www.ymca.int/who-we-are/mission/paris-basis-1855> (Retrieved13.9.2012); Binfield, p.161.

61 Binfield, pp.267-8

62 SC 27.9.1862, p.4.

63 The writer is grateful to Dr. Christopher French for this information.

64 James Morgan Strachan grave monument details, grave number 162438 St Mary with St Alban's Church Teddington, <http://www.gravestonephotos.com> (Retrieved 5.12.2012).

65 SC. 27.9.1862, p.4.

66 SC. 28.4.1877 p.5.

67 SC. 27.9.1862, p.4.

68 SC. 31.1.1863 p.1.

69 SC. 5. 4. 1864 p.1.

70 Figures collated from Reports mentioned in the Surrey Comet newspaper.

71 Feldman, D., 'Migration', in Dauntion, M., (ed) *The Cambridge Urban History of Britain, Volume III*

1840-1950, (Cambridge: Cambridge University Press, 2000), p.185.

72 M. Dawn, John de Fraine, The Family Tree Forum. has been replaced by *The Autobiography of John De Fraine: Or Forty Years of Public Lecturing Work.* <https://archive.org/details/autobiographyjo))faigoog> (Retrieved 8.3.2015).

73 S.C. 21.3.1863, p.4.

74 SC 26.9.1863, p.4.

75 Power, Politics & Protest: The Growth of Political Rights in Britain in the 19th Century, The National Archives <http://www.nationalarchives.gov.uk/education/politics/g7/> (Retrieved 23.9.2012); History Zone Chartist Lives: Henry Vincent <https://richardjohnbr.wordpress.com/2007/09/05/chartist-lives-henry-vincent> (Retrieved 4 6.2011).;John Taylor writes 'In 1848, he (Vincent) lectured for the Peace Society. Vincent's own religious sympathies were with the Society of Friends, though he was never formally received into membership. In addition to his public lectures, his strong advocacy of the North in the American Civil War made him a welcome visitor when he arrived in the United States.'

76 SC. 30.1.1864, p.4.

77 SC. 9.4.1864, p.4.

78 SC. 6.8.1864, p.4; 15.10.1864, p.4.

79 Garibaldi was an Italian revolutionary who united Italy.

80 Garibaldi in London - Karl Blind, in F*raser's Magazine*, Published in *The New York Times* October 8, 1882, <http://www.nytimes.com/> (Retrieved 8.3.2015).

81 Alessandro Gavazzi - <http://en.wikipedia.org/wiki/Alessandro_Gavazzi > (Retrieved 3.11.2012 14:33.)

82 SC 12.11.1864, p.1.

83 Alessandro Gavazzi, Wikipedia.

84 SC 6.11.1865, p.4.

85 SC. 12.10.1867, p.4.

86 SC 29.9.1866, p.4.

87 Reading, pp.101-2.

88 R.W.C. Richardson, *Thirty-Two Years of Local Self-Government, 1855-1887,* (Surbiton: Bull and Son, Victoria Road, 1888), pp.18-21.

89 Reading, p.101.

90 Reading, p.99.

91 A. Giles, *Surbiton: The Development of a Middle Class Suburb,* Unpublished Kingston University M.A. Dissertation, (2002); Census 1861 - 1891.

92 SC. 6.10.1866, p.4.

93 Reading, p.99.

94 SC. 12.10.1867, p.4.

95 SC. 14.11.1868, p.4.

96 SC. 19.12.1868, p.4.

97 SC. 1.5.1869 , p.5.

98 Sturney, p.38.

99 Sturney, p.38.

100 SC. 14.3.1868, p.4.

101 SC. 16.9.1871, p.3.

102 SC. 19.2.1876, p.3. A small notice at the bottom of the page announced that Lydia Byrnes had recently died, a date was not given.

103 Congregational Churches and Churches of Bristol, based on research by Neil Marchant, <http:// www.churchcrawler.pwp.blueyonder.co.uk/ htm.> (Retrieved 24.10.2012 14:01).

104 Cleal, pp.188-90.

105 Binfield, pp.262-3.

106 SC. 26.2.1870, p. 2.

107 Houghton pp.102-6: SC 2.8.1870: The History of Phrenology, John van Wyhe, History & Philosophy of Science, Cambridge University. <http://www.victorianweb.org/science/ phrenology/intro.html> (Retrieved 7.8.2011). It was believed that by examining the shape and unevenness of a head or skull, one could discover the development of the particular cerebral 'organs' responsible for different intellectual aptitudes and character traits.

108 SC. 2.4 1870, p.2.

109 SC. 22.10.1870, p.2.

110 SC. 7.1.1871, p.1.

111 Urban Dictionary, Penny Readings, These were entertainments consisting of readings, singing, piano playing by local people coming together in a hall, the price of admission being a penny. They commenced in 1859, and were common but are now less heard of, Victorian London – Publications <http:// www.victorianlondon.org/publications/ habits-10.htm> (Retrieved 1.6.2015). It has been said that they were introduced into Kingston by the Y.M.C.A. in September 1866. However in March 1866 the Congregational Schools were entertained by 'Poets and Humerists of America,' the event being entitled 'Penny Readings,' S.C. 31.3.1866 p.4. The Association only held them once, as they were considered non-spiritual and the members were criticized for starting them.

112 SC. 25.11.1871, p.3.

113 Obituary – William Edwyn Shipton, <http:// www.nytimes.com/> (Retrieved 8.3.2015).

114 Bernd W. Hildebrandt, It Can Be! 150 Years German YMCA in London 1860 – 2010 < http:// www.german-ymca.org.uk/about-us-history.html> (Retrieved 9.3.2015)

115 Binfield, pp.128-9.

116 Binfield, pp.273-5.

117 SC 1.6.1861, p.4.

118 Binfield, p.278-9.

119 SC. 16.7.1864, p 4.

120 Binfield, p.286-7.

121 Bayless, pp.21-2.

122. Bayless, p.9.

123 SC. 2.12.1871 p.4.

124 SC. 5.9.1874, p.3.

125 SC. 6.10.1877, p.3.

126 Binfield, pp.278-83.

127 SC. 30.10.1880 p.3.

128 Y.M.C.A. Minutes 10.1.1874 – 25.9.1879, p.11.

129 Y.M.C.A. Minutes 10.1.1874 – 25.9.1879, pp. 10-1.

130 Y.M.C.A. Minutes 10.1.1874 – 25.9.1879, pp. 41-2.

131 Y.M.C.A. Minutes 10.1.1874 – 25.9.1879, pp. 1-2.

132 Reading, p.82-3, Butters p.137.

133 Y.M.C.A. Minutes 10.1.1874 – 25.9.1879, pp. 1-10.

134 *Kingston Young Men's Christian Association Memoirs in the Centenary year 1874-1979*, YMCA Archive.

135 List of Members, Number 1. P. 1., Y.M.C.A. Archive.

136 The 1881 census shows Frank Hertslet as Frank Hunslet. His occupation is listed on the census as 'Officer Metropolitan Board of Works.'

137 Y.M.C.A. Minutes 10.1.1874-25.9.1879, P. 13.

138 Y.M.C.A. Minutes 10.1.1874-25.9.1879, p.13.

139 Y.M.C.A. Minutes 10.1.1874-25.9.1879, pp. 14-6.

140 Y.M.C.A. Minutes 10.1.1874-25.9.1879, pp. 21-2.

141 Y.M.C.A. Minutes 10.1.1874-25.9.1879, pp. 27-30.

142 Sturney, p.14; *Phillipson's Almanack and Directory 1876* lists Zoar Chapel as the first building in Brick Lane east from Eden Street, whilst the 1880 Edition refers to this building as the Y.M.C.A. Ayliffe looks at Brick Lane from the other direction. He writes, 'Next to the Watch House was the old Baptist Chapel, which was an extremely uninviting building, very different from the present handsome structure…Beyond the chapel was Ash's cooperage and Leney's dairy, and then came a garden belonging to Mr. Walker, of the Apple-market, and a building rented by Mr. Warren, of Hampton Court, who for many years conducted religious services there. This building was the first home of the Y.M.C.A. in Kingston, and ultimately came into the possession of Mr. C. Burrows,' p.27. The new

Baptist Chapel was built during the 1860s, the Y.M.C.A. took the lease on Zoar Chapel in 1876.

143. Holmes, pp.146-8.

144 Some of Mr. Burrows' neighbours both in 1881 and 1891 remain in the same locations, giving the impression that he had not moved premises. It is possible that Mr. Burrows shop backed onto the side of the Y.M.C.A. Rooms. Details of his renting the cellars is in Minute Book, May 1885-December 1887 pp.94-95, 102.

145 Y.M.C.A. Minutes 10.1.1874-25.9.1879, pp. 31-2.

146 Y.M.C.A. Minutes 10.1.1874-25.9.1879, p.34.

147 Bayless, pp.24-5.

148 Y.M.C.A. Minutes 10.1.1874-25.9.1879, p.38.

149 Y.M.C.A. Minutes 10.1.1874-25.9.1879, p.38.

150 Y.M.C.A. Minutes 10.1.1874-25.9.1879, pp. 103-4.

151 Y.M.C.A. Minutes 10.1.1874-25.9.1879, pp.33, 92, 107.

152 Y.M.C.A. Minutes 13.6.1882-3.2.882, pp.101, 106.

153 Y.M.C.A. Minutes 10.1.1874-25.9.1879, p.35.

154 Y.M.C.A. Minutes 10.1.1874-25.9.1879, PP.41-6.

155 SC. 10.3.1877, P. 3; Y.M.C.A. Minutes 10.1.1874-25.9.1879, p.44.

156 Y.M.C.A. Minutes 10.1.1874-25.9.1879, p.49.

157 Y.M.C.A. Minutes 10.1.1874-25.9.1879, pp.62, 77.

158 Y.M.C.A. Minutes 10.1.1874-25.9.1879, p.52.

159 Y.M.C.A. Minutes 10.1.1874-25.9.1879, p.67.

160 Y.M.C.A. Minutes 10.1.1874-25.9.1879, p.77.

161 Y.M.C.A. Minutes 10.1.1874-25.9.1879, pp. 68-71.

162 Y.M.C.A. Minutes 10.1.1874-25.9.1879, pp. 73-88.

163 Y.M.C.A. Minutes 10.1.1874-25.9.1879, p.95.

164 Y.M.C.A. Minutes, 2.10.79-3.2.82 pp.1-3.

165 Y.M.C.A. Minutes 2.10.79-3.2.82, p.8.

166 The London City Mission was founded in May 1835 by David Nasmith. Sharing Jesus Christ with all London, Our History, <http://www.infed.org/socialaction/london_city_mission.htm> (Retrieved 8.3.2015).

167 SC. 20.12.1873, p.3: C. French,'Housing the middle classes in late Victorian and Edwardian Surbiton,' *The Local Historian: Journal of the British Association for Local History,* vol. 45 (2) April 2015, pp. 128–136: A.C. Giles, *Surbiton: The Development of a Middle Class Suburb,* (M.A. dissertation, Kingston University 2002).

168 Butters, *The Book of Kingston,* pp.122-5;

169 YMCA Minutes 2.10.79-3.2.1982, pp.3, 5.

170 The Open-Air Mission was started in Holborn, London in 1853 by a barrister called John MacGregor, <http://www.oamission.com/index.html> (Retrieved 14.12.2011).

171 SC. 9.11.1878, p.3.

172 Y.M.C.A. 2.10.79-3.2.82, p.5.

173 SC. 4.10.1879 p.2,

174 SC. 15.9.1883, p3.

175 YMCA Minutes 2.10.79 – 3.2.81, p13.

176 YMCA Minutes 2.10.79 – 3.2.81, pp.10-1.

177 YMCA Minutes 2.10.79 – 3.2.81, pp.15-6.

178 YMCA Minutes 2.10.79 – 3.2.81, p.23.

179 YMCA Minutes 2.10.79 – 3.2.81, pp.25-30.

180 YMCA Minutes 2.10.79 – 3.2.81, pp.32-40.

181 Binfield, p.274.

182 SC 19.12.1868, p.4. The Vicar of Kingston would have been the vicar of All Saints Church in Kingston Market Place. From the 10 April 1867 until his death on the 26 April 1877 this would have been the Rev. Alfred Williams.

183 History of the National Secular Society, <http://www.secularism.org.uk/about.html> (Retrieved 8.3.2015)

184 U.C.L. Bentham Project, 'Who Was Jeremy Bentham?' http://www.ucl.ac.uk/Bentham-Project/who (Retrieved 7.7.2014): Born in 1748 Bentham was a child prodigy who at the age of twelve entered Queen's College Oxford as a student. Throughout most of his life, his aim was to test and re-evaluate the usefulness of existing institutions, practices and beliefs. At the time of his death in 1832 he had become a respected figure although his work, tens of thousands of manuscripts, remained mostly unpublished. He also left a large estate which financed the new University College, London, allowing university

education to non-conformists, Catholics and Jews.

185 V.A.C. Gatrell, Introduction, *Robert Owen, Report to the County of Lanark: A New View of Society* (London: Pelican, 1970), p.41; T. Hindle, Robert Owen, *The Economist,* <http://www.economist.com/node/12499674> (Retrieved 18.3.2015). Born in 1771, by his late twenties Robert Owen had become a partner and manager of a cotton mill in New Lanark on the River Clyde. A 'benevolent entrepreneur', he educated the factory children, shortened labour hours and improved working conditions. Instead of showing a loss his mill showed very large annual returns. Visitors included the future Tsar of Russia, Bentham and despite Owen dismissing all religion as false, the Archbishop of Canterbury, and William Wilberforce. From 1813 he started to urge his ideas not only on the ruling classes of Britain but also on those in Europe and America. After the collapse of his model cooperative community "New Harmony' in America he returned home. His ideas spread through the trade unions and in 1844 a movement was started in Lancashire that developed into the modern Co-operative Movement.

186 E.P. Thompson *The Making of the English Working Class,* Reprint, (Harmondsworth: Penguin, 1974), pp. 814-6, 818, 830-31, 838-46. Richard Carlile was born into poverty in 1790, and was fortunate in receiving education from a Church of England school, but it was poverty that took him later to political meetings and a career in publishing a radical newspaper. He was to write an eye witness report of the details of the Peterloo Massacre on August 16, 1819, describing how the cavalry with sabres drawn had charged a demonstration killing eleven people and injuring about four hundred. His criticism of the government resulted in his being sentenced under the 'seditious libel laws.' He supported many working class issues including women's rights and the campaign against child labour and spent

the last few years of his life again in extreme poverty, dying in 1843

187 *Parish Records, Vestry Books Esher 1809-1852,* Surrey Record Office. Esher is approximately five miles south west of Kingston.

188 Butters, *The Book of Kingston,* pp.89-110.

189 SC. 30.1.1864, p.4.

190 SC. 16.1.1869, p. 5; *The Bible,* Genesis, Chapters 6-9, commonly called the Story of Noah's Ark and the Flood. It appears probable that the discussion about the Noachian Deluge took place at one of the London Associations as there is no mention of this in connection with the Kingston movement. . Noah and the Flood are mentioned in Rabbinic Judaism, Christianity, Islam and in other religions, the story dates back many thousands of years to an actual flood that covered a wide area of the then known world. For more detail see: *The Westminster Dictionary of the Bible,* (London: Collins, 1944) pp.429-30.

191 The National Secular Society, <http://www.secularism.org.uk/> (Retrieved 8.3.2015)

192 SC 13.2.1869, p.4.

193 SC 20.2.69 p.4.

194 SC. 23.1.1869, p.5.

195 SC. 23.1.1869, p.5.

196 Binfield, p.310; J. Simpkin, Spartacus Educational, Charles Bradlaugh, <http://spartacus-educational.com/PRbradlaugh.htm> (Retrieved 8.3.2015); History of the National Secular Society, <http://www.secularism.org.uk/> (Retrieved 8.3.2015)

197 SC.25.8.1888, p.4.

198 SC. 15.3.1873, p.5.

199 SC. 12.4.1873

200 SC. 17.5.1873, p.4.

201 SC 7.10.1876, p.3.

202 SC. 17.10.1868, p.5.

203 SC 1.6.1861, p.4.

204 SC. 21.11.1874 , p.3.

205 Binfield p.310.

206 SC. 19.10.1867, p 4.

207 SC. 16.10.1875, p.3.

208 YMCA Minutes 2.10.79-3.2.1882, p.217.

209 John Bunyan Church Kingston 'Bringing people together History at 125 years in 2007' <http://www.jbckingston.org.uk/history.htm > (Retrieved 26.12.2011).

210 Kingston U.R.C. History provided by John Fisher, United Reformed Church archivist <http://www.kingstonurc.orgkurc_aboutourchurch.html> (Retrieved 26.12.2011).

211 G. Clifton, *Professionalism, Patronage and Public Services in Victorian London: The Staff of the Metropolitan Board of Works 1856 - 1889* (London: Athrone Press, 1992) cited in <http://en.wikipedia.org/wiki/Metropolitan_Board_of_Works > (Retrieved 8.1.2012).

212 Joseph Bazalgette, <BBC History, Joseph Bazalgette (1819-1891), <http://www.bbc.co.uk/history/historic_figures/bazalgette_joseph.shtml> (Retrieved 28.7.2012). On the 1901 Census Frank Hertslet is shown living in Islington, his four eldest children born in Kingston upon Thames but his youngest Cyril E. Hertslet aged 2 born in Islington, London.

213 G.W. Gale, Obituary, Dr. L.E. Hertslet, South African Medical Journal, HMPG, Obituary reads: [H]is wide and profound knowledge of Native life particularly, in all its phases, from remotest kraal to heart of city slum, made him an accurate diagnostician and skilled therapist. In him, the Abantu of South Africa have lost a discerning friend and wise counsellor; and the profession to which he belonged has lost a pioneer who blazed a trail which increasingly it must follow. 21 May 1949, p.412. <http://archive.samj.org.za> (Retrieved 23.1.2015).

214 YMCA Minutes 2.10.79-3.2.1882, pp.43, 65.

215 YMCA Minutes 2.10.79-3.2.1882, p.217.

216 YMCA Minutes 2.10.79-3.2.1882, pp.40-1.

217 YMCA Minutes 2.10.79-3.2.1882, pp.38-217.

218 It is not possible to locate Mr. Newson's home as the name of the house was changed between 1881 and 1891.

219 YMCA Minutes 2.10.79-3.2.1882, p.45.

220 Binfield, pp.268, 286.

221 YMCA Minutes 2.10.79-3.2.1882, p.43.

222 YMCA Minutes 2.10.79-3.2.1882, pp.89-90.

223 Binfield, pp.230, 286

224 YMCA Minutes 2.10.79-3.2. 1882, pp.50-1.

225 YMCA Minutes 2.10.79-3.2.1882 pp.52-3.

226 YMCA Minutes 2.10.79-3.2.1882, p.55.

227 YMCA Minutes 2.10.79-3.2.1882, p.58.

228 YMCA Minutes 2.10.79-3.2.1882, pp.62-3.

229 YMCA Minutes 2.10.79-3.2.1882, pp.63.

230 YMCA Minutes 2.10.79-3.2.1882, p.68.

231 YMCA Minutes 2.10.79-3.2.1882, pp.93-4.

232 YMCA Minutes 2.10.79-3.2.1882, pp.103-6.

233 YMCA Minutes 2.10.79-3.2.1882, pp.119-20.

234 YMCA Minutes 2.10.79-3.2.1882, pp.161-2.

235 YMCA Minutes 2.10.79-3.2.1882, pp.190-1.

236 YMCA Minutes 2.10.79-3.2.1882, pp.91-4.

237 YMCA Minutes 2.10.79-3.2.1882, pp.120-5.

238 YMCA Minutes 2.10.79-3.2.1882, pp.132-7.

239 YMCA Minutes 2 10.1879 – 3.2.1882, pp.140-1.

240 YMCA Minutes 2.10.79-3.2.1882, pp.160-1.

241 SC. 24.8.1872 p.4.

242 Samuel Fry – Brighton Photographer 1835-1890, <http://photohistory-sussex.co.uk/ BTNFrySamuel.htm >(Retrieved 8.3.2015).

243 Samuel Fry – Brighton Photographer 1835-1890

244 YMCA Minutes 2.10.79-3.2.1882, p.169.

245 SC. 27.10.1862, p.4.

246 SC. 25.9.1880 p.4.

247 YMCA Minutes 2.10.79-3.2.1882, p.208.

248 YMCA Minutes 2.10.79-3.2.1882 pp.168-9.

249 YMCA Minutes 2.10.79-3.2.1882, pp.170-1.

250 SC 3.2.1881, p.3. The Surrey Comet reports this remark as: it was a common thing to speak of the associations in the country as being isolated societies, whereas they were branches of the London head association.

251 YMCA Minutes 2.10.79-3.2.1882, pp.171-2.

252 Y.M.C.A. Minutes, 3.3.1882-8.9.1884, pp.7-8.

253 Binfield, pp.268-9.

254 Y.M.C.A. Minutes, 3.3.1882-8.9.1884, pp.14-7.

255 SC. 10.3.1877, p.3.

256 Bayless, pp.25-6.

257 Binfield pp.312-3; The Dictionary of Victorian London – Buildings Monuments and Museums – Exeter Hall <http://www.victorianlondon.org/ buildings/exeterhall.htm>; <http:// en.wikipedia.org/wiki/Exeter_Hall> < http:// en.wikipedia.org/wiki/Anti-Corn_Law_League> (Retrieved 28.9.2012).

258 YMCA Minutes 2.10.79-3.2.1882, p.97.

259 SC. 22.9.1877, p.3.

260 SC 26.11.1878 p.3.

261 Going to School: The 1870 Education Act, <http://www.parliament.uk> (Retrieved 3.6.2015)

262 YMCA Minutes 2.10.79-3.2.1882, pp.97-8.

263 SC 4.9.1880 p.5.

264 YMCA Minutes 2.10.79-3.2.1882, pp.142-4.

265 YMCA Minutes 2.10.79-3.2.1882, p.147.

266 YMCA Minutes 2.10.79-3.2.1882, pp.148-52.

267 YMCA Minutes 2.10.79-3.2.1882, p.157.

268 YMCA Minutes 2.10.79-3.2.1882, pp.214-5.

269 YMCA Minutes 2.10.79-3.2.1882, p.166.

270 YMCA Minutes 2.10.79-3.2.1882, p.183.

271 Butters, *That Famous Place*, pp.166-8; Richardson p.3.

272 The Queen's Royal Surrey Regiment 1661-1966, Col A.C.Ward OBE DL, <http:// www.queensroyalsurreys.org.uk/chapels/ all_saints_1.html> (Retrieved 19.3.2012).

273 The Queen's Royal Surrey Regiment 1661-1966 <http:// www.queensroyalsurreys.org.uk/index.shtml> (Retrieved 29.9.2012).

274 SC. 27.5.1876, p.3.

275 YMCA Minutes 2 10.1879 – 3.2.1882, p.184.

276 SC. 16.7.1881, p.3; In 1881 the 1st Royal Surrey Militia became the 3rd Battalion of The East Surrey Regiment. The Queen's Royal Surrey Regiment 1661-1966, Col A.C. Ward OBE DL, <http://www.queensroyalsurreys.org.uk/ militia_vol_territorial/mvt38_1.html> (Retrieved 19.3.2012).

277 YMCA Minutes 2 10.1879 – 3.2.1882, pp.183-4.

278 YMCA Minutes 2 10.1879 – 3.2.1882, pp.197-8.

279 YMCA Minutes 2 10.1879 – 3.2.1882. pp.205-6.
280 YMCA Minutes 2 10.1879 – 3.2.1882, pp.210-1.
281 YMCA Minutes 2 10.1879 – 3.2.1882, p.234.
282 YMCA Minutes 2 10.1879 – 3.2.1882, pp.244-5.
283 Y.M.C.A. Minutes, 3.3.1882-8.9.1884, pp.2-3.
284 J. Burnett, *The Social History of Housing 1815-1985* (London: Routledge, 1986), pp.156-7; H. Hobhouse, *Thomas Cubitt Master Builder*, (London: Macmillan, 1971), p.114.
285 Y.M.C.A. Minutes, 3.3.1882-8.9.1884, p.7.
286 Y.M.C.A. Minutes, 3.3.1882-8.9.1884, p.46.
287 Y.M.C.A. Minutes, 3.3.1882-8.9.1884, pp.101-11.
288 Y.M.C.A. Minutes, 3.3.1882-8.9.1884, pp.107-8.
289 R. F. Holmes, *Pubs, Inns and Taverns of Kingston*, (Wildhern Press: 2009), p.146.
290 Y.M.C.A. Minutes, 3.3.1882-8.9.1884, p.116.
291 Y.M.C.A. Minutes, 3.3.1882-8.9.1884, pp.151, 154.
292 Y.M.C.A. Minutes, 3.3.1882-8.9.1884, pp.164, 169.
293 YMCA Minutes 2.10.1879-3.2.1882, p.229.
294 YMCA Minutes 3.3.1882-8.9.1884, pp.1,13.
295 YMCA Minutes 3.3.1882-8.9.1884 p.37.
296 YMCA Minutes 3.3.1882-8.9.1884, pp.52, 54, 68.
297 YMCA Minutes 3.3.1882-8.9.1884, pp.45, 56-7.
298 YMCA Minutes 3.3.1882-8.9.1884, p.79.
299 YMCA Minutes 3.3.1882-8.9.1884, pp.90, 137.
300 YMCA Minutes 3.3.1882-8.9.1884, p.95.
301 YMCA Minutes 3.3.1882-8.9.1884, pp.105, 124.
302 YMCA Minutes 3.3.1882-8.9.1884, pp.109, 122, 123.
303 John Bunyan Church Kingston <http://www.jbckingston.org.uk/history.htm > (Retrieved 24.1.2012).
304 SC. 19.11.1881, p.3.
305 SC. 24.6.1882, p.3.The *Surrey Comet* refers to the meeting place as the Wood-street schools.
306 SC. 24.6.1882, p.3.
307 SC. 23.10.1886, p.3.
308 SC. 7.5.1887 p.3.
309 SC. 27.8.1887 p 4.
310 YMCA Minutes 2 10.1879 – 3.2.1882, pp. 216-22.
311 YMCA Minutes 2.10.1879-3.2.1882, p.235.
312 YMCA Minutes 2 10.1879 – 3.2.1882, pp.241-5.
313 YMCA Minutes 2.10.1879-3.2.1882, pp.224-8.
314 YMCA Minutes 3.3.1882-8.9.1884, p.2
315 Archives Hub at the Centre of Great Research based at The University of Manchester. <http://archiveshub.ac.uk/features/0701ymca.html> (Retrieved 11.3.2012).
316 YMCA Minutes 3.3.1882-8.9.1884, p.8.
317 YMCA Minutes 3.3.1882-8.9.1884, pp.11-2.
318 YMCA Minutes 3.3.1882-8.9.1884, pp.14-5.
319 YMCA Minutes 3.3.1882-8.9.1884, pp34, 51.
320 YMCA Minutes 3.3.1882-8.9.1884, pp84-5.
321 YMCA Minutes 3.3.1882-8.9.1884, p88.
322 YMCA Minutes 3.3.1882-8.9.1884, p118.
323 YMCA Minutes 3.3.1882-8.9.1884, p155.
324 YMCA Minutes 3.3.1882-8.9.1884, p.159.
325 YMCA Minutes 3.3.1882-8.9.1884, pp166-7.
326 Y.M.C.A. Minutes, 3.3.1882-8.9.1884, pp.39, 63.
327 Y.M.C.A. Minutes, 3.3.1882-8.9.1884, pp.102-7.
328 Y.M.C.A. Minutes, 3.3.1882-8.9.1884, pp.102-7.
329 SC 8.10.1881 p.3.
330 SC 24.2.1883 p.5.
331 SC 24.2.1883 p.5.
332 Y.M.C.A. Minutes, 9.5.1885-5.12.1887, p.196.
333 SC. 2.9.1882 p.5.
334 Y.M.C.A. Minutes, 3.3.1882-8.9.1884, p.124.
335 Y.M.C.A. Minutes, 3.3.1882-8.9.1884, pp. 177-83.
336 Y.M.C.A. Minutes, 3.3.1882-8.9.1884, p. 202; Mr. Knapp lived in Clarence Street and was the son of Mary Knapp the Newspaper Proprietor Printer & Stationer who employed 11 Men, 4 Apprentices & 3 Boys.
337 *The Victoria History of the County of Surrey* (1911) H.E. Malden, Vol.3. p.494; Richardson p. 2.
338 J. Wakeford, *Kingston's Past Rediscovered*, (1990: Phillimore for Kingston upon Thames Archaeological Society and Surrey History Council), p. 73-4; Holmes, p. 133. Holmes writes that in 1831 the Waggon and Horses was leased to Young's Brewery and Ayliffe describes it as "a real

old-fashoned public house", which indicates that it was in situ long before 1800. A pair of indentures, those of 'grant and fee farm' dated 1775 mention that a piece of waste near Surbiton Common between the road from Kingston to Ewell…abuts on the premises of Chas Jemmett. Kingston History Centre KC1/1/271-272, (LHR) KC1/1.273.

339 Richardson, p. 3.

340 Richardson, p. 8, 'furze' – the *Oxford Dictionary Ninth Edition* – gorse (Old English unknown origin).

341 Law Commission Statute Law Repeals: Nineteenth Report Draft Statute Law (Repeals) Bill, 5.62 p.163. <lawcommission.justice.gov.uk/docs/19th_statute_law_repeals_report.pdf>, (Retrieved 10.3.2015).

342 Richardson, p. 8.

343 A.C. Giles, *The Failure of a Speculative Builder: The Downfall of Thomas Pooley of Surbiton, 1838-1844*, Issue 1 2000, Occasional Paper, Number 1/03, Centre for Local History Studies.

344 Richardson, p.142.

345 Amy Sycamore, The Parish is Formed, *100 Years The Story of the Parish of Christ Church, Surbiton Hill, 1863-1963*, (Surbiton: Centenary Christ Church Edition,1963.) p 5.

346 A prebendary is an honorary canon whose stipend comes from a prebend, a portion of the revenues of a cathedral, *Oxford Dictionary of English.*

347 Wikipedia incorporates text from "Edward Garbett" from *The Dictionary of National Biography, 1885-1900*, Volume 20, Augustus R. Buckland, <http://en.wikipedia.org/wiki/Edward_Garbett> (Retrieved 1.10.2012).

348 John Hudson Tiner, Robert Boyle--Founder of Modern Chemistry <http://www.doesgodexist.org/MarApr03/RobertBoyleFounderOfModernChemistry.html> (Retrieved 2.5.2012).

349 T.H.R. Boyle, *The Christian Virtuoso: Shewing That by being addicted to Experimental Philosophy, a Man is rather Assisted than Indisposed, to be a Good Christian.* (Edw. Jones for John Taylor at the Ship in St. Paul's Church-yard: 1690). <http://archive.org/details/christianvirtu00boyluoft> pdf (Retrieved 8.3.2015).

350 M. Hunter, Robert Boyle: An Introduction (2004: Birkbeck College, University of London) <http://www.bbk.ac.uk/boyle/index.htm> (Retrieved 2.5.2012).

351 E. Garbett, *The Bible and its Critics: an Enquiry into the Objective Reality of Revealed Truths,* (1861: London, Seeley and Griffiths)

352 Project Canterbury, Bampton Lectures <http://anglicanhistory.org/england/bampton> (Retrieved 2.5.2012).

353 E. Garbett, *The Dogmatic Faith: An Inquiry into the Relation subsisting between Revelation and Dogma,* (London: Rivingtons London, Oxford and Cambridge 1867). <http://archive.org/stream/cu31924029181259#page/n5/mode/2up>(Retrieved 2.5.2012).

354 *The Fifth Report of the Surbiton Young Men's Christian Association, for Spiritual Improvement of Young Men 1871-1872*, Knapp, Steam Printer, Kingston, p. 9.

355 Garbett, *The Dogmatic Faith*, Preface.

356 SC. 27.11.1869, p. 5.

357 C. French, 'Housing the middle classes in late Victorian and Edwardian Surbiton.' p. 129: A.C. Giles, Surbiton: The Development of a Middle Class Suburb, pp.18-20. Unpublished M.A. Dissertation.

358 SC. 27.7.1878, p. 4.

359 E. Healey, *Emma Darwin: The Inspirational Wife of a Genius,* (London: Headline Book Publishing, 2001),Chapter 10, p. 214.

360 SC. 17.10.1868, p.5.

361 SC. 15.10.1864, p.4.

362 SC. 12.10.1867, p 4.

363 SC 27.11.1869, p.5.

364 Binfield, pp.119-23.

365 D.G. Smith, Halls and other Church Premises, *100 Years The Story of the Parish of Christ Church, Surbiton Hill, 1863-1963*, p.9.

366 SC. 17.10.1868, p.5.

367 SC. 17.10.1868, p.5.

368 SC. 17.10.1868, p.5.

369 SC. 27.11.1869, p.5.

370 SC. 27.11.1869, p.5.

371 SC. 27.11.1869, p.5.

372 SC.15.2.1873, p.4.

373 SC. 17.5.1873, p.4.

374 SC. 17.5.1873, p.4.

375 Surbiton YMCA Minutes 26.10.1876.

376 Surbiton YMCA Minutes 2.1.1877.

377 Surbiton Y.M.C.A. 6.2.1877.

378 Surbiton Y.M.C.A. 6.2.1877-10.4.1877.

379 Surbiton 25 5 1878.

It is uncertain what is meant by 'issue therefrom' but it could mean that a child had been born through the 'connection.'

380 Surbiton Y.M.C.A. 25.3.1878- 30.5.1878.

381 Surbiton Y.M.C.A. 20.11.1878.

382 SC. 24.2.1883, p.5.

383 Information obtained from the Exhibition held at Wimbledon Y.M.C.A. on November 28, 2012.

384 Surbiton Y.M.C.A. 1.10.1878-6.10.1879.

385 SC. 27.10.1862, p. 4.

386 Quakers in Britain, <http:// www.quaker.org.uk/IndividualInvolvement> (Retrieved 8.4.2012); Quaker and Temperance – Individual Involvement, <http:// www.quaker.org.uk/TemperanceIntro> (Retrieved 3 10. 2012).

387 SC 20.12.1873, p. 3.

388 SC. 25.11.1871, p. 3; Although a family with the surname of Fewkes have been found on the 1861 census a Mr. Thomas Fewkes is not included in their number.

389 Marles, H. *The Life and Labours of Rev. Jabez Tunnicliffe* (London: W. Tweedie, 1865), cited in <http://en.wikipedia.org/wiki/Jabez Tunnicliffe> (Retrieved 5.4.2012); Hunslet remembered, <http://www.hunslet.org/ Schools_and_religion.html> (3.10.2012).

390 Binfield, pp.268, 302.

391 Binfield, pp.298, 302-3.

392 Binfield, p. 326.

393 There is no indication of the actual area covered by the map.

394 A full account of this meeting can be found in SC. 16. 5.1874, p. 4.

395 *Alcohol and Temperance in Modern History, An International Encyclopedia*, Volume 1. edited by Jack S. Blocker, David M. Fahey, Ian R. Tyrrell, (Google eBook) (ABC CLIO: 2003) pp.107-9. <wwwGoogle.com> (Retrieved 10.3.2015).

396 Y.M.C.A. Minutes, 3.3.1882-8.9.1884, pp.78-9.

397 SC. 21.4.1883 Supplement.

398 R.W.C. Richardson, *Thirty-Two Years of Local Self-Government, 1855-1887*, (1888: Bull and Son, Victoria Road, Surbiton), pp.50, 131.

399 SC. 21.4.1883 Supplement

400 SC. 28.4.1883, p.5.

401 SC. 5.5.1883, p.3.

402 SC. 19.5.1883, p.5.

403 SC. 20 10.1883 p.3.

404 SC. 1.11.1884, p.3.

405 SC 16.2.1884 p.6: SC 19.7.1884 p.2: SC.1.11.1884 p.3: SC 24.1.1885 p.5: SC 3.5.1884 p.3: SC 24.5.1884 p.4: SC. 31.10.1885 p.3: SC 28.11.1885 p.5.

406 YMCA Minutes 3.3.1882-8.9.1884, p.8.

407 Surbiton Y.M.C.A. 12.5.1882

408 Surbiton Y.M.C.A. 16.5.1882.

409 Surbiton Y.M.C.A. 27.6.1882

410 Surbiton Y.M.C.A. 14.7.1882

411 K/S 1874 Archive Letter to Arthur Maxwell from James Cundy 11.7.1882.

412 Surbiton Y.M.C.A. 28.7.1882

413 Surbiton Y.M.C.A. 2.11.1882.

414 Surbiton Y.M.C.A. 30.11.1882.

415 Surbiton Y.M.C.A. 30.1.1883.

416 Surbiton Y.M.C.A. 6.2.1883

417 Surbiton Y.M.C.A. 1.3.1883.

418 Surbiton Y.M.C.A. 19.6.1883.

419 Surbiton Y.M.C.A. 19.6.1883.

420 Report for the Year Ending 30 September 1884, Printed by W. Prince, Surbiton Hill.

421 Surbiton Y.M.C.A. 3.10.1884.

422 Surbiton Y.M.C.A. 12.10.1883.

423 Surbiton Y.M.C.A. 23.11.1883-1.8.1884

424 Report for the Year Ending 30 September 1884, Printed by W. Prince, Surbiton Hill.

425 Report for the Year Ending 30 September 1884, Printed by W. Prince, Surbiton Hill.

426 Report for the Year Ending 30 September 1884, Printed by W. Prince, Surbiton Hill.

427 Surbiton Y.M.C.A. unattached papers within the book.

428 Surbiton Y.M.C.A. 16.12.1884.

429 Surbiton Y.M.C.A. 17.4.1885

430 K/S 1874 Archive Letter to Arthur Maxwell from James Cundy 11.7.1882.

431 Surbiton Y.M.C.A. 2.12.1884-28.4.1885.

432 Surbiton Y.M.C.A. 17.4.1885.

433 Y.M.C.A. Minutes, 9.5.1885-5.12.1887, p.2.

434 Y.M.C.A. Minutes, 9.5.1885-5.12.1887, pp.1-8.

435 Y.M.C.A. Minutes, 9.5.1885-5.12.1887, pp.12-3.

436 Y.M.C.A. Minutes, 9.5.1885-5.12.1887, pp.5-6.

437 Y.M.C.A. Minutes, 9.5.1885-5.12.1887, pp.16-7.

438 Y.M.C.A. Minutes, 9.5.1885-5.12.1887, p.23.

439 Y.M.C.A. Minutes, 9.5.1885-5.12.1887, pp.77-8.

440 Y.M.C.A. Minutes, 9.5.1885-5.12.1887, pp.28-9.

441 Y.M.C.A. Minutes, 9.5.1885-5.12.1887, pp.34-6.

442 1881 Census

443 Y.M.C.A. Minutes, 9.5.1885-5.12.1887, p. 43 SC. 15.8.1885

444 Y.M.C.A. Minutes, 9.5.1885-5.12.1887, p.49, Book listing Members, (128)

445 The date each house was built can be found engraved on the stonework near the roof.

446 Y.M.C.A. Minutes, 9.5.1885-5.12.1887, p.41.

447 Samuel Fry – Brighton Photographer - Samuel Fry (1835-1890) Samuel Fry, the photographer, father of Samuel Herbert Fry, remained an active member of the Kingston Bicycle Club in 1887 even although he was over 50 by this time. <http://photohistory-sussex.co.uk/BTNFrySamuel.htm> (Retrieved 8.3.2015).

448 Y.M.C.A. Minutes, 9.5.1885-5.12.1887, pp. 46-50.

449 Y.M.C.A. Minutes, 9.5.1885-5.12.1887, p.75.

450 Y.M.C.A. Minutes, 9.5.1885-5.12.1887, pp. 144-7.

451 Y.M.C.A. Football Committee Minutes, pp. 18-9.

452 Y.M.C.A. Minutes, 9.5.1885-5.12.1887, pp. 153-4.

453 Y.M.C.A. Minutes, 9.5.1885-5.12.1887, pp.61-3.

454 Y.M.C.A. Minutes, 9.5.1885-5.12.1887, pp.80, 95-6.

455 Y.M.C.A. Minutes, 9.5.1885-5.12.1887, pp. 102-3.

456 Y.M.C.A. Minutes, 9.5.1885-5.12.1887, p.93.

45728 Y.M.C.A. Minutes, 9.5.1885-5.12.1887, pp. 106-7, 118-9

458 SC. 2.1.1886 p.2; SC. 9.1.1886 p.3.

459 Y.M.C.A. Minutes, 9.5.1885-5.12.1887, pp. 172-182.

460 Y.M.C.A. Minutes, 9.5.1885-5.12.1887, pp. 188-9.

461 Y.M.C.A. Minutes, 9.5.1885-5.12.1887, pp. 181-2, 209-10.

462 Y.M.C.A. Minutes, 9.5.1885-5.12.1887, pp.204, 211.

463 Y.M.C.A. Minutes, 9.5.1885-5.12.1887, pp.223, 229, 245-6.

464 Y.M.C.A. Minutes, 9.5.1885-5.12.1887, pp. 241-2.

465 Y.M.C.A. Minutes, 9.5.1885-5.12.1887, p.254.

466 Y.M.C.A. Minutes, 9.5.1885-5.12.1887, pp. 255-6.

467 Sir Charles Douglas Fox and Mary Wright: A Tale of Downward Social Mobility Posted by Justin Kirby in Fox, Kirby and Portraits, Scrapbook of an Edwardian Lady, 2012, <http://descentfromadam.wordpress.com/2012/01/29/sir-charles-douglas-fox-and-mary-wright/> (Retrieved 21.3.2015); Victoria Falls Bridge Construction <http://www.victoriafalls-guide.net/victoria-falls-bridge-construction.html> (Retrieved 15.1.2013);

468 Y.M.C.A. Minutes, 9.5.1885-5.12.1887, pp. 262-3.

469 Y.M.C.A. Minutes, 9.5.1885-5.12.1887, pp. 306-8.

470. SC.. 2.7.1887, p.3.

471. C. French, 'Housing the middle classes in late Victorian and Edwardian Surbiton,' pp.

134–5: S. Williams, London Gardens on Line: Hillcroft College, Kingston, <http.// www.londongardensonline.org.uk/gardens-online-record.asp?ID=KIN021> (Retrieved 10.9.2012).

472 L. Raw, *Striking A Light: The Bryant and May Matchwomen and their Place in History,* Revised 2011, (London: The Continium International Publishing Group, 2009), pp.96-7.

473 B. Williams, *Quakers in Reigate 1655-1955*, (Self published: 1980), pp.72-6

474 *The Encyclopaedia of Plymouth History*, cited an article about Mr. Francis May found in *The Oxford Dictionary of National Biography*, (<www.oxforddnb.com/> (Retrieved 8.3.2015).

475 Minute Book 9 May 1885 – 5 December 1887, p.126.

476 SC. 3.12.87, p.7.

477 BBC History, Joseph Bazalgette. (1819 - 1891) <http://www.bbc.co.uk/history/ historic_figures/bazalgette_joseph.shtml> (Retrieved 28.7.2012).

478 Baker, C, *Development Governor: A Biography of Sir Geoffrey Colby*, p.5. <books.google.co.uk/ books> (Retrieved 22.9.2014).

479 London Parks & Gardens Trust, London Gardens On Line, <http:// www.londongardensonline.org.uk/gardens-online-record.asp?ID=KIN021> (Retrieved 9.10.2012).

480 SC. 27.3.1886, p.2.

481 Y.M.C.A. Minutes, 9.5.1885-5.12.1887, pp.183, 191, 205-6, 213-4, 258.

482 SC. 2.10.2012, p. 3, 29.1.1887, p. 3, 1.10.1887, p. 2. 29.9.1888, p. 5.

483 Raw, p. 158.

484 Raw, pp.97-9.

485 A. Bessant White slavery in London, *The Link: A Journal for the Servants of Man*, printed and published for the Proprietor by Annie Bessant, 34

Bouverie Street, Fleet Street, E.C.. From: Issue No. 21 (Saturday, June 23, 1888,) <http:// www.mernick.org.uk/thhol/thelink.html> (Retrieved 9.10.2012).

486 Raw, 98-9, 100-1.The early friction matches consisted of a coating of potassium chloride, gum Arabic, starch and antimony sulphide on the end of a stick. The invention was a fire hazard and banned in France and Germany but later, modification was to result in the 'Lucifer' sold in cardboard boxes. In 1831 a French chemist Charles Sauria substituted white phosphorus for antimony sulphide making matches that were able to be ignited on any hard surface and therefore far more popular. However this modification was to result in the disfiguration and subsequent death of countless matchworkers. Various strikes by the workers were unsuccessful as the Company managed to convince the public through journals such as *Cassell's Saturday Journal* that they were caring employers, and that the factory was safe.

487 Raw, p.126.

488 SC. 21.7.1888, p.7.

489 Roots Web Genbrit –L- Archives Bryant and May Match Company. <http:// archiver.rootsweb.ancestry.com/th/read/ GENBRIT/1998-05/0895041837>

490 Raw, p.94.

491 R. Hattersley, *Blood & Fire*, <https:// www.littlebrown.co.uk/Books/detail.page? isbn=9780349112817> (Retrieved 8.3.2015).

492 Baker, p.5. <books.google.co.uk/books?> (Retrieved 22.9.2014).

493 Pugh, P., *Stoke Park: The First 1,000 Years,* Chapter 5, Wealthy Victorians, (Cambridge: Icon Books Ltd., 2008) <http://www.stokepark.com/ book/chapter5.>pdf (Retrieved 9.10.2012).

494 Y.M.C.A. Minutes, 3.3.1882-8.9.1884, p.195.

495 Y.M.C.A. Minutes, 3.3.1882-8.9.1884, pp.195-6.

496 Binfield, pp.228-9.

497 Y.M.C.A. Minutes, 3.3.1882-8.9.1884, pp.198-9.

498 Y.M.C.A. Minutes, 3.3.1882-8.9.1884, p.216.

499 Y.M.C.A. Minutes, 9.5.1885-5.12.1887, pp.70-1.

500 Y.M.C.A. Minutes, 9.5.1885-5.12.1887, pp. 197-8.

501 Y.M.C.A. Minutes, 9.5.1885-5.12.1887, pp. 200-2.

502 Y.M.C.A. Minutes, 9.5.1885-5.12.1887, p.218.

503 Y.M.C.A. Minutes, 9.5.1885-5.12.1887, p.220.

504 Y.M.C.A. Minutes, 9.5.1885-5.12.1887, p.231.

505 Y.M.C.A. Minutes, 9.5.1885-5.12.1887, pp. 237-9.

506 Y.M.C.A. Minutes, 9.5.1885-5.12.1887, pp. 249-50.

507 Y.M.C.A. Minutes, 9.5.1885-5.12.1887, pp. 251-3.

508 Y.M.C.A. Minutes, 9.5.1885-5.12.1887, pp. 262-4. The terminology 'Misses' was used in the minutes and indicates that there was more than one Miss Butler involved.

509 Samuel Fry Brighton Photographer, *The Times*, Thursday 25 May 1882 <http://photohistory-sussex.co.uk/BTNFrySamuel.htm> (Retrieved 8.3.2015 22.24.)

510 Y.M.C.A. Minutes, 9.5.1885-5.12.1887, pp. 264-6.

511 An Ancestry Community, hosted by rootsweb, <http:// freepages.genealogy.rootsweb.ancestry.com/ ~agene/census/wickhammkt.htm> (Retrieved 12.10.2012)

512 Y.M.C.A. Minutes, 9.5.1885-5.12.1887, pp. 277-9.

513 Y.M.C.A. Minutes, 9.5.1885-5.12.1887, pp. 284-5.

514 Y.M.C.A. Minutes, 9.5.1885-5.12.1887, pp. 285-8.

515 Y.M.C.A. Minutes, 9.5.1885-5.12.1887, pp. 298-302.

516 Y.M.C.A. Minutes, 9.5.1885-5.12.1887, pp. 334-7.

517 Y.M.C.A. Minutes, 9.5.1885-5.12.1887, p.355.

518 Y.M.C.A. Minutes, 20.1.1888-15.9.1890, p.12.

519 Y.M.C.A. Minutes, 20.1.1888-15.9.1890, pp. 16-9.

Messrs G. Constable 5 The Terrace Hampton Wick; Messrs Oldridge & Sons, London Road, Norbiton; Messrs Hanley & Sons, London Road, Kingston Hill, Mr. W. Lane, London Street, Kingston;

Messrs R. Scrase & Son, Ewell Road, S.H. Mr. J.J. Collings, Victoria Road, Norbiton, Mr. H. Snelling, Hawks Road, Norbiton, Mr. J.S. Havell, Eden Street, Kingston in conjunction with London Bull.

520 Y.M.C.A. Minutes, 20.1.1888-15.9.1890, p.25.

521 Y.M.C.A. Minutes, 20.1.1888-15.9.1890, pp. 25-7.

522 Y.M.C.A. Minutes, 20.1.1888-15.9.1890, pp. 34-6.

523 Y.M.C.A. Minutes, 20.1.1888-15.9.1890, pp. 39-46.

524 This probably refers to the basins and towels, costing 17/6 in October 1886 bought as the Footballers used the Y.M.C.A. rooms as dressing rooms. Minute Book of the Young Men's Christian Association Cricket Club and of the Y.M.C.A. Football Club "Saxons F.C." 28.10.86; Y.M.C.A. Minutes, 20.1.1888-15.9.1890, pp.47-56. Further details of the removal from the Y.M.C.A. of the football club can be found in an article 'Forty-Five Years of Football in Kingston', written by Councillor W.E. Blake Carn found in the *Surrey Comet* in January 1831. Despite the apparent disconnection with the Association, football is mentioned as being provided by the Athletic Club in the 1895-6 Annual Report, see page 229. A member of the Carn family continued to support the Y.M.C.A. with an annual donation in later years.

525 Y.M.C.A. Minutes, 20.1.1888-15.9.1890, pp.9, 15, 22-5.

526 Y.M.C.A. Minutes, 20.1.1888-15.9.1890, p.20.

527 Y.M.C.A. Minutes, 20.1.1888-15.9.1890, pp. 21-24, 30, 31, 33-4, 37, 63.

528 Y.M.C.A. Minutes, 20.1.1888-15.9.1890, p.57.

529 Y.M.C.A. Minutes, 20.1.1888-15.9.1890, pp.62, 65-6.

530 Y.M.C.A. Minutes, 20.1.1888-15.9.1890, p.74.

531 The 'Specification of Works' shows more than one person's handwriting.

532 Butters p.126; Mike Baker, Slum or Suburb? The Development of The Forty Acres, Kingston upon Thames 1869-95, (Kingston University London Issue 11, Winter 2005), pp.3-4.

533 Y.M.C.A. Minutes, 20.1.1888-15.9.1890, pp. 85-6.

534 Y.M.C.A. Minutes, 20.1.1888-15.9.1890, pp.100, 109, 115, 120-2.

535 Bedford House is a Grade II Listed Building I.D: 206583.

536 Gentle Author, Spitalfields Life - At Bedford House, 29 September 2011, <http:// spitalfieldslife.com/2011/09/29/at-bedford-house/>(Retrieved 1 1.2013).

537 Undated Pamplet relating to the proposed New Building Y.M.C.A. Archives.

538 Y.M.C.A. Minutes, 20.1.1888-15.9.1890, pp. 188-9, 123.

539 Y.M.C.A. Minutes, 20.1.1888-15.9.1890, p. 66.

540 Y.M.C.A. Minutes, 20.1.1888-15.9.1890, pp.67, 69, 71, 72, 75.

541 Y.M.C.A. Minutes, 20.1.1888-15.9.1890, p.161.

542 Y.M.C.A. Minutes, 20.1.1888-15.9.1890, pp. 97-8.

543 Y.M.C.A. Minutes, 20.1.1888-15.9.1890, p.107.

544 Y.M.C.A. Minutes, 20.1.1888-15.9.1890, p.113.

545 Subcommittee Minute Book, October 22, 1889.

546 Y.M.C.A. Minutes, 20.1.1888-15.9.1890, pp. 150-7.

547 Y.M.C.A. Minutes, 20.1.1888-15.9.1890, pp. 132-2.

548 Y.M.C.A. Minutes, 20.1.1888-15.9.1890, p.146.

549 Y.M.C.A. Minutes, 20.1.1888-15.9.1890, p.137.

550 Y. M.C.A. Minutes, 20.1.1888-15.9.1890, pp. 151, 157-8.

551 Y.M.C.A. Minutes, 20.1.1888-15.9.1890, pp.170, 179.

552 Y.M.C.A. Minutes, 20.1.1888-15.9.1890, pp. 104-5.

553 Y.M.C.A. Minutes, 20.1.1888-15.9.1890, p.127.

554 Y.M.C.A. Minutes, 20.1.1888-15.9.1890, pp.164, 168.

555 Y.M.C.A. Minutes, 20.1.1888-15.9.1890, pp. 139-40.

556 Y.M.C.A. Minutes, 20.1.1888-15.9.1890, pp. 164-5.

557 Y.M.C.A. Minutes, 20.1.1888-15.9.1890, pp. 165-6.

558 *The Coffee Public-House and Temperance Hotel Journal*, 1 November 1883, p. 134, <http:// books.google.co.uk/ > (Retrieved 8.3.2015).

559 Y.M.C.A. Minutes, 20.1.1888-15.9.1890, p.169.

560 Y.M.C.A. Minutes, 20.1.1888-15.9.1890, pp. 173-4

561 Y.M.C.A. Minutes, 20.1.1888-15.9.1890, p.180.

562 Y.M.C.A. Minutes 20.1.1888-15.9.1890, pp. 184-189.

563 Y.M.C.A. Minutes, 20.1.1888-15.9.1890, pp. 191-2.

564 SC. 10.5.1890, p.3.

565 SC. 10.5.1890, p.3.

566 SC. 31.5.1890, p.5.

567 SC. 7.6.1890, p.3.

568 J.A.Kay, C.N. Morris, S.M. Jaffer, S.A. Meadowcroft, *The Regulation of Retail Trading Hours*, The Institute for Fiscal Studies, 1-2 Castle Lane, London S.W.1 E .D.R. <http:// www.ifs.org.uk/comms/r13.pdf> (Retrieved 23.3.2012).

569 Y.M.C.A. Minutes 20.1.1890-15.9.1890, pp.195, 205.

570 'That the proposed draft Deed of Assignment as submitted be adopted' subject to the insertion on the covenant of the assignors for payment of the £30 per annum, of the words "That the said George Clifton Sherrard and Edward Wilmott will pay and discharge all rent and other outgoings and observe and perform the covenants and conditions in the said recited lease contained up to and including the 29th day of September next and that some arrangement be made if possible as to an apportionment of the rates and taxes and that the 2 guineas costs be allowed." Y.M.C.A. Minutes 20.1.1890-15.9.1890, pp.196-7.

571 Y.M.C.A. Minutes, 20.1.1888-15.9.1890, p.203.

572 Subcommittee Minutes 30, July 1890.

573 Subcommittee Minutes 18, August 1890.

574 Y.M.C.A. Minutes, 20.1.1888-15.9.1890, p198.

575 SC. 16.8.1890, p.2.

576 SC. 16.8.1890, p.2.

577 Annual Report, 1902-3, pp. 4-5.

578 Y.M.C.A. Minutes, 20.1.1888-15.9.1890, pp. 204-212.

579 Kingston & Surbiton, Annual Report 1892-3, pp.3-4.

580 Kingston & Surbiton, Annual Report 1899-1900, p.1.

581 Sub Committee Minutes July 1895.

582 W. Hill, Kingston Young Men's Christian Association: *Memoirs in the Centenary Year 1874-1974*, pp.2-3.

583 This is incorrect. Mr. W.G. Carn who was the first Captain of the YMCA Football Club was the father of W.E.Blake Carn who was Mayor of Kingston in 1928. Thanks are expressed to Richard Coulthard for pointing this out to me.

584 Y.M.C.A. Archive, Hill, p.4.

585 Y.M.C.A. Archive, Eggleton.

586 Kingston & Surbiton, Annual Report 1898-99, p.9.

587 Kingston & Surbiton Annual Report 1895-6, pp.9-14.

588 Thirty-Seventh Report for the year ending March 31 1882, Y.M.C.A., Exeter Hall, p.25; Kingston & Surbiton Annual Report 1899-1900.

589 Binfield pp.305-6.

590 K/S 1874 Archive

591 SC. 26.2.1859 p.6.

592 SC. 16. 9.1871, p.3.

593 Cleal, pp.188-90.

594 SC. 17.10.1868, p.5.

595 R. Bentall, *My Store of Memories*, (London: W.H.Allen, 1974), pp.97-9.

596 Bayless, pp.21-2; Binfield, p.163.

597 My duties included putting margarine on the bread, (butter was rationed), washing up and other duties. Every one who ordered a meal was given a number and when the meal was ready the number was called out.

598 The Mission Statement can be found in 'Empowering Young People' http://www.ymca.int/who-we-are/mission/ (Retrieved 12.4.2014).

599 The Y.M.C.A. S.W. has also three residential care homes, Landown House, Rodney House and The Summers.

600 *The Bible* St. Mark Chapter 12 Verse 31.

BIBLIOGRAPHY

Primary Sources

Y.M.C.A. Minute Books

Kingston Minute Book - January 1874 to September 1879.

Kingston Minute Book - 2 October 1879 to 13 January 1882.

Surbiton Minute Book - 26 October 1876 to 16 October 1879
12 May 1882 - 28 April 1885.

Kingston Minute Book - 3 March 1882 to 8 September 1884.

Kingston & Surbiton Minute Book - 9 May 1885 to 5 December 1887.

Cricket Club Minute Book - 19 May 1886 to 1 October 1886.

Cricket Club and Football Club Minute Book 1884 to 1888.

Kingston & Surbiton Minute Book - 20 January 1888 to 15 September 1890.

Athletic Club - 29 April 1901 to 6 September 1904.

Sub Committee Minutes - 26 October 1887 to 30 September 1897.

List of Members

Y.M.C.A. Annual Reports

The Fifth Report of the Surbiton Young Men's Christian Association for the Spiritual Improvement of Young Men 1871-72. (Kingston: Knapp, Steam Printer, 1872).

Thirty-Seventh Report for the year ending March 31 1882, Young Men's Christian Association Exeter Hall.
Surbiton Y.M.C.A. Annual Report Year dated 30th September 1884, Printed by W. Prince, Surbiton Hill.

Kingston and Surbiton District Young Men's Christian Association, Twenty-Seventh Annual Report, 1899-1900, (Knapp Typ, Kingston, Surbiton and Wimbledon).

Report of the Committee of Management of the Kingston & Surbiton District Young Men's Christian Association for the Year 1892; Kingston upon Thames Printed by Drewetts "Kingston and Surbiton News" Office Market Place, 1892.

Report of the Committee of Management of the Kingston & Surbiton District Young Men's Christian Association for the Year 1893-4; Kingston upon Thames Printed by Knapps Steam Printing Works, Clarence Street, 1894.

The Twenty-Third Annnual Report of the Kingston & Surbiton District Young Men's Christian Association, 1895-6.

The Twenty-Fourth Annual Report Kingston & Surbiton District Young Men's Christian Assocation, 1896-7.

The Twenty-Fifth Kingston and Surbiton Annual Report Young Men's Christian Association 1897-8,

The Twenty-Sixth Kingston and Surbiton Annual Report Young Men's Christian Association 1898-9.

The Twenty-Seventh Kingston and Surbiton Annual Report Young Men's Christian Association 1899-1900.

Kingston on Thames and Surbiton District Young Men's Christian Association; An Abstract of the Thirtieth Annual Report 1902-3.

Y.M.C.A. Papers

Kingston, Surbiton & District Y.M.C.A. Reception of Local Y.M.C.A. War Helpers at the The Guildhall, Kingston upon Thames, Wednesday, April 10th 1946.

Kingston Young Men's Christian Association, Memoirs in the Centenary Year Y.M.C.A.

Papers relating to the building of the premises in Denmark Road together with papers relating to various sites visited, Saunders, Rutland, (Architect & Surveyor) Specification of Works, 6 Bishopsgate Street, Without E.C. K/S 1874 Archive.

Undated Pamplet relating to the proposed New Building.

Y.M.C.A. Kingston and Surbiton District Abstract Report 1917-18.

Secondary Sources – Books and Articles

Baker, M., 'Slum or Suburb? The Development of The Forty Acres, Kingston upon Thames, 1869-95,' *Kingston University London Centre For Local History Studies*, Issue 11, Winter 2005. (Kingston upon Thames, History Room).

Bayless, P., *The Y.M.C.A. at 150: A History of the YMCA of Greater New York, 1852-2002* (New York: YMCA of Greater New York, 2002).

Bentall, R., *My Store of Memories*, (London: W.H.Allen, 1974),

Binfield, C., *George Williams and the Y.M.C.A: A Study in Victorian Social Atttitudes* (London: Heinemann, 1973).

Blocker, J. S., Fahey, D. M. Ian R. Tyrrell, I. R., (eds.) *Alcohol and Temperance in Modern History*, Volume 1, (ABC-CLIO Ltd: 2003)

Burnett, J. *The Social History of Housing 1815 – 1985*, (London: Routledge, 1986.)

Butters, S., *The Book of Kingston*, (Oxon: Barron for Quotes, Finmere, 1995).

Butters S., *That Famous Place: A History Of Kingston Upon Thames*, (Kingston: Kingston University Press, 2013)

Cleal, E.E., *The Story of Congregationalism in Surrey*, (London: James Clarke & Co., 1908)

Davis, J.R., *The Great Exhibition*, (Gloucestershire: Sutton Publishing Ltd., 1999).

Feldman, D., Migration, in Daunton, M., (ed) *The Cambridge Urban History of Britain*, Volume III 1840-1950, (Cambridge: Cambridge University Press, 2000).

Freeman, M., *Railways and the Victorian Imagination*, (London: Yale university Press, 1999).

French, C., 'Housing the middle classes in late Victorian and Edwardian Surbiton,' *The Local Historian: Journal of the British Association for Local History*, vol. 45 (2) April 2015, pp. 126–142.

Garbett, E., *The Bible and its Critics: an Enquiry into the Objective Reality of Revealed Truths*, (London: Seeley and Griffiths, 1861)

Garbett, E., *The Dogmatic Faith: An Inquiry into the Relation subsisting between Revelation and Dogma*, (London, Oxford and Cambridge: Rivingtons, 1867).

Healey, E., *Emma Darwin: The Inspirational Wife of a Genius*, (London: Headline Book Publishing, 2001)

Hobhouse, H., *Thomas Cubitt Master Builder*, (London: Macmillan, 1971)

Holmes, R.F., *Pubs, Inns and Taverns of Kingston*, (Wildhern Press: 2009).

Houghton, W.E. *The Victorian Frame of Mind 1830-1870*, (New Haven and London: Yale University Press:1957).

Morris, P. *The Chapel on the Hill: A History of Surbiton Hill Methodist Church 1882-1982*, (Wimbledon: CF Ltd., Wimbledon SW19 2SE, 1981).

Owen, R., *Report to the County of Lanark A New View of Society*, (Harmondsworth: Pelican Books Ltd,1970)

Phillipson's Almanack and Directory 1876 (Kingston upon Thames, History Room)

Pugh, P., *Stoke Park: The First 1,000 Years*, Chapter 5 Wealthy Victorians, (Cambridge: Icon Books Ltd., 2008).

Raw, L., *Striking A Light: The Bryant and May Matchwomen and their Place in History*, Revised 2011, (London: The Continium International Publishing Group, 2009).

Richardson, R.W.C., *Thirty-Two Years of Local Self-Government, 1855-1887*, (Surbiton: Bull and Son, Victoria Road,1888).

Smith, D.G., Halls and other Church Premises, *100 Years The Story of the Parish of Christ Church, Surbiton Hill, 1863-1963*. (Surbiton: Centenary Christ Church Edition,1963.)

Sturney, A.C., *The Story of Kingston Congregational Church*, (Stourbridge: Mark & Moody,1955).

Sycamore A., The Parish is Formed, *100 Years The Story of the Parish of Christ Church, Surbiton Hill, 1863-1963*. (Surbiton: Centenary Christ Church Edition:1963).

The Victoria History of the County of Surrey (1911) H.E. Malden, Vol.3.

The Westminster Dictionary of the Bible, (London: Collins, 1944).

Thompson, E.P., *The Making of the English Working Class*, (Harmondsworth: Penguin Books Ltd: 1968).

Tiller, K., *English Local History: An Introduction*, (Gloucestershire: Alan Sutton Publishing, 1992).

Tosh, J., *The Pursuit of History*, 3rd. ed. (Harrow: Longman, 2000)

Wakeford, J., *Kingston's Past Rediscovered*, (Phillimore for Kingston upon Thames Archaeological Society and Surrey History Council: 1990.)

Williams, B, *Quakers in Reigate 1655 – 1955*, (Redhill: Self Published, 1980).

Newspaper

Surrey Comet 1858-1890. (History Room, Kingston upon Thames).

Internet

Alcohol and Temperance in Modern History, An International Encyclopedia, Volume 1. edited by Blocker, J.S., Fahey, D.M., Tyrrell, I. R., (Google eBook) (ABC CLIO: 2003) pp.107-9. <wwwGoogle.com> (Retrieved 10.3.2015).

Archives Hub based at The University of Manchester. <http://archiveshub.ac.uk/features/0701ymca.html> (Retrieved 11.3.2012).

Baker, C, Development Governor: A Biography of Sir Geoffrey Colby, p.5. <books.google.co.uk/books> (Retrieved 22.9.2014).

Bampton, J., Extract from the Last Will and Testament of the Late John Bampton, Canon of Salisbury, (Project Canterbury 2006, managed by Richard Mammana). <http://anglicanhistory.org/england/bampton> (Retrieved 2.5.2012).

BBC History, Joseph Bazalgette (1819-1891), <http://www.bbc.co.uk/history/historic_figures/bazalgette_joseph.shtml> (Retrieved 28.7.2012).

Bentham Project, 'U.C.L. Who Was Jeremy Bentham?' http://www.ucl.ac.uk/Bentham-Project/who (Retrieved 7.7.2014):
Bessant, A., White slavery in London, The Link: A Journal for the Servants of Man, printed and published for the Proprietor by Annie Bessant, 34 Bouverie Street, Fleet Street, E.C. Issue No. 21 (Saturday, June 23, 1888,) <http://www.mernick.org.uk/thhol/thelink.html> (Retrieved 9.10.2012).

Blind, K., Garibaldi in London, Fraser's Magazine, published in The New York Times October 8, 1882, <http://www.nytimes.com/> (Retrieved 8.3.2015).

Bournemouth YMCA 'Christian Faith in Action' <http://www.bournemouthymca.org.uk/about-us/history-of-the-ymca/> (Retrieved 23.2.3014).

Boyle, H.R. The Christian Virtuoso: Shewing That by being addicted to Experimental Philosophy, a Man is rather Assisted than Indisposed, to be a Good Christian. (Edw. Jones for John Taylor at the Ship in St. Paul's Church-yard, 1690) <http://archive.org/details/christianvirtu00boyluoft> pdf (Retrieved 8.3.2015).

Chambers, R., Vestiges of the Natural History of Creation: The Bodies of Space, Their Arrangements and Formation, <www.gutenberg.org/dirs/etext04/vstc10h.htm> (Retrieved 8.12.2011).
<//en.wikipedia.org/wiki/Vestiges_of_the_Natural_History_of_Creation#cite_note-Darwin> (Retrieved 2.3.2013).

Cheshunt College, <www.british-history.ac.uk/report.aspx?compid=66624> (Retrieved 27.4.2011);

Clifton, G., Professionalism, Patronage and Public Services in Victorian London: The Staff of the Metropolitan Board of Works, 1856-1889, (London: Athlone Press, 1992) cited in Wikipedia <http://en.wikipedia.org/wiki/Metropolitan_Board_of_Works > (Retrieved 8.1.2012).

Cobham United Reformed Church, About Us <http://www.cobhamurc.org.uk/about-us/> (Retrieved 27.4.2015)
Congregational Churches and Churches of Bristol, based on research by Neil Marchant, <http://www.churchcrawler.pwp.blueyonder.co.uk/htm.> (Retrieved 24.10.2012 14:01)

Cook, G.C., Construction of London's Victorian sewers: the vital role of Joseph Bazalgette, Postgraduate Medical Journal, (2001;77:802 doi: 10.1136) <http://pmj.bmj.com/content/77/914/802.full> (Retrieved 21.3.2015)

De Fraine, J., The Autobiography of John De Fraine: Or Forty Years of Public Lecturing Work. <https://archive.org/details/autobiographyjo00fraigoog> (8.3.2015).

Fry, D., Fry, N., Samuel Fry Brighton Photographer, 1835 – 1890,: <http://photohistory-sussex.co.uk/BTNFrySamuel.htm> (Retrieved 8.3.2015);

Fullerton, W.Y., The Spurgeon Archive, Charles Haddon Spurgeon: A Biography, <http://www.spurgeon.org/misc/bio11.htm> (Retrieved 11.9.2012).

Gale, G.W., Obituary, Dr. L.E. Hertslet, South African Medical Journal, HMPG, 21 May 1949, p. 412. <http://archive.samj.org.za> (Retrieved 23.1.2015).

Garbett, E., The Dogmatic Faith: An Inquiry into the Relation subsisting between Revelation and Dogma, (London, Oxford and Cambridge: Rivingtons, 1867). <http://archive.org/stream/cu31924029181259#page/n5/mode/2up> (Retrieved 2.5.2012).

Garbett, E, Dictionary of National Biography, London, Smith, Elder & Co. 1885-1900, cited in Wikipedia, <http://en.wikipedia.org/wiki/Edward_Garbett> (Retrieved 1.10.2012).

Gavazzi, A., - <http://en.wikipedia.org/wiki/Alessandro_Gavazzi > (Retrieved 3.11.2012).

Going to School: The 1870 Education Act, <http://www.parliament.uk> (Retrieved 3.6.2015)

Hart, T.E., The Victorian Web, Natural Theology of Paley, <http://www.ucmp.berkeley.edu/history/paley.html>(Retrieved 27.4.2015).

Hattersley, R., Blood & Fire: William and Catherine Booth and the Salvation Army, (London: Little, Brown & Co., 1999) <https://www.littlebrown.co.uk/Books/detail.page?isbn=9780349112817> (Retrieved 8.3.2015).

B.W. Hildebrandt, It Can Be! 150 Years German YMCA in London 1860 – 2010 < http://www.german-ymca.org.uk/about-us-history.html> (Retrieved 9.3.2015).

Hillcroft College, Gardens on Line, Kingston, London Parks & Gardens Trust, (Williams, S., Keeper of the Inventory, 2002). <http://www.londongardensonline.org.uk/index.html> (Retrieved 21.3.2015).

Hindle, T., Robert Owen, The Economist, Oct 31, 2008, (http://www.economist.com/node/12499674), (Retrieved 18.3.2015)

History in Focus: The Open University, What is History? Arthur Marwick, The Fundamentals of History. <www.history.ac.uk/ihr/Focus/Whatishistory/marwick1.html> (Retrieved 6.2.2012).

Hunslet remembered, compiled by chris@Hunslet.org, <http://www.hunslet.org/Schools_and_religion.html> (3.10.2012).

Hunter, M., Robert Boyle: An Introduction (2004: Birkbeck College, University of London) <http://www.bbk.ac.uk/boyle/index.htm> (Retrieved 2.5.2012).

John Bunyan Church Kingston <http://www.jbckingston.org.uk/history.htm > (Retrieved 26.12.2011). (

Kay, J.A., Morris, C.N., Jaffer, S.M. Meadowcroft, S.A., The Regulation of Retail Trading Hours, The Institute for Fiscal Studies, 1-2 Castle Lane, London S.W.1 E 6.D.R. <http://www.ifs.org.uk/comms/r13.pdf>(Retrieved 23.3.2012).

Kingston U.R.C. History provided by John Fisher, United Reformed Church archivist <http://www.kingstonurc.orgkurc_aboutourchurch.html> (Retrieved 26.12.2011).

Kirby J. in Fox, Places and Portraits, Scrapbook of an Edwardian Lady, 2012, Sir Charles Douglas Fox, and Mary Wright: A Tale of Downward Social Mobility, <http://descentfromadam.wordpress.com/2012/01/29/sir-charles-douglas-fox-and-mary-wright/> (Retrieved 21.3.2015).

Law Commission Statute Law Repeals: Nineteenth Report Draft Statute Law (Repeals) Bill, 5.62 p.163. <lawcommission.justice.gov.uk/docs/19th_statute_law_repeals_report.pdf>, (Retrieved 10.3.2015).

MacDermot, E.T., History of the Great Western Railway 1833-1863., Appendix 1 volume 1 (London: Great Western Railway reprinted Ian Allan:1982), pp.130-1. <//en.wikipedia.org/wiki/Great_Western_Railway#cite_note-12> (Retrieved 18.8.2012).

Marchant, N., Congregational Churches and Churches of Bristol <http://www.churchcrawler.pwp.blueyonder.co.uk/htm.> (Retrieved 24.10.2012).

Marles, H. The Life and Labours of Rev. Jabez Tunnicliff, (London: W. Tweedie, 1865) cited in Wikipedia, < http://en.wikipedia.org/wiki/Jabez_Tunnicliff > (Retrieved 5.4.2012).

Paley, W., A View of the Evidences of Christianity, 1794, <www.wmcarey.edu/carey/paley/paley.htm> (Retrieved 12.6.2011);

Penny Readings, Victorian London — Publications <http://www.victorianlondon.org/publications/habits-10.htm> (Retrieved 1.6.2015).

Pugh, P., Stoke Park: The First 1,000 Years, Chapter 5, Wealthy Victorians, (Cambridge: Icon Books Ltd., 2008) <http:// www.stokepark.com/book/chapter5.>pdf (Retrieved 9.10.2012).

Quakers in Britain, <http://www.quaker.org.uk/IndividualInvolvement> (Retrieved 8.4.2012);

Roots Web Genbrit –L- Archives Bryant and May Match Company. <http://archiver.rootsweb.ancestry.com/th/read/GENBRIT/1998-05/0895041837>

Simpkin J., Spartacus Educational, Charles Bradlaugh, <http://spartacus-educational.com/PRbradlaugh.htm> (Retrieved 8.3.2015);

Strachan, James Morgan grave monument details, grave number 162438 St Mary with St Alban's Church Teddington, <http://www.gravestonephotos.com> (Retrieved 5.12.2012).

Surman, C. The Surman Index On-Line, <www.english.qmul.ac.uk/drwilliams/surman/intro.html> (Retrieved 8.3.2015).

Taylor, J., History Zone, Chartist Lives: Henry Vincent <https://richardjohnbr.wordpress.com/2007/09/05/chartist-lives-henry-vincent> (Retrieved 4 6.2011).

The Coffee Public-House and Temperance Hotel Journal, 1 November 1883, p. 134, <http://books.google.co.uk/ > (Retrieved 8.3.2015).

The Dictionary of Victorian London – Buildings Monuments and Museums – Exeter Hall <http://www.victorianlondon.org/buildings/exeterhall.htm>; <http://en.wikipedia.org/wiki/Exeter_Hall> <http://en.wikipedia.org/wiki/Anti-Corn_Law_League> (Retrieved 28.9.2012)

The Encyclopaedia of Plymouth History, cited an article about Mr. Francis May found in the Oxford Dictionary of National Biography, (<www.oxforddnb.com/> (Retrieved 8.3.2015).

The Gentle Author, Spitalfields Life - At Bedford House, 29 September 2011, <http://spitalfieldslife.com/2011/09/29/at-bedford-house/>(Retrieved 1. 1.2013).

The History of Phrenology, John van Wyhe, History & Philosophy of Science, Cambridge University. <http://www.victorianweb.org/science/phrenology/intro.html>

The London City Mission, Evangelism and Philanthropy, cited Thompson, P., To the Heart of the City, (London: Hodder and Stoughton, 1985) <http://www.infed.org/socialaction/london_city_mission.htm> (Retrieved 8.3.2015).

The National Archives, Chartism - Power, Politics & Protest: The Growth of Political Rights in Britain in the 19th Century, <http://www.nationalarchives.gov.uk/education/politics/g7/> (Retrieved 23.9.2012)

The New York Times, Obituary – William Edwyn Shipton, <http://www.nytimes.com/> (Retrieved 8.3.2015).

The Open-Air Mission <http://www.oamission.com/index.html> (Retrieved 14.12.2011).

The National Secular Society, <http://www.secularism.org.uk/about.html> (Retrieved 8.3.2015).

Tiner, J.H., Robert Boyle - Founder of Modern Chemistry <http://www.doesgodexist.org/MarApr03/RobertBoyleFounderOfModernChemistry.html> (Retrieved 2.5.2012).

Van Wyhe, J., History & Philosophy of Science, Cambridge University. <http://www.victorianweb.org/science/phrenology/intro.html> (Retrieved 7.8. 2011).

Victoria Falls Guide, Victoria Falls Bridge Construction <http://www.victoriafalls-guide.net/victoria-falls-bridge-construction.html> (Retrieved 15.1.2013)

Ward, Col. A.C. OBE DL., The Queen's Royal Surrey Regiment, 1661-1966, <http://www.queensroyalsurreys.org.uk/index.shtml> (Retrieved 19.3.2012).

Watts, Isaac, 1674-1748 <//www.wholesomewords.org/biography/biorpwatts.html> (Retrieved 4.9.2012).

Williams, S., London Parks & Gardens Trust, London Gardens On Line, Hillcroft College, Kingston, <http://www.londongardensonline.org.uk/gardens-online-record.asp?ID=KIN021> (Retrieved 9.10.2012).

World YMCA Empowering Young People <http://www.ymca.int/who-we-are/mission/paris-basis-1855> (Retrieved13.9.2012).

Unpublished Thesis and Dissertations

Giles, A.C. Railway Influence in Kingston upon Thames: paternalism, 'welfarism', and nineteenth century society, 1838–1912, (PhD thesis Kingston University: 2007).

Giles, A.C., *The Failure of a Speculative Builder: The Downfall of Thomas Pooley of Surbiton, 1838-1844*, Centre for Local History Studies, Issue 1 2000, Occasional Paper, Number 1/03 (History Room).

Giles, A.C., *Surbiton: The Development of a Middle Class Suburb,* (M.A. dissertation, Kingston University 2002).

Goepel, H., Children of the poor of Kingston-upon-Thames, 1834–1882 (PhD thesis Kingston University: 2010).

Reading, P., Reluctant Reformers: Politics and Society in Kingston upon Thames, 1830-1900, (PhD thesis Kingston University: 2008).

INDEX

Old Currency

1 shilling (1/-) = 12 old pennies (d)

£1 = 20 shillings (20/-) = 240 old pennies (d)

£1. 1s. 0d = a guinea = 21 shillings

New Currency

100 new pennies (p) = £1